THE Small GARDEN

THE Small GARDEN

JENNY PLUCKNETT

Abbeydale Press

This edition published in 2002 by
Abbeydale Press
An imprint of Bookmart Limited
Desford Road, Enderby,
Leicester
LE9 5AD

© Bookmart 1999

All rights reserved. No part of this publication may be
reproduced, stored in a retrieval system, or transmitted
in any way or by any means, electronic, mechanical,
photocopying, recording or otherwise, without the prior
permission of the copyright holder.

ISBN 1-86147-055-X

Printed and bound in Italy

CONTENTS

Garden designers' names are shown in italics

HOW TO USE THIS BOOK

For ease of use this book is divided into two main parts.

CHAPTERS 1 – 4 (pages 9–99)

This section provides both the inspiration and the know-how to help you design your garden, whatever its shape or situation. Top garden designers show how, with flair and ingenuity, they have dealt with some of the problems you may experience along the way.

Chapter 1 contains the background information to help you measure your garden accurately and draw up a plan. The next three chapters show how garden designers have tackled the designing of small gardens of every shape and in every situation so that you can pick out those that most nearly relate to your particular plot. Gardens with a specific theme are also covered.

For each garden there is a problem solver box which shows the main problems that were encountered and how they were solved and in each case there is one plan which shows the basic design used for the garden and a second to highlight the planting. The following pages show photographs of the finished garden and close-ups of some of the plants it contains.

CHAPTERS 5 – 9 (pages 101–189)

This section supplies the nuts and bolts for turning the design into reality on the ground.

Chapter 5 shows how to identify the type of soil you have and what you can do to improve its condition. There are lots of tips on the best way to water plants so that they develop strong, deep root systems as well as information on installing garden lighting and power.

Chapter 6 provides the choices available for use in creating the ground surfaces and structures that form the garden's main design shapes. It also covers the ornamental extras like water features, arches and pergolas, garden furniture, containers and lighting for both safety and security as well as for decorative effect.

The final three chapters cover some of the huge range of plants available for every situation, with both descriptive information and practical planting details.

Throughout the book there are illustrated tips on both practical garden projects and plant care, and also on decorative effects to delight the eye.

Jenny Plucknett

INTRODUCTION

Small Gardens have always been of great interest to me, firstly because that's where most of my own gardening has been done and, secondly, because professionally I know that the vast majority of my readers and viewers have small gardens – about 85% of people in this country have a garden half the size of a tennis court.

I am also very interested in garden design and a great admirer of garden designers for their ability to look at a space and come up with a design – often very simple in concept – that I know I would never have dreamed up myself, no matter how long I'd tried.

Not so long ago, many people thought that garden design was only for those with rolling acres to play with, but now they realise that it's just as important in a small garden, if not more so. In a large space you have the room to try out all sorts of different ideas and styles, and include all the features you'd like, but in a small garden you don't have that luxury. You have to make the most of the space you have and often that means one strong basic idea – turning the axis through 45 degrees

GAY SEARCH

in a square garden to emphasise the diagonal, for example, or dividing a long thin garden into 'rooms'

This book is full of good ideas for gardens of all shapes and situations and to my mind, the most successful designs are those that are bold and simple, using strong geometric shapes, and where there are curves, making them broad and sweeping. Once you have a good strong, clear structure in the garden you can begin to soften it with exuberant planing and decoration.

If you're about to tackle a brand new garden, or want to revamp an existing one, you'll find plenty of ideas in this book. Just looking at all the different gardens featured will help you to decide what kind of garden you want and also give you some underlying design principles and practical knowledge to turn your ideas into reality.

gay Search

CHAPTER 1

WORKING OUT YOUR OWN DESIGN

You may be starting a garden from scratch, in which case you have the freedom to arrange the elements you want within it in almost any form, bearing in mind aspect, prevailing wind, views (both pleasing and ugly), and privacy. Alternatively, you may want to replan a garden that you have planted and arranged without originally giving a lot of thought to its overall design, or to redesign a garden you have inherited when moving house. If you have just taken over an established garden it would be wise to wait a year before planning it so that you can assess its present design and planting before you decide which factors you want to retain and which you would prefer to change.

Before working on a design it is best to make an accurate scaled plan of the garden, even if this seems rather complicated. Also some thought needs to be given to what you want the garden to provide as well as how you want it to look. Once your garden plan has been drawn up you can use it to arrange the various areas that you require and plan the planting, bearing in mind some of the clever tricks that an expert uses to change the space visually, add excitement and deal with the problems encountered in your particular spot.

Making a plan to scale

Information to include

Aspect

The direction your garden faces, together with the position of the house, surrounding walls, trees, and fences, affects the amount of sun or shade it gets. Use a compass to get an accurate position for north and mark this on your plan. Make a note of sunny and shady areas at different times of the day. This will help you to position both structures and plants in your garden.

Views

You will want to show off a good view. Framing it with trees or shrubs will highlight it. At the same time an ugly view is best hidden. Mark this on your plan so that you remember to design in a concealing barrier.

Overlooked areas

Privacy can be provided by trees, pergolas and frameworks for climbing plants, so show on the plan the areas where the garden is overlooked.

Noise

An area thickly planted with evergreen shrubs or trees will help to deaden noise, so mark in the position of a busy road or other sources of noise.

The first thing you need to do when designing your garden is to measure the area accurately and make a detailed, scaled plan of it. Omit anything you do not want to include in the new design but show the position of anything you want to keep, such as an old tree or specimen shrub. You will also need to show the positions of other fixtures, as these can influence your design. Mark the site of manholes, overhead cables (so that you don't plan a tree in their path), and underground drain lines and cables and their depth (so that you don't cut through them when digging a pond or other excavations).

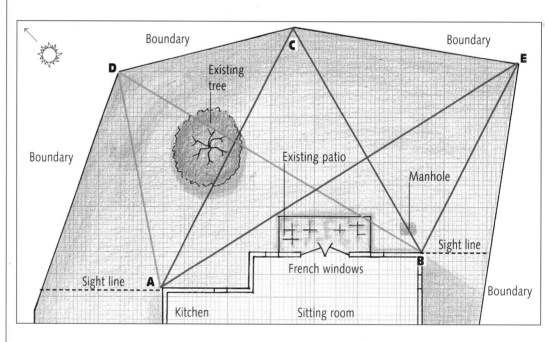

Stages in drawing up a plan

1 Do a rough sketch on a large piece of paper first. A long tape, 30m/100ft will make measuring easier and more accurate. Start by marking in the area of the house, which should be included in the plan. Mark the positions of doors and windows. To measure the distance of the boundary at each side of the house use a sight line from the house. To do this, stand so that you can look directly along the house wall and with one eye line up a point on the boundary along the same line. Mark this spot with a cane and then take a measurement from the nearest house corner to this point. Then do the same on the opposite side.

2 Now move on to the garden. By using triangulation, positions can accurately be plotted. Measure from one house corner, A, to the end of the garden to a point such as a

boundary corner, C. Then measure the distance of C from the opposite house corner, B. Mark these two distances on the plan. Do the same from A and B to the opposite boundary corner D (or any other boundary corners). If the house and garden are wide you may need to measure from a number of points along the house to a range of boundary points – see lines from A and B to D, C and E on the plan, above.

3 Once the boundary distances are recorded, move on to those items in the garden that cannot be moved, such as manholes, oil tanks, and trees or shrubs that you wish to keep. Use triangulation as described in step 2 to plot the positions of each of these. Heating vents, rainwater barrels and garden tap positions also need to be shown. To avoid confusion you may find it easiest to use a different colour for lines and measurements to each point. For large trees, you will also need to measure the

approximate diameter of the trunk and radius of the canopy and mark these on the plan.

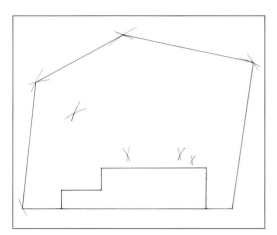

4 Now you can move on to making a proper scale plan. You will need a large piece of graph paper for this. First work out the scale you need to use to fit the complete garden onto the paper: a scale of 2.5cm to 3m or 1in to 10ft is a usually a good size. Note the scale used on the plan itself, and also show the north point. To mark each pair of measurements use compasses, set to each recorded scaled-down distance, and draw a short curve (see diagram, above). The point at which the curves from two measurements cross is the accurate position. Draw in the boundary lines by connecting these points. Mark the positions of the items such as manholes, trees, shrubs (see step 3) within the garden in the same way and show a rough circle for a tree or shrub canopy.

5 (See diagram, above right.) Mark on the plan the positions of any views to be accentuated or blocked out (making it clear which is which), any overlooked areas of the garden, any wet areas, slopes, and the main wind direction. All of this information is important in helping you design the garden.

6 When the plan is drawn up in outline, arrange the elements you wish to include in the design. Use two sheets of tracing paper, one to show the basic structure and one for the planting. Design the basic structure first, then overlay the second sheet on top and position the planting on this.

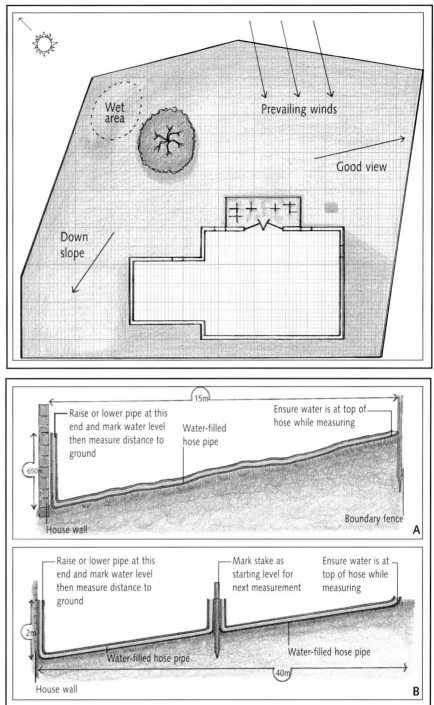

MEASURING A SLOPE

A simple way to measure a slope is to use the Egyptian method, which uses a garden hose (see diagram A). Lay one end of the hose, filled with water, at the top of the slope and run it down the slope, holding the second end in the air to avoid water loss and ensuring that the water remains in the pipe end at the higher level.

Gently lower the second end until you can see the water just reaching the top of the pipe. Measure the distance from this water level to the ground and this will give you the drop on the slope.

On a long slope you may need to take two or more measurements, then add them together (see diagram B for how to do this).

Designing the garden

The list below gives some of the factors you may wish to include in your design. Pick out those that you would like to incorporate and make your own check-list, grading it in order of priority. In a small garden you are unlikely to be able to fit in everything you would like to include, so less vital choices may have to disappear.

Lifestyle
- Areas for outdoor living/BBQ
- Children's play areas
- Pets
- Clothes line/airer

Structures and fittings
- Boundary wall, fence or hedge
- Patios and paths
- Lawns
- Gates
- Dustbin
- Coal bunker/wood shed
- Greenhouse/cold frame
- Lighting
- Rainwater tanks
- Compost bins
- Pergola/arbour
- Moving water feature/pond

Ornamental extras
- Pots/statues
- Sundial/bird table
- Decorative natural materials

Planting
- Ornamental plants
- Herbaceous border
- Rock or gravel garden
- Vegetables/herbs/fruit
- Cut flowers
- Raised beds
- Trees
- Wild area
- Wildlife area to attract birds/mammals/butterflies/bees

There are several points to consider before you put pencil to paper and plan your design, work out the materials you need to implement it and decide on the planting. First of all consider the style of the house – its period, shape and the materials used in its construction, so that house and garden will blend visually. Then think what style of garden you want to create – the following pages will give you some ideas and help you to decide what you prefer.

Formal gardens, with centrally positioned features and sides that form mirror images, match well with symmetrical houses and square or rectangular gardens, but even here most people opt for an easier and more natural-looking informal style.

A wild garden with a naturally shaped pond, areas of long grass, fallen timber, wild flowers, and native plants for hedging will bring in the wildlife that help to keep pests at bay. This type of garden appeals to the organic gardener. A wild garden can also be incorporated as part of an informal garden.

The minimalist design of a Japanese garden with its raked gravel, and carefully positioned sculptural plants and boulders works well in a small space and is easily maintained. But if you enjoy working in the garden you may prefer the abundantly planted cottage-garden style with intermingled vegetables and flowers and plants spilling over paths.

A strong skeleton

If you look through the gardens that follow you will notice that they are based on a simple, strongly shaped skeleton, which ensures that the garden looks good at all times of the year, both when overflowing with greenery and flowers and when growth is more restricted. The pattern may be based on curves, geometric shapes or a mixture of both. A series of interlocking circles or of squares and rectangles both provide a clean, distinctive background. Squares and rectangles do not have to be set straight but can also be used very effectively across the diagonal.

Tricks of the trade

In a small rectangular garden a series of centrally positioned circles that decrease in size away from the house can increase the apparent size of the garden. Lines that run away from you make an area appear longer and you can cleverly accentuate this by creating paths that narrow towards the distance.

A long narrow space looks more interesting if the length is broken up into a series of separate 'rooms', which can be divided with pergolas, hedges, trained trees or trellis-work. Allow a view down the garden through the separate sections by way of a path or matching archways. Create a focal point at the end if there is not a natural one. This can be formed by any eye-catching seat, urn or specimen tree or shrub. Provide interest at a range of levels by fixing structures for plants to grow up, such as trellis, arches, pergolas, corkscrews and obelisks.

A secret corner which is not immediately visible gives interest, as does a garden that tricks you into believing that it continues beyond the boundary by the use of an arch, doorway, mural or mirror. Frame a view with trees and shrubs or with an archway; create privacy with a plant-covered arbour; provide shelter from wind with trellis screens and more climbers, and help to blank out noise with areas of thick shrubs.

Creating a series of terraces is the best way of dealing with a sloping garden. This will require quite a lot of initial work but the resulting series of levels, held in place by retaining walls or banks and linked by steps or paths, can look very attractive. Use a small slope to make a rock garden.

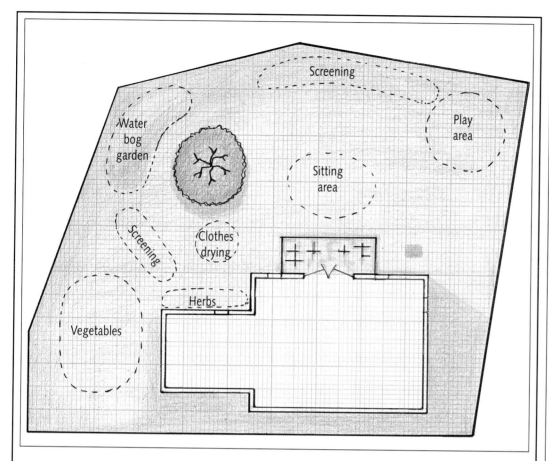

Labels in diagram: Screening, Play area, Water bog garden, Sitting area, Screening, Clothes drying, Herbs, Vegetables

THE STAGES OF DESIGN

1 Bearing in mind sunny and shady areas, wind, views, privacy, noise, and practicalities of access roughly mark in areas for each of the uses you want to include in your design.

2 Now integrate the marked areas, using the basic pattern you have chosen of straight or curved lines or a mixture of both. You can, of course, use a number of overlays to try out a range of patterns. Once you are satisfied with the basic design go over this in pen.

3 Place the planting sheet over the construction plan and, bearing in mind all the points mentioned in step 1 which will affect your choice of plants, plan the areas to be planted in more detail.

A poorly drained garden shows up in constantly wet or puddled areas. Improving the condition of the soil will greatly improve drainage. Low-lying areas can be used for a pond or bog garden. However, if the problem is severe laying drains may be the only answer.

Budgeting

Constructing a garden from scratch can be expensive in terms of materials and hired labour. An extension to your mortgage may be available if you want to complete the construction and planting in one go. If you can do much of the work yourselves the cost will be considerably reduced. For example, it is possible to hire earth moving equipment that will make the work easier.

Alternatively draw up a work time schedule so that you can pay for the work in instalments. Start with the basic construction jobs of installing any electricity, forming the boundary, building a patio and making paths. As a second stage add areas of lawn and some of the key plants plus quick-growing climbers and annuals. Decorative features such as ponds, moving water features, arches, pergolas, and arbours can be added later.

Time-saving considerations

As well as soil and situation, altitude, rainfall, and wind are contributory factors to what will grown well in your garden. Wherever your garden is situated there will be plants that flourish and others that will be hard to grow. Local garden centres are a good source for plants that thrive locally. Growing these will be much less time consuming than choosing unsuitable alternatives.

Terracing

When terracing it is important to remove the topsoil temporarily during construction, then level the subsoil before replacing the topsoil. If you do not do this the depth of topsoil will vary considerably at different points on each terrace.

See also:
- *Identifying and improving soil, Chapter 5*
- *Laying drains, page 103*
- *Form and shape, Chapter 6*
- *Electricity in the garden, page 112*

CHAPTER 2

DESIGNS FOR SPECIFIC SHAPES AND AREAS

The shape and situation of a garden have a great bearing on the best type of design to create to ensure that it becomes interesting. Even the plainest and smallest garden is enhanced by a few surprises, and a long, narrow strip always benefits from being divided into a series of garden 'rooms'.

In this chapter top garden designers have created innovative solutions to some common problems that arise due to a garden's shape, and factors such as land gradient or situation.

Courtyard garden

This tiny garden, designed by Jean Goldberry, is packed with interesting features. From the house a small pergola acts as an arched entrance to the garden and a pathway leads off to the right to a circular terrace with a central statue. Then it turns left to step up to the main terrace shaded by an eye-catching wisteria which clothes the pergola and from which long, falling streamers of lilac-blue flowers appear in late spring. The path then curves around to join up with the original terrace by the house, on its way passing the central raised circular water feature on the left, where a low fountain splashes a collection of pebbles to highlight their subtle colourings. Tall grasses echo the shape of the falling water. To the right of the path stepping stones, each softened by a frame of ground-hugging plants, line up to lead off to the right on a mysterious journey to a spot that is discreetly hidden by shrubs.

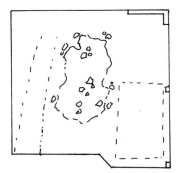

▲ **Before conversion** *the garden had a flowerbed on the left-hand side, a pile of rubble in the centre, a lower area on the right where possibly an old shed or greenhouse stood, and the space was outlined by a fence and walling*

▼ **The planting scheme** *was cleverly arranged to give this tiny area depth, perspective and a lush feel*

THE GARDEN'S PROBLEMS

Pile of rubble in the centre of the garden.

The garden was not only small, but also flat and uninteresting.

Wind, mainly from the right-hand side, was a problem in this small space.

An unattractive view of a huge expanse of a neighbour's wall to the right.

The owner was very keen to have a water feature but was concerned about the safety of visiting small grandchildren.

HOW THEY WERE SOLVED

This rubble, utilized for hardcore, created a base for the brick terrace, so forming a raised area to the right of the garden which would provide additional interest.

A design was created to include a range of levels which would give the space more interesting contours.

A collection of trees were planted which would provide shelter, most particularly for the raised sitting area. A solid wall or fence would simply have provided more turbulence.

The pergola over the sitting area was constructed to blot out some of the wall and raising the terrace also helped. With seating facing towards the garden the view could be controlled to provide plenty to look at.

A raised brick-edged water feature with a shallow layer of pebbles and a low geyser was constructed in the centre of the garden to form a bold statement. The height, and the fact that the water only bubbles over the pebbles makes it safe for small children.

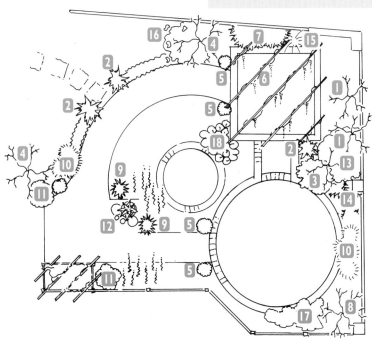

DESIGNER'S PLANTING SCHEME

Key plants

1 *Sorbus commixta* 'Embley'
2 *Rosmarinus officinalis* 'Miss Jessopp's Upright'
3 *Cistus* x *purpureus*
4 *Cornus controversa* 'Variegata'
5 Box, *Buxus sempervirens* – clipped into a globe
6 *Wisteria floribunda* 'Macrobotrys'
7 Japanese fatsia, *Fatsia japonica* 'Variegata'
8 Crab apple, *Malus* 'Van Eseltine'
9 Juniper, *Juniperus communis* 'Hibernica'
10 Lavender, *Lavandula* x *intermedia*
11 *Hebe* 'Caledonia'
12 *Yucca gloriosa*

Decorative detail

13 *Geranium psilostemon*
14 Globe artichoke, *Cynara scolymus*
15 *Miscanthus tinctoria* 'Nanus Variegatus'
16 *Geranium pratense* 'Mrs Kendall Clark'
17 *Penstemon* 'Alice Hindley'
18 *Astilboides tabularis*

Plants for added colour

Morning glory, *Ipomoea purpurea*
Nemesia strumosa 'KLM'
Lobelia 'Riviera Blue Splash'
Larkspur, *Consolida ajacis*
Blue daisy, *Felicia heterophylla* 'Spring Marchen'
Antirrhinum – tall white variety in sunny spaces

Slabs with ground-
hugging planting
in between

Curved, pressure-
treated timber
edging

Solar energy path
lights on either
side of path

Slabs with pea
gravel to finish

Raised brick
geyser fountain
water feature,
with boulders
and pebbles

Solar energy path lights on
either side of brick-edged,
paved path

Uplight below
Miscanthus sinensis

Pergola over raised
terrace

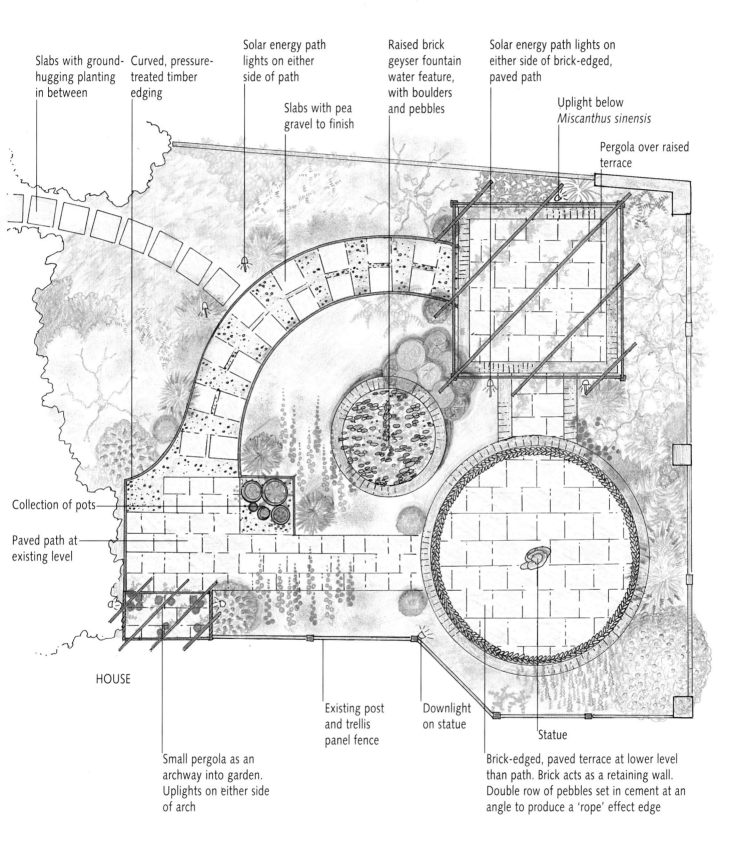

Collection of pots

Paved path at
existing level

HOUSE

Small pergola as an
archway into garden.
Uplights on either side
of arch

Existing post
and trellis
panel fence

Downlight
on statue

Statue

Brick-edged, paved terrace at lower level
than path. Brick acts as a retaining wall.
Double row of pebbles set in cement at an
angle to produce a 'rope' effect edge

CONSTRUCTION

There is so much to look at in this tiny garden that the space appears much larger than it really is. Clever use of a large variety of hard surface materials also helps to break up the space, as do the subtly changing levels.

Flagstones, not all of the same size, are used for the area next to the house with a step down to the brick-edged circular paved area, where pebbles are used to make a rope edging that acts as a defining line between areas of brick and paving. The path and square sitting-out area also use the same materials but the curved path mixes gravel and paving with an edge of timber to hold the gravel in place. More slabs, surrounded by creeping plants, form another, slightly different-looking walkway that leads away from the initial path and through the area to the left.

▲ The view along the side of the house looking towards the circular terrace and statue, with the water feature, grasses and pots on the left.
On entering the garden the eye is arrested by this central grouping, so giving the courtyard depth and perspective. Sorbus trees at the back help to break up the wind and provide late summer berries and some autumn colouring. In summer the garden becomes a haze of pinks, blues and lilacs

PLANTING

Jean gave the seating area an oriental feel with wisteria on the pergola backed by bamboos and a variegated *Fatsia japonica*. She also used junipers to reflect yet soften the upright pergola posts. Junipers, still small in these pictures but which will grow to over 3m/10ft, are also planted to form a frame for the pots by the water feature.

KEY PLANTS

▲ The wonderful magenta flowers, each with an inky black centre, of this cranesbill, *Geranium psilostemon* form a brilliant area of colour planted next to the *Cistus* x *purpureus* (not shown). The leaves also provide colour in spring, when they are pink tinted, and in autumn, when they turn a rich red.

◄ The leaves of *Miscanthus tinctoria* 'Nanus Variegatus' add highlights with their cream and bright green stripes. This dwarf clump-forming grass grows to 45cm/18in.

The pergola over the sitting area, and the smaller one used to form an archway to the garden entrance, persuade the eye upwards and provide the opportunity to introduce climbing plants. The raised water feature introduces yet another level, while the mixed boulders and pebbles on which the water splashes provide a contrasting and varied kind of hard surface.

Lighting is used to create a different look for the garden in evening. A downlighter, fixed to the house wall, is trained to pinpoint the statue in the centre of the circular terrace and solar energy path lights, that involve no wiring, herald the start of the stepping-stone path and highlight the pergola-covered terrace. This lighting focuses the eye on nearby plants and makes the path safe to use at night.

▲ The curving path that leads back towards the house from the pergola-covered sitting area uses paving surrounded with gravel to soften the effect and the slightly raised edging prevents soil spilling onto the path. Plants fall over the path's edge to soften the outline. The mystery path can be seen leading off into the background in the centre top of the picture.

FOR EXTRA COLOUR

Rock roses display very decorative flowers and *Cistus x purpureus* is specially stunning. The decorative tissue-paper thin, magenta pink flowers are highlighted by yellow centres and evenly distributed splashes of dark purple-maroon. Plants of the Mediterranean region, cistus grow well in dry, well-drained soil and this hybrid will grow to about 1–1.2m/3-4ft in both height and spread. They also have a long flowering season. Flowers appear in late May and continue well into July.

Special effect

A raised water feature The type of water feature, top, with a raised brick edge allows you to sit on the rim of the pool and enjoy the water from close at hand. The low central geyser-like waterfall mimics the sound of a gurgling stream to create a relaxing atmosphere.

In the same way, water spills out of an upside-down pot, (above), to coat the container with a flowing golden glaze. Both these features provide an additional eye-catching focus in winter as well as summer for any area of the garden that lacks other interest.

▲ Forming a background to the circular terrace, a group of tall penstemon 'Alice Hindley' with their bell-shaped pale lilac flowers, frill-edged in a deeper tone, bloom right through from mid-summer to early autumn.

Square garden

A square garden has many advantages. It does not beg to be visually shortened with horizontal divisions, as a long garden often does, nor does it need to be broken up with vertical or diagonal lines in the way a short but wide garden may need. However, a strong defining central shape that brings the eye towards the garden's centre can transform the space as is clearly shown in this garden designed by Jean Goldberry, which uses a circle as its theme within the square.

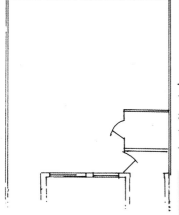

▲ **Before conversion** *the garden shed and workshop provided the main focal point and the plain geometric shape of the garden was clearly emphasized*

▼ **The planting scheme** *was kept to two main areas over opposite corners of the garden, with pots on the terraces to provide extra colour*

THE GARDEN'S PROBLEMS

A downward slope from the end of the garden towards the house.

An ugly fence at the end of the garden.

The harsh shape of a rectangular area of paving by the house which the owner was keen to retain.

A large tree from next door overhangs the bottom left-hand corner of the garden.

An uninteresting side alley with a not particularly. attractive view of neighbouring houses.

HOW THEY WERE SOLVED

A raised patio was built at the end of the garden above the slope. This is much easier than digging out a flat area. The lawn and the beds at the sides follow the natural slope and flatten out at the terrace.

Raised beds in front of the fence help to hide it and provide an attractive view from the house. The height ensures that they are easy to maintain.

The terrace was extended and curved to give a more attractive shape. This also created a solid walkway between the house and garden shed.

As little would grow beneath the tree this space was chosen to site a summer house which looked from shade into sun and took the scale from tree to ground level gently downwards.

Two wide wire arches planted with clematis, sweet peas and a trachelospermum help to hide the view.

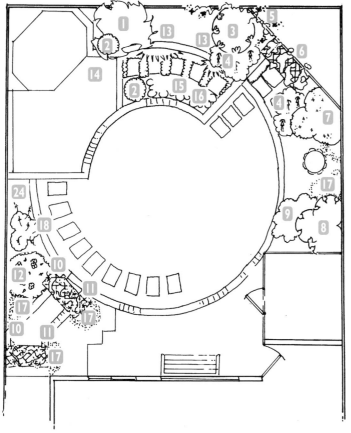

DESIGNER'S PLANTING SCHEME

Key plants
1 Bamboo, *Indocalamus latifolius*
2 Box, *Buxus sempervirens* 'Elegantissima'
3 *Choisya ternanta* 'Sundance'
4 *Fuchsia* 'Tom Thumb'
5 *Clematis armandii*
6 *Rosa* 'Kathleen Harrop'
7 *Daphne odora* 'Aureomarginata'
8 *Viburnum davidii*
9 *Phlomis italiça*
10 *Trachelospermum asiaticum* – over arches
11 *Clematis viticella* 'Alba Luxurians' – over arches
12 *Cistus purpureus*

Decorative detail
13 *Sisyrinchium striatum*
14 *Geranium cinereum* subsp. *subcaulescens* – between slabs
15 *Bergenia ciliata*
16 *Geranium pyrenaicum* 'Bill Wallace'
17 Bronze fennel, *Foeniculum vulgare* 'Bronze'
18 *Erysimum* 'Bowles' Mauve'

Plants for added colour
Antirrhinum 'Black Prince'
Osteospermum 'Nairobi Purple'
Maurandya scandens in purple – in spaces on the fence
Petunia – trailing in deep purple, burgundy and red – in pots and baskets
Convolvulus 'Star of Yelta' – on fences and arches where space
Stock, *Matthiola* 'Giant Excelsior' – in mixed colours

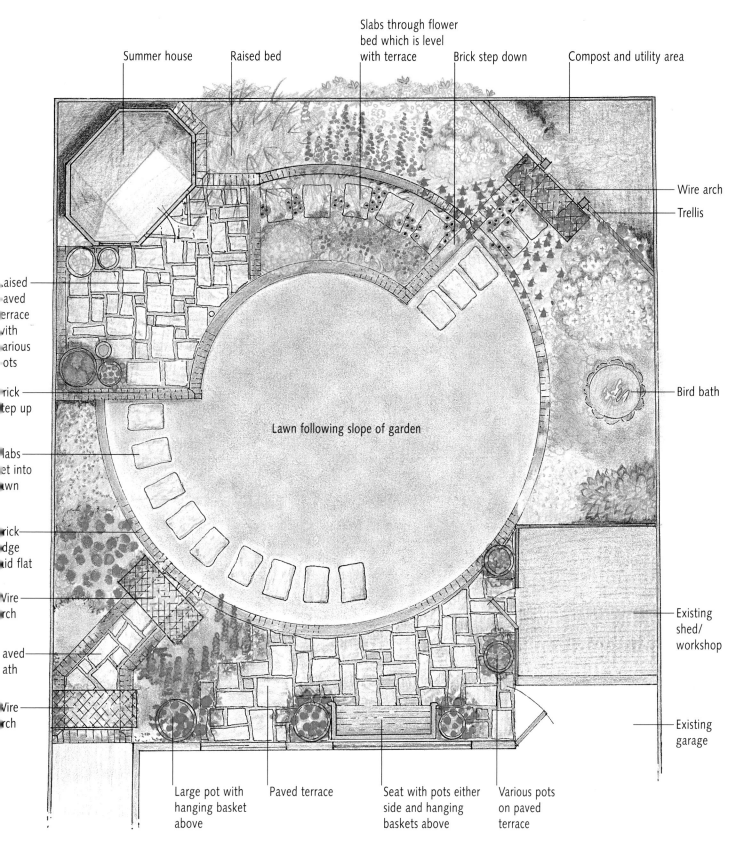

Summer house

Raised bed

Slabs through flower
bed which is level
with terrace

Brick step down

Compost and utility area

Wire arch

Trellis

Raised
paved
terrace
with
various
pots

Brick
step up

Slabs
set into
lawn

Brick
edge
laid flat

Wire
arch

Paved
path

Wire
arch

Bird bath

Lawn following slope of garden

Existing
shed/
workshop

Existing
garage

Large pot with
hanging basket
above

Paved terrace

Seat with pots either
side and hanging
baskets above

Various pots
on paved
terrace

HOUSE

CONSTRUCTION

The circular central lawn is outlined around its circumference with brick and paving to strengthen the simple, strong shape which is the key to the transformation of this plain square garden. The raised paved terrace at the end of the garden follows the curve and overlaps the lawn, and on the same higher level slabs run through the flower bed so that the raised bed behind, edged in stone, is easily reached.

Slabs laid in the lawn follow the shape or lead through an archway into the neatly concealed compost area. Square trellis clothes the fences to break up the harsh outlines and provide a framework for attaching climbers.

The summer house, positioned diagonally across a corner, is in an ideal position to view the complete garden, while the path from the side of the

▲ Siting a summer house under the branches of a large tree, extending over the corner from next door, turns an unsuitable spot for plants into a decorative and enjoyable feature

PLANTING

Jean used a range of grasses, bamboo, a clipped box and shrubs to provide a good basic round-the-year evergreen structure. Striking rich pink and purple perennials and annuals provide most of the summer colour: petunias, the osteospermum 'Nairobi Purple', the fuchsias and the climbing *Maurandya scandens* amongst them.

KEY PLANTS

▲ A trellis and archway mask the compost area, entered through a wrought iron gate. These also provide a framework for honeysuckle and the evergreen *Clematis armandii* with its early, scented white flowers. Pinks and purples are mirrored each side of the gateway.

◀ A range of gold and cream-splashed ivies, *Hedera helix* cultivars, break up the edge of the raised stone bed at the end of the garden, backed by the rich red, pink and purple flowers of the fuchsia 'Tom Thumb'.

◀ *From the end of the garden the view includes the plant-covered arches which straddle the path that curves round from the side of the house and help to hide the house next door*

house, edged with bricks to define its route, is angled to reach the slab path around the lawn. With its wire arches smothered in climbers, this creates a division between the terrace by the

house and the flower bed on the left.

The terraced areas in front of the house and the summer house are broken up with pots of evergreens, for round-the-year interest, and colourful annuals.

▲ Plants with a range of leaf colours fill the raised bed by the arch. Creamy yellow spikes of *Sisyrinchium striatum* are echoed in the golden leaves of *Choisya ternata* 'Sundance' behind. *Fuchsia* 'Tom Thumb' adds colour at the front and the rose 'Kathleen Harrop' covers the arch.

FOR EXTRA COLOUR

Begonias and fuchsias fill a pot to bursting with their dark purple and green leaves and pink, red and white flowers. This mixture is a good choice for a more shaded area of the terrace. Begonia tubers can be lifted in autumn and dried off then replanted in spring. In frost-prone areas many fuchsias will survive if the stem base is planted 5cm/2in below the soil surface and a deep layer of mulch is added. Alternatively bring pots indoors.

Special effect

Raised flower beds are used almost everywhere in this garden. These both help to contain the soil and are easier to maintain. The lower beds are edged in a framework of neatly laid bricks. The taller bed, at the end of the garden, has large golden-grey rocks laid in the jig-saw-like manner of a country stone wall. The taller stone-edged bed, at 45cm/18in, means that little bending is necessary when gardening, and larger, smoother stones provide a seat when a little quiet contemplation is required.

See also:
- *Raised beds, page 108*
- *Building a low brick wall, page 120*
- *Arches, page 132*

Short, wide garden

The owners of this garden, attached to a 1930s house, wanted it to be, above all, modern, minimalist and a bit different. They turned to sculptor and garden designer Paul Cooper to use his combined creative talents to conceive a garden that was both modern and formal.

Over years the garden, originally large, had been sold off as plots, leaving a piece of land that was wide and very short with a line of tall conifer trees along the end that dominated and brought the boundary even closer. As these were planted in the adjoining garden they could not be removed, so Paul decided to create a strong feature to detract from them.

▲ **Before conversion** *the garden was laid out with a central lawn and beds around the edges, highlighting its short length and its width*

Trellis panels _____

THE GARDEN'S PROBLEMS

A line of 6m/20ft conifers at the end of the garden and growing in the adjoining garden.

The owners wanted to be able to look down on the garden from the top windows of the house and see precise and clear geometric patterns.

The short length of the garden.

Old basic concrete paving slabs were to be retained.

HOW THEY WERE SOLVED

▶ Paul designed a bold structure that mimicked a gateway to imply extra space beyond. Adjoining this he created a pergola and both were painted white to draw the eye to these and so detract from the line of trees beyond.

▶ By using a wide range of hard surface materials plus grass and forming strong, juxtapositioned shapes Paul has formed an eyecatching minimalist and modern design.

▶ Lines that run towards the structure at the end of the garden narrow as they reach the boundary, thereby creating an impression of greater length. The wide range of hard materials and the shapes they create also give a sense of extra space.

▶ By edging the original paved area with brick and introducing other materials the original paving became part of a wider scheme of clearly defined shapes.

Buff chippings, timber edge

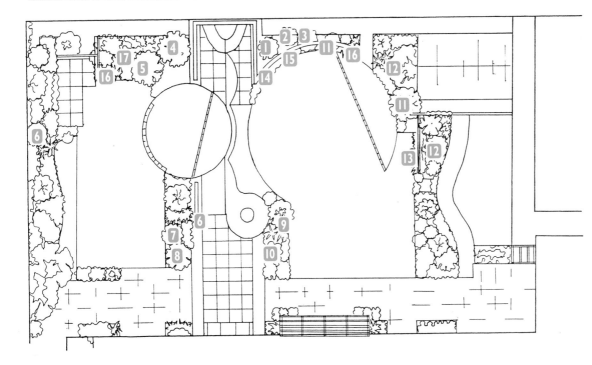

◀ **The planting scheme** *was deliberately tidy and compact with most of the shrubs clipped to form neat globes. Low plants are either ground hugging or form tight hummock shapes*

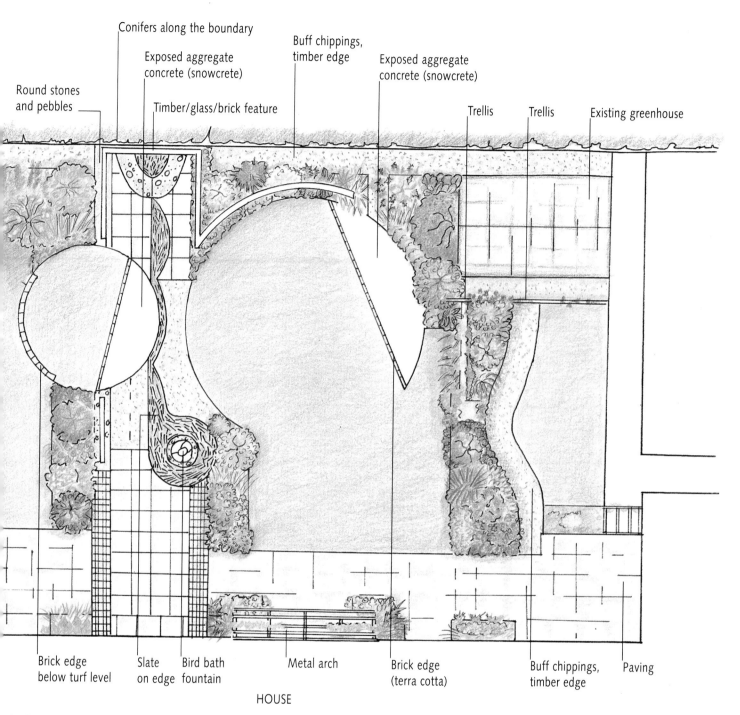

Round stones
and pebbles

Conifers along the boundary

Exposed aggregate
concrete (snowcrete)

Timber/glass/brick feature

Buff chippings,
timber edge

Exposed aggregate
concrete (snowcrete)

Trellis   Trellis   Existing greenhouse

Brick edge
below turf level

Slate
on edge

Bird bath
fountain

Metal arch

Brick edge
(terra cotta)

Buff chippings,
timber edge

Paving

HOUSE

DESIGNER'S PLANTING SCHEME

Key plants

1 Myrtle, *Myrtus communis* 'Variegata'
2 *Mahonia* x *media* 'Charity'
3 Golden Mexican orange blossom, *Choisya ternata* 'Sundance'
4 Privet, *Ligustrum ovalifolium* 'Argenteum'
5 *Rosa xanthina* 'Canary Bird'
6 *Viburnum tinus*
7 *Abelia* x *grandiflora*
8 *Photinia* x *fraseri* 'Red Robin'
9 *Elaeagnus* x *ebbingei*

10 *Viburnum* x *carlcephalum*
11 *Viburnum davidii*
12 *Ceanothus dentatus*

Decorative detail

13 *Agapanthus africanus*
14 Cranesbills, *Geranium macrorrhizum* 'Album' and *G.* 'Johnson's Blue'
15 Foam flower, *Tiarella cordifolia*
16 Iris – tall bearded species and varieties
17 Sage, *Salvia officinalis* 'Icterina'

Plants for added colour

Campanula carpatica – in blue
Coral flower, *Heuchera* 'Palace Purple'
Dianthus 'Doris'
Ceratostigma willmottianum
Red-hot poker, *Kniphofia rooperi*
Eryngium bourgatii

▲ Looking from the house towards the end of the garden. The main structure and water feature, together with the pergola to the right, take the eye off the line of conifers behind

CONSTRUCTION

Designer Paul Cooper has used white for the main structures, arches, pergola and ground surfaces, to highlight the patterns he has formed with the hard landscaping that mixes curves and straight lines. Structures are kept deliberately clear of climbers which would hide the clean lines and eventually blend in colour with the background, so loosing the strong outline they are intended to create.

Where trellis has been used, to either side of the central structure, some of the spaces have been blocked in with plywood and then painted green or black to enhance the modern feel of this garden.

The main giant white structure at the end of the garden is in fact a water feature with water tumbling from the centre top down over glass bricks. Two semi-circles of mirror reflect the same-shaped pool below, creating a mirror image of the

PLANTING

This is a garden where man shows his control over nature. Shrubs are kept neatly trimmed in a series of globes, boxes and tidy hummocks. In each space created by the post and rail pergola a shrub, chosen for its colour or leaf shape, forms a simple sculptural silhouette, an unusual alternative to screening the timber with climbing plants.

KEY PLANTS

▲ Long tooth-edged bracts, tinged with pink, create a ruff of silvery spikes that surround and protect the grey-blue flowers of *Eryngium varifolium*. The strong shape and silvery tints of eryngiums create a perfect foil for the clean lines maintained in this modern garden.

◀ Cranesbill, *Geranium* 'Johnson's Blue', with its bright green leaves and pink-tinged blue flowers, forms good ground cover.

◄ *The water feature and central paving seen from the side and looking across a section of lawn. The square arches create strong images against the clipped shrubs and the rest of the planting*

water that turns it into a full circle. From this pool flows a series of part circles of broken slate used on edge to mimic water. The flow of slate completes its journey near the house as a circle with a

bird bath and fountain as a centrepiece.

Ground surfaces are cleverly mixed to create a range of colours and textures that highlight the strong shapes that are such an important part of the design.

▲ Another sculptural plant that highlights the simple architectural shapes of the garden's outlines is the silk-tassel bush, *Garrya elliptica*. In winter the grey-green catkins hang like silvery tree decorations and give the bush its common name.

FOR EXTRA COLOUR

An excellent plant to provide flashes of colour in autumn is the bulbous nerine from South Africa. *N. bowdenii* has faintly scented and lily-shaped pink flowers with long drooping stamens. It also comes in white, tinted palest pink, as f. *alba*. *Nerine filifolia* has smaller pink and white flowers with frilled edges.

Special effects

Mixing ground surfaces In this garden Paul Cooper has used a very wide range of hard surfaces to highlight the shapes that he wanted to bring into focus. Amongst these are square paving stones and smaller pavers, which line up on either side of the paving, to outline the pathway leading to the water feature.

This is a clever way of incorporating the retained areas of paving with those that are new and it also introduces a range of textures and colours that provide further interest.

Brick and timber edgings create clean-cut shapes for the circular lawns, while white-finished concrete, and light buff-coloured chippings highlight and mimic the shapes of the main structures. Slates fixed on edge, together with cobbles, provide a rougher finish that contrasts well with the smoother concrete and paving.

See also:
• *Moving water, page 128*
• *Trellis, pages 47, and 123*

Long, narrow garden

This garden was bordered by long, narrow beds which tended to increase its apparent length. There were unattractive views at the end and to the right of the garden and a new conservatory and terrace of hexagonal paving would need to be integrated into the scheme for the garden, which was required to provide a place to entertain friends and a large extended family. Finally, two small boys wanted to be able to enjoy and use the garden as well as the adults.

Designer Sally Court decided to divide the length into separate sections. The space nearest to the house became an area for family gatherings with a view of a triangular pool on the left that has a simple waterfall system with water falling into a shallow pebble-lined pool below. The second section is reserved for the boys' use, and at the end of the garden, which lies in the path of the morning sun, there would be a place for a relaxed breakfast as well as a screened utility area.

▲ **Before conversion** *the garden was lined along both sides with narrow borders which made the space appear even longer and narrower than it actually was*

THE GARDEN'S PROBLEMS

Ugly views, of a block of concrete garages at the end of the garden and a new block of flats on the right.

The garden's long and narrow shape.

A new conservatory and a terrace beyond it with octagonal paving needed to be considered in the choice of materials used in the garden.

HOW THEY WERE SOLVED

Raised beds, the pond, and tall planting part way down the garden hide the views from the terrace close to the house and evergreen planting helps further. Luxuriant climbers, grown along the fence on the right-hand side of the garden, also act as a decorative screen.

Sally dealt with this problem by dividing the garden into three separate 'rooms' and providing only a hint of what was beyond from each section. A trip down the garden was therefore a constant journey of discovery.

The geometric shape of the paving used for the terrace meant that curves would not have been a suitable choice for the rest of the garden. Instead Sally used straight lines for paths and created a triangular pond, which were more in keeping.

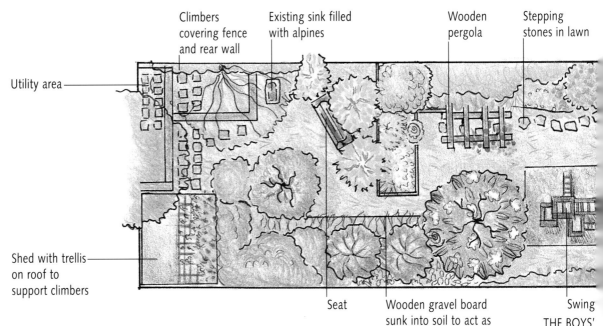

Climbers covering fence and rear wall

Existing sink filled with alpines

Wooden pergola

Stepping stones in lawn

Utility area

Shed with trellis on roof to support climbers

Seat

THE WILD GARDEN

Wooden gravel board sunk into soil to act as edging to border and lawn

Swing

THE BOYS' GARDEN

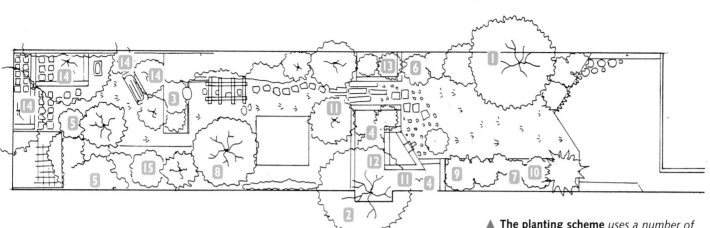

▲ **The planting scheme** *uses a number of plants that were already in the garden, mainly rhododendrons and camellias, which were repositioned nearer to the house*

DESIGNER'S PLANTING SCHEME

Key plants

Already existing

1 Tree of heaven, *Ailanthus altissima*
2 Mountain ash, *Sorbus aucuparia*
3 *Pittosporum tenuifolium*
4 Selection of rhododendrons and camellias – relocated
5 Conifers

New

6 *Malus* 'Golden Hornet'
7 *Prunus virginiana*
8 *Magnolia grandiflora*
9 *Pittosporum tobira*
10 *Ceanothus* 'Puget Blue'
11 New Zealand flax, *Phormium tenax* 'Purpureum'
12 *Photinia* x *fraseri* 'Red Robin'
13 Strawberry tree, *Arbutus unedo*
14 Himalyan birch, *Betula utilis*
15 *Osmanthus delavayi*

Decorative Detail

Clematis macropetala
Japanese maple, *Acer palmatum* var. *dissectum*
Lamium 'White Nancy'
Pulmonaria saccharata
Bergenia silberlicht
Hosta 'Royal Standard'
Romneya hybrid
Ornamental hop, *Humulus lupulus* 'Aurea'
Hydrangea arborescens 'Annabelle'
Paeonia delavayi

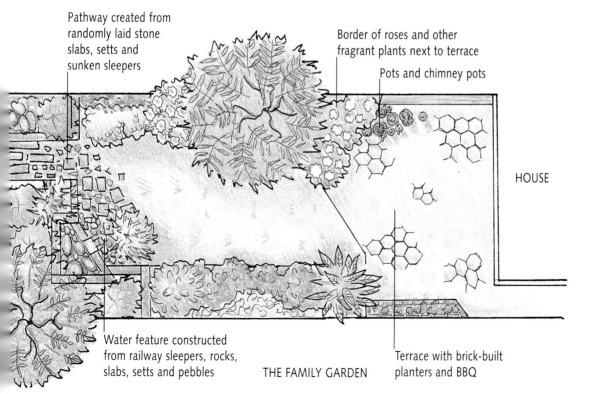

Pathway created from randomly laid stone slabs, setts and sunken sleepers

Border of roses and other fragrant plants next to terrace

Pots and chimney pots

HOUSE

Water feature constructed from railway sleepers, rocks, slabs, setts and pebbles

THE FAMILY GARDEN

Terrace with brick-built planters and BBQ

▲ *The conservatory and the paved terrace in front of it were the starting point for the garden's design*

Long, narrow garden

CONSTRUCTION

Apart from being long and narrow, the garden was also very flat. This led Sally to add height at the end of the first section by constructing slightly raised beds, edged in railway sleepers, together with a raised pool. These provide an interesting view from the house and terrace.

The upper pool, constructed of railway sleepers and a flexible liner, has a centrally placed funnel that spills water down into a shallow, pebble-lined pool below. The water is then recirculated back into the top pond. The raised beds and pond also divide off the next section, reached by a gravel path, broken up with stepping stones and partly buried sleepers.

The second section is given over to the boys with swings, plenty of space to kick a ball and a bed where they can try out their gardening skills. A pergola and evergreen planting screen the end of the garden,

Long, narrow garden

PLANTING

A number of plants already in the garden were retained, some being moved to a new home. A tree of heaven, *Ailanthus altissima* was resited close to the terrace to provide a backdrop, and a mature *Pittosporum tenuifolium* adds privacy to the end of the garden and has been joined by another specimen tree, a *Magnolia grandiflora*.

KEY PLANTS

▲ As a background to the pond a mountain ash, *Sorbus aucuparia*, provides a decorative round-the-year view from the house. In spring clusters of white flowers appear, later followed by bright red berries. In autumn the leaves turn yellow and red before they fall.

◄ Next to the raised bed a bear's breeches, *Acanthus spinosus*, banked on either side by roses, shows off its tall spires of purple-pink and white-throated flowers and attractive large, dark green, spiny, divided leaves.

◄ *Looking down the garden from the top terrace. On the left are the triangular pond and raised bed that divide this section off from the next*

▼ *The unusual triangular raised pool with its overspill into a shallow pebble-lined pond below*

where shrubs create a den for the boys.

This section has areas of rough grass, mature shrubs and trees, and a seat positioned to face the early morning sun. The mature planting and trellis-work over which climbers grow give privacy and screen the utility part of the garden.

▲ The bell-shaped white flowers of a *Pittosporum tobira* along the garden path flourish in late spring to early summer. They are scented and gradually turn more creamy yellow with age. The leathery dark green shiny leaves are paler on the underside.

FOR EXTRA COLOUR

For colourful early flowers that brighten a shady position the perennial pulmonaria with its blue, pink or white flowers and white- or silver-spotted leaves is a good choice. *Pulmonaria saccharata*, shown, has unusual lilac to pink flowers whereas the variety *P. saccharata* 'Frühlingshimmel' has bright pastel blue flowers with a darker blue centre.

Pulmonaria likes humus-rich and moist soil, as well as full or partial shade.

Special effects

Mixing path materials By mixing the materials used in creating a path much more interesting effects can be achieved. This also allows you to curve a path made from rigid materials such as paving by introducing gravel or stone chippings and then setting the paving with gaps, like stepping stones, along the length.

With paving for the main walkway other ornate and less resilient materials can also be used, such as bark chippings, broken slate or even shells.

Here Sally has mixed larger paving slabs, smaller setts and sunken sleepers, all laid in gravel. The slabs continue on as stepping stones through the lawn that the path leads to.

See also:
- *Paths steps and edgings, page 118*
- *Children's play space, page 138*

Split-level garden

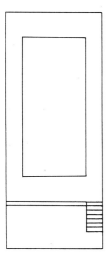

▲ **Before conversion** *the lower rooms of this tall town house were below garden level with a narrow paved strip adjoining the house and a blank wall between this and the garden*

The owners of this garden on two levels had quite different views of what they would like it to look like. One, who dislikes clutter, wanted a modern, simple and stylish outdoor room, the other preferred a romantic, traditional country-garden look. It was therefore designer Sally Court's job to bring these two rather opposing requirements together in a garden that both would like.

Originally the house, on a lower level, was faced from the main downstairs rooms with a blank wall, with the main area of the garden above this. The first thing that Sally did was to extend the narrow paved areas next to the house outwards so that it became wide enough to use as a sitting and eating area.

The paving and retaining wall were extended in a series of curves, and brick steps up to the top section of the garden follow the same curves. The wall has also been used as a backdrop for a moving water feature to break up the length of the wall and create sound and visual interest on the patio.

Trellis fixed along the boundary fences was stained green so that it would blend into the background, as was a decoratively designed garden shed at the end of the garden that looks more like a gazebo.

THE GARDEN'S PROBLEMS

The large kitchen and family room set below the main garden and facing a blank wall.

Drainage problems in a garden where the house is on a lower level.

Squirrels constantly dug up the garden to store nuts and seeds collected nearby.

HOW THEY WERE SOLVED

By extending the lower terrace and making it a much more interesting shape the views from the lower rooms became much more exciting. Sandstone floors inside the house were reflected in the paving material chosen for the terrace outside and with sliding patio doors onto the terrace the inside and space outdoors became visually linked.

Sally introduced a gully that runs along the edge of the house and terrace and leads to a sump. In wet weather this allows any rainwater to run away safely.

The owners set up a special squirrel feeder in the garden as well as birds-only feeders. Soon the squirrels were using the feeder and this curtailed their digging activities.

DESIGNER'S PLANTING SCHEME

Key plants

1 Strawberry tree, *Arbutus* x *andrachnoides*
2 Jelly palm, *Butia capitata*
3 Dwarf fan palm, *Chamaerops humulis*
4 Cabbage palm, *Cordyline australis*
5 Daphne odora 'Aureomarginata'
6 Loquat, *Eriobotrya japonica*
7 *Magnolia grandiflora* 'Samuel Sommer'
8 New Zealand flax, *Phormium tenax*
9 Black bamboo, *Phyllostachys nigra*
10 Japanese mock orange, *Pittosporum tobira*

Decorative detail

11 *Cistus* x *skanbergii*
12 Cardoon, *Cynara cardunculus*
13 Alexandrian laurel, *Danae racemosa*
14 *Dianella tasmanica*
15 Woodrush, *Luzula sylvatica* 'Marginata'
16 Lilyturf, *Ophiopogon planiscapus* 'Nigrescens'
17 Soft shield fern, *Polystichum setiferum*
18 Prostrate rosemary, *Rosmarinus lavandulaceus*
19 *Parthenocissus henryana*
20 *Wisteria* 'Snow Showers'

◀ **The planting scheme** *was planned to use plants that are unusual in this area and very architectural in form*

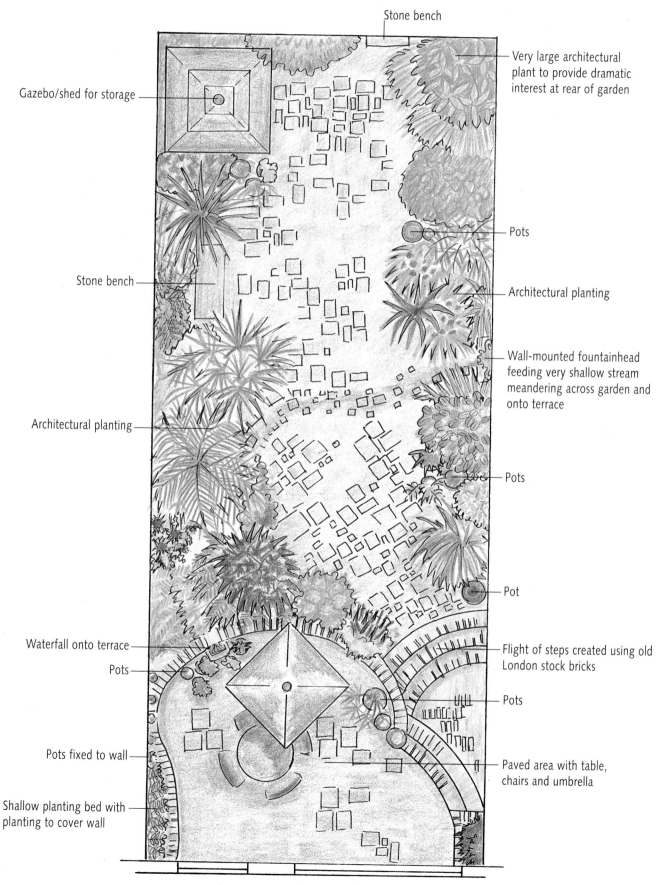

Stone bench

Very large architectural plant to provide dramatic interest at rear of garden

Gazebo/shed for storage

Pots

Stone bench

Architectural planting

Architectural planting

Wall-mounted fountainhead feeding very shallow stream meandering across garden and onto terrace

Pots

Pot

Waterfall onto terrace

Flight of steps created using old London stock bricks

Pots

Pots

Pots fixed to wall

Paved area with table, chairs and umbrella

Shallow planting bed with planting to cover wall

HOUSE

See also:
• Ornamental extras page 136
• Moving water page 128

▲ *The water feature creates a perfect focal point on the wall of the lower terrace. This and the giant pots containing evergreen shrubs placed on either side break up the expanse of plain wall*

Split-level garden
CONSTRUCTION

The major work in the garden was to open up the terrace close to the house and replace the 1m/39in retaining wall with a new one that followed a series of decorative curves.

Both the lower terrace and most of the garden above this were paved in a range of slabs of different sizes with gravel between to give a uniform look throughout. Reclaimed honey-coloured bricks were used for the wall and steps.

To create an attractive view from the house, and break up the retaining wall, pots were fixed to the surface around the wall. A fountain was positioned on the wall with a stone water-garden trough placed below it. Three beautiful giant lizards sculpted by Lucy Smith were commissioned, two to act as spouts for the fountain and a third for the top of the wall.

Other features have been introduced

Split-level garden
PLANTING

A modern theme of structural plants, most of which provide interest around the year, is used here with a range of palms, black-stemmed bamboo, cardoon and New Zealand flax. These blend with verdant climbers to cover the walls, fences and trellis. In frost-prone areas alternative species of these plants may be better suited to winter outside.

KEY PLANTS

▲ In a large pot on the terrace an evergreen viburnum, *Viburnum davidii*, with its three-veined dark green leaves provides round-the-year interest. It has small, white, slim, bell-shaped flowers in late spring followed by sprays of metallic, almost black fruit.

◄ A mat of brilliant yellow is created by the stonecrop, *Sedum acre* which has star-shaped yellow flowers throughout summer. It grows to form a low bun shape 5cm/2in high by about 60cm/24in across.

◀ *The view from the upper terrace looking back towards the house. This area is a happy mix of paving and greenery when seen from the house*

▼ *The panorama from the lower terrace looking towards the garden shed, masked by trellis and climbers, and the stone seat set in the sunshine that looks over the garden*

throughout the garden to provide focal points. On the right-hand side, and part way down, a second fountain tumbles into a shallow stream that meanders its way across to the terrace. A stone bench on the opposite side of the garden provides a good view.

▲An umbrella plant, *Cyperus* species, flourishes in the damp conditions of the water feature and makes a natural home for two of the three basking lizards. Water spouting from the lizards' mouths spatters decoratively onto large pebbles before falling into the stone sink below.

FOR EXTRA COLOUR

Container evergreens may not be very colourful but they provide interest around the year. The bay tree, *Laurus nobilis* not only has aromatic leaves but can be clipped into interesting topiary shapes. In an exposed spot or in a frost-prone area it is best taken indoors for the colder months. Grown close to the house, its leaves can easily be picked for use.

Special effects

A garden ornament is a very personal thing. Ornaments can be ornate and classical, fun and frivolous or simple and streamline. They may be mass-produced or, as here, specially designed for their location.

Siting is all-important. Here a giant maroon fish stands on its tail to view passers by, its positioning amongst the planting at the side of the path creating a surprise.

Paved town garden

Garden designer Sally Court inherited a very small town garden on a slight slope that she considered was overplanted. Laurel, privet and Scots pine, as well as some inappropriately large shrubs, made it dark and unappealing.

Sally decided to remove everything that was there and start again, paving the area throughout and allowing space for wider beds. She took advantage of the slope to create the new garden on slightly different levels so that shallow steps take you up onto the terrace immediately adjacent to the house and then up again from this

section to the terrace with the water feature provided by the fountain and pool.

Changing the garden's design also allowed Sally to move the back gate from the centre of the end fence and position it at one side, making room for a shed. Climbers soon covered the fences on all sides of the garden to provide colour and greenery on a second level, and a groups of pots and a sink garden provide extra space for yet more plants.

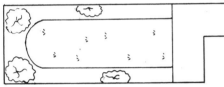

◀ **Before conversion** *there were pathways up both sides, and narrow borders, a small lawn and large trees and bushes*

THE GARDEN'S PROBLEMS

Surrounded by houses in almost every direction the garden had no privacy.

Straight paths and beds which ran from the house to the end of the garden and which made the small space appear ever narrower.

Poor soil condition.

No birds visited the garden.

HOW THEY WERE SOLVED

The multistem birch planted at the end of the garden screens it from the houses at the back. Rampant climbers like the evergreen clematis, *Clematis armandii* clothe the side fences, which were topped with trellis to add height for extra privacy.

The paths, beds and lawn were removed and a water feature was positioned centrally, part way down the garden, to divide off the area.

Debris had to be removed before manure and compost could be added to improve the soil, which is constantly topped up to maintain and improve its condition.

Planting was deliberately chosen to provide birds with berries and seeds.

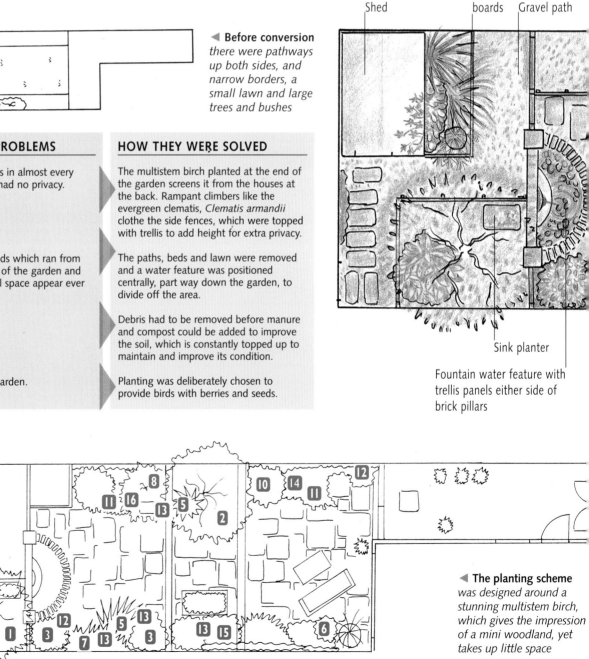

Shed　Gravel boards　Gravel path

Sink planter

Fountain water feature with trellis panels either side of brick pillars

◀ **The planting scheme** *was designed around a stunning multistem birch, which gives the impression of a mini woodland, yet takes up little space*

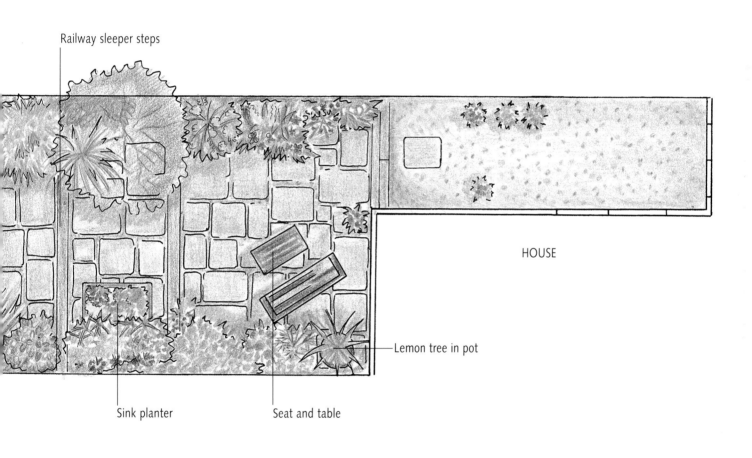

Railway sleeper steps

HOUSE

Lemon tree in pot

Sink planter

Seat and table

DESIGNER'S PLANTING SCHEME

Key plants
1 Birch, *Betula utilis* – multistem
2 *Ceanothus* 'A. T. Johnson'
3 *Pittosporum tobira* – standard
4 *Pittosporum tobira* 'Variegatum' – shrub
5 New Zealand flax, *Phormium tenax*
6 *Pinus mugo* var. *pumilio*
7 *Trachycarpus fortunei*
8 *Elaeagnus ebbingei*
9 *Aucuba japonica* 'Crotonifolia'
10 *Rosa* x *hugonis* – weeping standard

Decorative detail
11 *Astrantia major rubra*, 'Sunningdale'
12 *Hosta fortunei* 'Albopicta', 'Halcyon', *H. sieboldiana*, *H. undulata* and others
13 *Tradescantia* – a mixture of varieties
14 *Trachelospermum jasminoides*
15 *Trachelospermum jasminoides* 'Variegatum'
16 *Rosa* Heritage, Gertrude Jekyll and Tradescant

Plants for added colour
Clematis macropetala, *C. cirrhosa*, *C. armandii*, *C.* 'Vyvyan Pennell', *C. texensis*, *C. viticella*
Cranesbill, *Geranium*- ten species, including *G. renardii* and 'Johnson's Blue'
Paeonia x 'Bowl of Beauty'
Paeonia lutea var. *ludlowii*

CONSTRUCTION

Sally used reclaimed York stone to pave the major part of the garden, immediately giving it a mature finish. Railway sleepers are used to create the wide, shallow steps that take you onto the slightly different levels of the garden.

To increase the garden's privacy without losing too much light, and to turn it into a very sheltered spot where she could grow exotics, she added trellis to the top of all the boundary fences.

Two-thirds of the way down the garden she built a centrally positioned low wall from old honey-coloured bricks, with pillars at each end and space at the sides. This is part of the water feature with a lion-head fountain centrally positioned and a deep, semi circular pool below into which the water splashes. This makes an eye-catching centrepiece from the terrace near to the house and

▲ *The stunning white bark of the multistemmed birch,* Betula utilis, *together with the lion fountain set in the wall in front of it, catch the light and draw the eye to the end of the garden*

PLANTING

Simplicity is the keynote to Sally's planting in a small space. She uses a theme, which may be based on colour or a few specimen plants, then repeats it through the garden to create harmony.

Here she chose the birch as the star of the garden and planned the rest of the planting around this to include a range of textures and round-the-year interest.

KEY PLANTS

▲ A large terra-cotta jar gives height and further interest to a group of containers that hold colourful pelargoniums, a trailing fuchsia and a miniature citrus grown as a standard. By removing and replacing pots as the seasons change, Sally can provide round-the-year colour in this small space.

◀ A sink garden comes into its own in a small space, bringing the miniature and very decorative plants it holds up to a higher level and enabling good drainage to be provided.

◄ *The view from the house, showing the steps that lead onto the terrace. The courtyard is crammed with pots and the boundary fences are smothered in climbers to give a verdant effect*

▼ *Looking towards the end of the garden, where the garden shed can only just be seen amongst the greenery*

partially masks the end of the garden.

The beds are irregular in size, following the staggered edges of the stone paving and together with this groups of pots, carefully positioned, create a wide and curving pathway through the entire garden.

▲ A lemon tree, *Citrus limon* 'Meyer', grown in a container provides an exotic touch with its fragrant flowers in early summer followed by fruit. It has been positioned in a corner where it is out of the wind and gets the sunshine throughout the day.

FOR EXTRA COLOUR

Cranesbills, members of the geranium family, are easy to grow and flourish in sun or partial shade and in almost any soil except very wet. The flowers in pink, blue, purple and white appear in summer.

Compact perennial species grow to only about 15cm/6in tall, and are ideal for use in a sink garden. Taller clump-forming species look effective grown in a flower border or amongst shrubs.

Special effect

Wall fountains can give visual interest and provide the relaxing sound of moving water to the smallest of outdoor spaces and many are suitable for fixing indoors too. They are ideal for use where there are small children.

Many designs are available, from traditional-looking lion or human heads to figures and animals of stone, concrete or lighter metal resin to simple spouts and modern shapes.

Small front garden

Like many front gardens that run alongside busy streets or line the roadside on housing estates, this narrow strip of land lacked any imagination in its design. It was simply made up of a pathway leading along the front of the house, with a bed between this and the house and a strip of grass with some larger shrubs dotted around between the path and the road. By using a zig-zag shape for the path and introducing triangular beds the designer Jean Goldberry transformed the space into an eye-catching and luxuriant seaside garden.

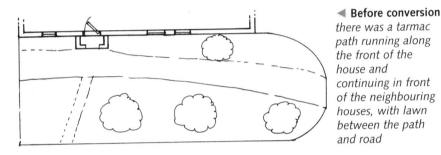

◀ **Before conversion** there was a tarmac path running along the front of the house and continuing in front of the neighbouring houses, with lawn between the path and road

THE GARDEN'S PROBLEMS

The garden was a very long and thin strip of land in front of the house.

Although this front strip is private, local kids on bicycles used the front path as a short-cut making it hazardous for others.

Guests and tradespeople took the quick straight option to the front door, cutting across lawn and through plants.

The owners wanted some privacy but were precluded by local regulations from using a fence or hedge.

HOW THEY WERE SOLVED

Strong diagonal shapes were used for beds and paving to break up the length.

The zig-zag raised beds and the uneven surface of pebbles and paving remove an easy short-cut and low posts and swagged ropes divide the garden off from the road.

It was decided to use this route as the sensible option for the new path to the front door.

Tall posts and swagged ropes provide an unusual pergola framework for climbers, which will give privacy when established.

Wire beside and above windows

HOUSE

Large pot

▼ **The planting scheme** As this house is near the sea it was given a coastal planting scheme in strong seaside colours

Water-washed pebbles on impacted hardcore

Paving slabs

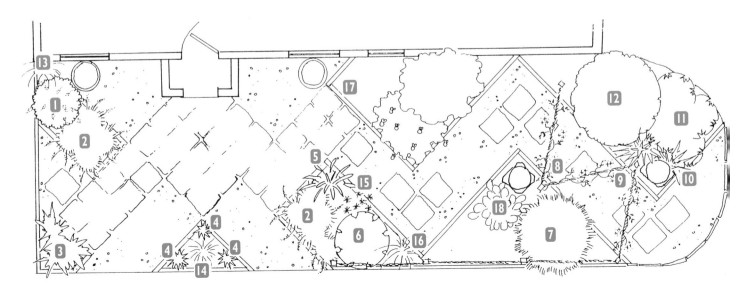

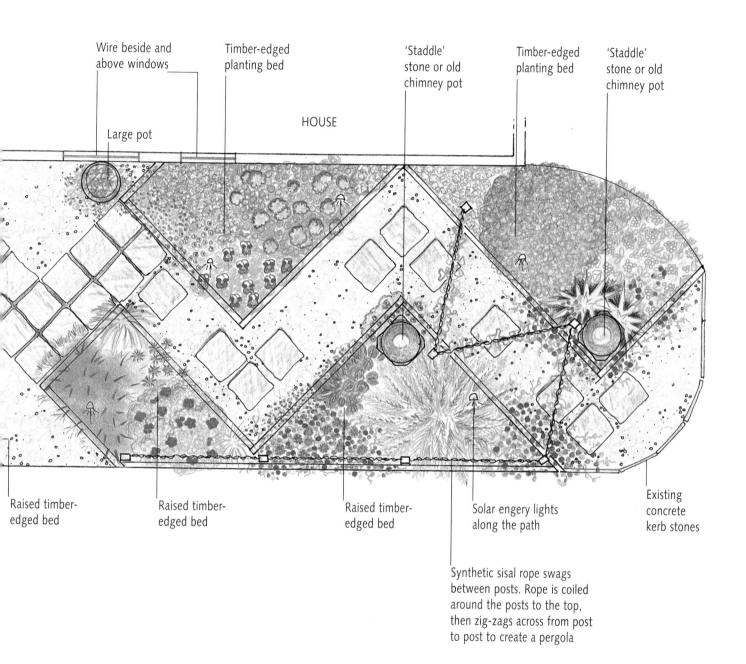

Wire beside and above windows

Timber-edged planting bed

'Staddle' stone or old chimney pot

Timber-edged planting bed

'Staddle' stone or old chimney pot

Large pot

HOUSE

Raised timber-edged bed

Raised timber-edged bed

Raised timber-edged bed

Solar engery lights along the path

Existing concrete kerb stones

Synthetic sisal rope swags between posts. Rope is coiled around the posts to the top, then zig-zags across from post to post to create a pergola

DESIGNER'S PLANTING SCHEME

Key plants

1   *Hebe* x *andersonii* 'Variegata'
2   Lavender, *Lavandula angustifolia* 'Twickel Purple'
3   Rosemary, *Rosmarinus officinalis* 'Miss Jessopp's Upright'
4   Juniper, *Juniperus scopulorum* 'Skyrocket'
5   *Phormium* ssp. *hookeri* 'Cream Delight'
6   *Cistus* x *cyprius*
7   *Fabiana imbricata violacea*
8   Potato vine, *Solanum jasminoides*
9   *Clematis florida* 'Sieboldii'

10 *Yucca filamentosa* 'Variegata'
11 *Skimmia japonica* 'Fructu Albo'
12 *Pittosporum crassifolium* 'Variegatum'

Decorative detail

13 *Pennisetum setaceum* 'Purpureum'
14 *Festuca glauca*
15 *Eryngium variifolium*
16 *Miscanthus sinensis* 'Variegatus'
17 *Viola cornuta*
18 *Bergenia* 'Bressingham White'

Plants for added colour

Pansy, *Viola* x *wittrockiana* 'Cornetto'
Nemophila maculata
Lobelia – in blue and white
Impatiens walleriana Super Elfin Series in violet blue – in shady spots
Cornflower, *Centaurea cyanus* – in blue
Lathyrus 'Snoopea' – trailing over ground

CONSTRUCTION

The cleverly designed zig-zag path of pebbles inset with paving slabs allows the slabs to be laid close together around the front door and main walkway while continuing the theme with less regularly placed slabs along the rest of the path. The pebbles are laid, as are the slabs, on a bed of compacted hardcore to stop weeds from encroaching.

The beds are all outlined with white-painted timber, to continue the clean lines introduced by the path. Along the roadside raised beds provide some privacy and a verdant view from the house. Wire and timber trellis to support climbers has been fixed to the house walls around windows and the doorway.

To divide off the private land from the public routes beyond it white timber posts 1m/39in high with swags of synthetic rope have been introduced.

▲ Tall posts, linked by rope, create a pergola to add interest to the zig-zag pathway and provide a framework for climbing plants

▲ As a finishing touch the end of the rope is curled around the final post and tied at the bottom

Small front garden
PLANTING

This garden is designed to be colourful and interesting around the year, with a basis of evergreen shrubs, many with variegated foliage, that require a minimum of maintenance. Strong summer colour is provided by annuals such as lobelia, cornflowers, sweet peas and busy lizzies. The bright blues, purples, reds and white show up well in the clear coastal light.

KEY PLANTS

▲ The arching leaves of grasses form decorative fountains of green along the pathway. Here the blue-green leaves of *Miscanthus sinensis* (in front) balance the cream-streaked leaves of *M. sinensis* 'Variegatus' (behind).

◄ In specific areas of the pebble-lined path planting spaces have been left to soften the background. Here the grass *Festuca glauca* creates a blue tussock while the golden variegated thyme, *Thymus* 'Aureus' adds sunshine to the surface.

The same idea has been used for the taller posts that make up a pergola at one end. Here the ropes criss-cross above the pathway. They run through large rings fixed to the top or side of each post and wind decoratively around the taller posts where they begin and end their run. This all lends to the sunny, seaside atmosphere which has been deliberately created to match the location.

Solar-powered lights line the pathway to show the route at night. Using stored energy from sunlight these lights avoid the expense of buying and installing electricity cables beneath the surface of the garden, as well as the upheaval this inevitably involves.

◀ *Looking along the length of this unusual and dramatic front garden, the widening effect of the use of diagonal lines can be clearly seen. A similar garden to the original appears beyond it*

▲ An Adam's needle, *Yucca filamentosa* stands sentinel beside the pergola and persuades visitors to follow the pathway to the house.

FOR EXTRA COLOUR

The large bright blue summer flowers of cornflowers, *Centaurea cyanus* stand out against the scarlet poppies behind. Colour mix, as well as height, has been taken into consideration here.

Wildflower meadow seeds, grown in a sunny spot, create a colourful wildflower edge or miniature meadow.

Special effect

Swagged rope makes a very effective alternative to horizontal timber rails and a more unusual option than plastic-coated chain link. When using natural hemp rope buy extra length and soak it well first, then leave to dry. If the rope is fixed without this being done it will almost certainly shrink when it dries out after the first rainstorm and the swagged effect will be lost. Once the rope is fixed unwind the ends and comb them out for a tasselled effect. Bind the rope with twine to stop it unravelling further.

Rope also gives an opportunity to use a wide range of fixings and introduce decorative boat knots and curls, an ideal complement to a seaside garden.

See also:
• *Pergolas page 132*
• *Lighting page 144*

Roof garden

The owner of this roof space is a keen gardener with a country garden out of town and when she took over this apartment, with doors leading out onto the roof, her first thought was to turn the roof to good use as a place to enjoy in summer and to look out on through winter. The space was overlooked from almost every direction, providing no privacy, and, furthermore, an unattractive office block was positioned in the prime spot, spoiling what could otherwise have been a stunning view over the city. Another problem was that the roof is also a fire escape route for neighbouring apartments, so gates would have to be inserted and the escape route kept free.

She enlisted the help of garden designer Sally Court, who set to work to produce a design for a high-level haven. As structural information was lacking and the roof was over a block of garages, any weight was positioned along the edges of the roof and over

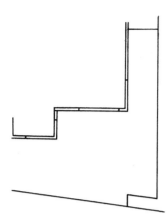

▲ **Before conversion** *this was an empty tarmac roof space which led straight out of double doors from the apartment*

THE GARDEN'S PROBLEMS

The roof space was overlooked in almost every direction by the windows of neighbouring apartments and adjoining buildings.

An ugly view of an adjacent office block.

Weight, which is always a problem in gardens that are above ground level.

Wind is a problem at this height.

HOW THEY WERE SOLVED

Sally used trellis to provide privacy and a decorative background. Wind-tolerant and rampant climbers adorn the trellis for further screening.

At the corner of the roof terrace a deep bed edged by railway sleepers was positioned and in the space a group of trees planted to create a decorative backdrop. A distinctive water feature in the foreground and the staggered planting all help to eclipse the view beyond.

Weight was kept to a minimum, with most plants being grown in light-weight pots. Timber decking was chosen for the ground surface as it is much lighter than paving slabs.

Choice of plants that are wind tolerant is vital for most roof gardens or balconies, which are usually subject to high winds. Evergreens were picked to provide privacy and these are regularly trimmed back to keep them small. Other shrubs have been selected for their natural low-level shapes.

▼ **The planting scheme** *includes a good evergreen backdrop. Other plants are used for their interesting sculptural shape or their vibrant seasonal colour*

DESIGNER'S PLANTING SCHEME

Key plants

1 *Abelia* x *grandiflora*
2 Himalyan birch, *Betula utilis* var. *jacquemontii*
3 *Camellia* 'Nobilissima'
4 Creeping ceanothus, *Ceanothus thrysiflorus* var. *repens*
5 *Convolvulus cneorum*
6 *Elaeagnus* x *ebbingei* 'Limelight'
7 Myrtle, *Myrtus communis* ssp. *tarentina*
8 Chusan palm, *Trachycarpus fortunei*
9 Juniper, *Juniperus* x *pfitzeriana* 'Mint Julep'
10 Juniper, *Juniperus squamata* 'Blue Carpet'

Decorative details

11 *Acer palmatum* var. *dissectum*
12 *Acer palmatum* 'Crimson Queen'
13 *Buddleia davidii* 'Black Knight'
14 Dogwood, *Cornus* 'Eddie's White Wonder'
15 *Viburnum farreri*
16 *Clematis* 'The President'
17 Climbing hydrangea, *Hydrangea petiolaris*
18 *Jasminum* x *stephanense*
19 *Passiflora caerulea*
20 Star jasmine, *Trachelospermum jasminoides*

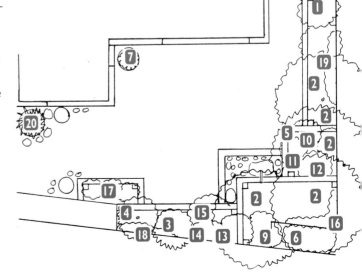

the main structural walls. The roof area was flat and therefore rather uninteresting so Sally decided to use raised beds and form a corner plant grouping so that the tallest shrubs and trees would form the centrepiece and help to mask the office block nearby.

She included a water feature, and fixed trellis along the roof's edges to help to cut down on the force of the wind and provide screening.

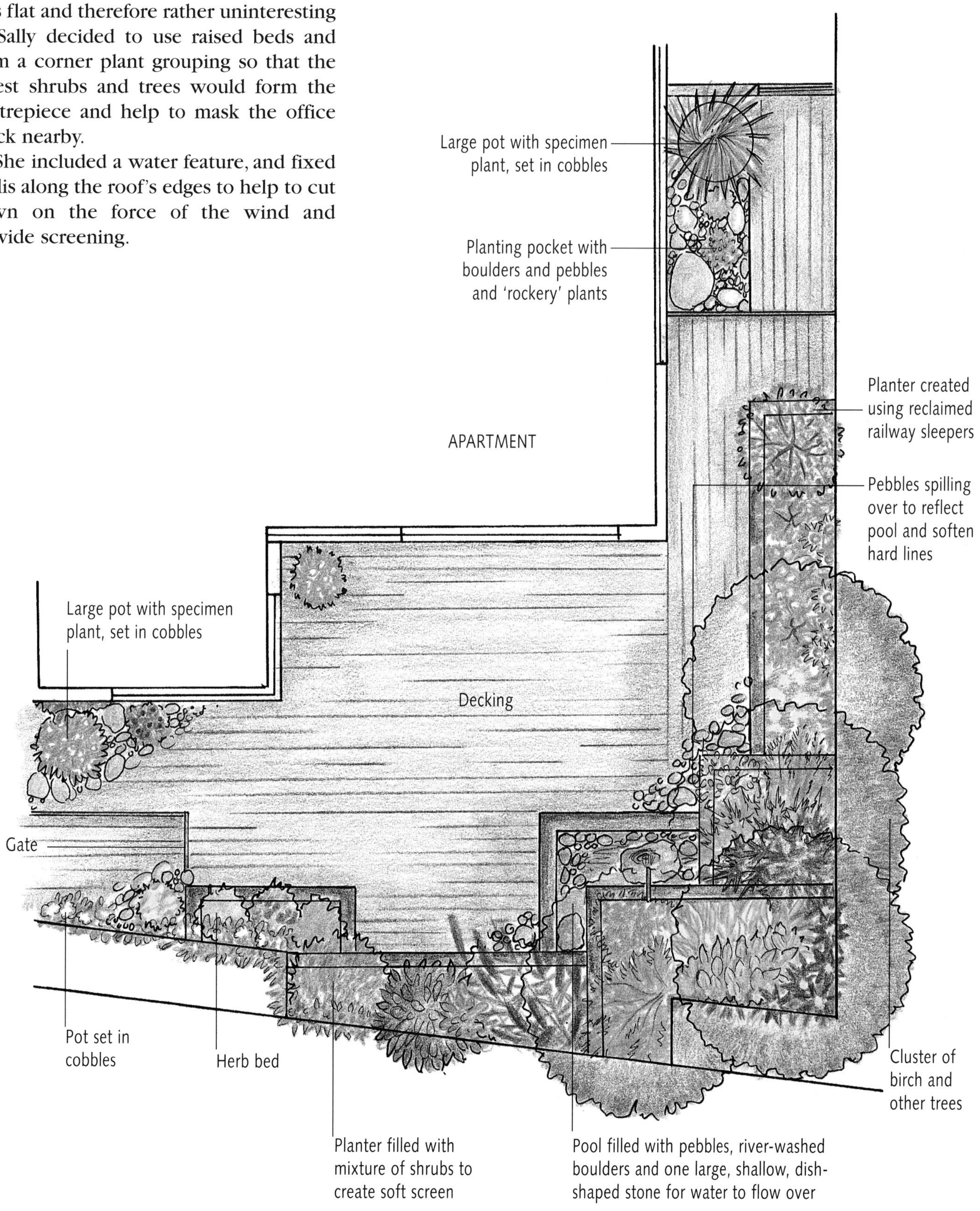

Large pot with specimen plant, set in cobbles

Planting pocket with boulders and pebbles and 'rockery' plants

Planter created using reclaimed railway sleepers

Pebbles spilling over to reflect pool and soften hard lines

APARTMENT

Large pot with specimen plant, set in cobbles

Decking

Gate

Pot set in cobbles

Herb bed

Planter filled with mixture of shrubs to create soft screen

Pool filled with pebbles, river-washed boulders and one large, shallow, dish-shaped stone for water to flow over

Cluster of birch and other trees

▲ *View of the corner of the roof garden showing the plants in the raised beds. Containers add colour and pebbles provide natural sculptures*

Roof garden
CONSTRUCTION

Sally picked natural honey-coloured pressure-treated New Zealand pine for the decking as it is light but tough and has a special grooved non-slip surface. The diamond-shaped trellis she uses as a screen is of a similar colouring to the flooring and looks so decorative that even the unadorned areas create an attractive backdrop.

Raised beds are built of railway sleepers and assembled at a range of heights so that, together with the climbers that clothe the trellis, a waterfall of planting has been created as viewed from the terrace. Light-weight containers have been chosen in a wide range of sizes and these are arranged in groups to complete the lush planting effect.

The pond is sited in the corner of the roof space and backed by the highest planting area. It is deliberately shallow to

See also:
- *Plants for wind, page 188*
- *Walls and screens, page 120*

Roof garden
PLANTING

Each plant picked for inclusion in this garden had to fulfil many requirements so that a minimum of planting would produce a maximum effect. Those growing in the beds provide a round-the-year backdrop, while most of the colourful seasonal planting is grown in pots that are easily removed and replaced with the next season's arrangements.

KEY PLANTS

▲ The passion flower, *Passiflora caerulea*, is a fast-growing climber which can grow up to 9m/30ft or even more. Towards the end of summer it produces large white flowers, sometimes tinged with pink, that have centres of a deep purple-blue. The flowers are followed by edible, orange-tinted, yellow fruit.

◀ Grasses and sedges take to life in a container surprisingly well and the leaves stand up to windy conditions. Here, a group of pebbles is an attractive complementary feature.

◄ *The pond, created within a framework of railway sleepers and lined with a flexible liner, is fed from above by a simple brass pipe fountain so that the water is always in movement*

▼ *A view along the roof terrace shows the step which leads to one of the small gates of the fire escape route*

keep down the weight but pebbles in a range of sizes make it visually interesting at all times of the year.

Finally the owner uses an automatic watering system operated by a timer switch so that at home or away the plants are always cared for.

▲ The highly coloured autumn leaves of Japanese maple, *Acer palmatum*, are equally attractive when they fall. For a roof garden or balcony it is wise to choose low-growing varieties such as *A. palmatum* var. *dissectum*.

FOR EXTRA COLOUR

Petunias are ideal pot plants to add extra summer colour wherever it is needed. They are easy to grow, reward you with a long flowering season, and come in almost every colour imaginable and in both upright and trailing varieties.

Grow petunias in light, well-drained soil in full sun. They need some protection from wind and are here placed in pots in positions protected by larger shrubs.

Grandiflora petunias are the ones with very large flowers; multiflora petunias are bushier with smaller flowers and are more tolerant of wet weather.

Special effect

Decorative trellis-work With the wide range of shapes now available, trellis need no longer be used only as a straight strip along the top of a fence to give additional height. It is simple to put together a design that creates a very attractive backdrop, whether clothed in climbers or deliberately left free of foliage.

Pre-constructed arches and arbours are also available and it is relatively easy to put together a pergola using a range of shapes and heights. Here the trellis boundary around the roof space consists of straight panels that have been topped with a stylish scalloped edge, while each post is finished with an ornate finial.

Trellis, square- or diamond-shaped, takes paint and wood stain well and is simple to customize for an original look. In the garden on pages 24-27 designer Paul Cooper has filled in some of the spaces in square trellis with plywood and painted these with a chequerboard effect to produce a modern alternative.

CHAPTER 3

DESIGNS FOR PROBLEM POSITIONS

Many gardens have a specific and overriding problem which has to be addressed as a major part of the design. With careful planning and the right planting, however, most problems can be considerably reduced or even eliminated.

Here our designers tackled six gardens, each with a commonly found but troublesome difficulty, and these have now been transformed into exciting and highly original outdoor spaces.

Garden on a new site

This garden, built on the site of what was previously a hotel car park, is long, narrow and sloping. The builders had produced long, thin beds along either side, and paths that followed the line of the beds with a further path crossing on the diagonal to join up the two independent routes. The result was an already long and thin area of ground which had been made to appear even longer and thinner. The owner, a keen gardener, wanted space to grow a wide range of plants and wished to concentrate on those with scent. She also wanted the length to be divided up so that the end of the garden was not immediately visible from the house at the top, and to end up with a design that would make the garden appear shorter and wider.

She turned to designer Antony Henn to solve the garden's problems. He started by shaping the lawn, already there, to form a long, lake-like outline that narrowed about one-third of the way down. This meant

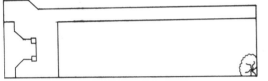

◀ **Before conversion** *the garden, created by the builders of the house, comprised lawn with a narrow bed and paths running along either side*

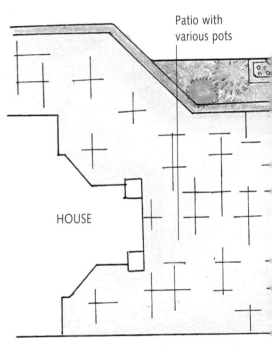

Patio with various pots

HOUSE

▲ **The planting scheme** *introduces a number of trees and shrubs for* *round-the-year interest, herbs and a range of scented plants*

THE GARDEN'S PROBLEMS

A downward slope away from the house.

The narrowness of the garden, which was emphasized by the shape and position of the present beds and lawn.

The flower bed was built over a previous car park and had a very shallow layer of topsoil so that nothing grew well.

HOW THEY WERE SOLVED

The lawn was allowed to slope but the terrace and arbour on the left were built on top of a flat platform and some beds were built up.

By curving the lawn and beds on either side the shape appears immediately much more interesting. The arbour to one side and square trellis to the other, where the lawn narrows part way down the garden, creates a division which breaks up the length.

Rather than endeavour to remove the tarmac, the bed on this side has been raised by 60cm/24in with more topsoil and well-rotted manure to provide the depth of soil that larger plants will require.

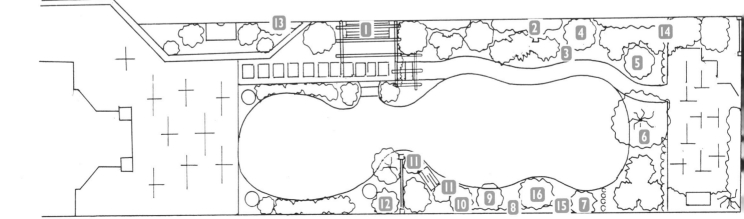

that, with the addition of strategically placed trellis and climbers, parts of the lower section of the garden would be out of view from the top end. However, a hint of what followed would appear through the narrow width of lawn in the centre.

On the left-hand side, where the lawn narrows, and which receives sun for most of the day, he introduced an arbour so that from here both the top and lower ends of the garden could be viewed simultaneously.

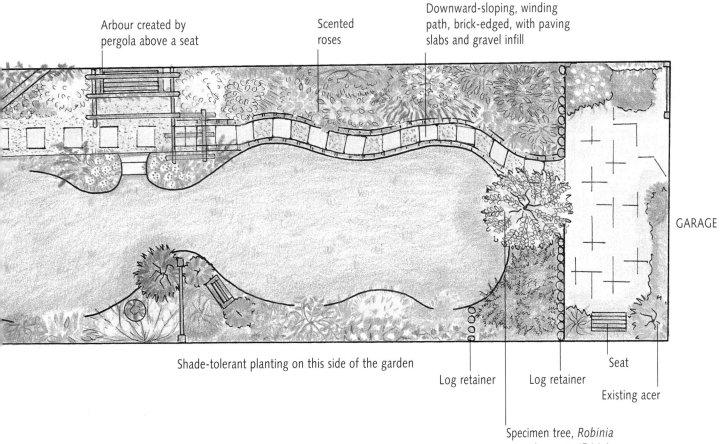

Arbour created by pergola above a seat

Scented roses

Downward-sloping, winding path, brick-edged, with paving slabs and gravel infill

GARAGE

Shade-tolerant planting on this side of the garden

Log retainer

Log retainer

Seat

Existing acer

Specimen tree, *Robinia psuedoacacia* 'Frisia'

DESIGNER'S PLANTING SCHEME

Key plants

1   *Wisteria sinensis* – over arbour
2   *Ceanothus* 'Concha'
3   French lavender, *Lavandula stoechas*
4   *Pittosporum tenuifolium* 'Silver Queen'
5   *Photinia* x *fraseri* 'Red Robin'
6   False acacia, *Robinia pseudoacacia* 'Frisia'
7   *Potentilla* 'Princess'
8   Climbing hydrangea, *Hydrangea petiolaris* – on fence
9   *Cotoneaster lacteus*

10   Sweet box, *Sarcococca confusa*
11   *Skimmia japonica* 'Rubella'
12   *Kerria japonica*

Decorative detail

13   *Clematis* 'Jackmanii'
14   Winter-flowering jasmine, *Jasminum nudiflorum*
15   Scarlet trumpet honeysuckle, *Lonicera* x *brownii* 'Dropmore Scarlet'
16   Spanish broom, *Spartium junceum*

Plants for fragrance

Daphne x *burkwoodii* 'Somerset'
Lonicera fragrantissima
Mock orange, *Philadelphus coronarius* 'Aureus'
Jasmine, *Jasminum* x *stephanense*
Scented roses including, climbers, *Rosa* 'New Dawn' and 'Compassion' plus 'Octavia Hill', Graham Thomas, and patio rose 'Rosy Future'

Garden on a new site
CONSTRUCTION

Once the lawn had been reshaped with an undulating edge, the main area of construction was on the left-hand side. Here, part way down the length and over a base of hardcore covered in paving, a pergola was constructed over a seat to form the arbour. A curving path, edged in bricks and of gravel over hardcore has paving stepping stones let into it and runs down the side of the lawn.

At the end of the garden a narrow paved path has been widened to create a larger terrace and working area and this is screened by trellis. In front of the lower terrace, on the opposite side, upended logs form a retaining wall for a flat bed which is built up above the paving. The planting, which includes a specimen *Robinia frisia*, helps to hide the wall of the garage from the house and to provide privacy for the terrace itself.

▲ *Looking up the garden towards the house, showing the curving path on the right leading to the arbour*

Garden on a new site
PLANTING

The owner of this garden wanted scented flowers. These include *Lonicera fragrantissima* with its creamy white flowers in winter and early spring, followed by *Daphne* x *burkwoodii* 'Somerset' with its purple-pink flowers and heady fragrance. *Philadelphus* 'Manteau d'Hermine' flowers in early summer, then roses and herbs take over.

See also:
- *Long, narrow garden, page 28*
- *Arbours, page 132*
- *Plants for moist shade, page 184*
- *Plants for full sun, page 186*

KEY PLANTS

▲ For winter interest evergreen shrubs with variegated foliage come into their own. The leaves of *Pittosporum tenuifolium* 'Silver Queen' have silvery white marbling.

◀ Using shrubs with brightly coloured berries adds autumn and winter colour. *Cotoneaster lacteus* has evergreen leaves that are dark on the topside, lighter underneath, and produces clumps of brilliant orange-red berries which remain through winter. These follow clusters of small white flowers that appear in summer.

◄ *The view from upstairs shows the soft shape of the lawn and path. A neighbouring garden hints at the design of the original garden*

The garden originally contained very poor soil. It also has extremes of temperature, one side being very sunny and the other cold and shady. The condition of the soil has been improved with the addition of plenty of well-rotted horse manure and this also helps to retain moisture in the soil on the sunny side and improve drainage on the cold and shady side of the garden.

▲ *The seat in the arbour, with a white-flowered cistus in the foreground. Steps lead onto the lawn in one direction while others follow the downward path*

▲ Ceanothus can be grown as a tree or shrub, or used to clothe a fence. *Ceanothus* 'Dark Star', shown, forms an arching shape and has scented, dark purple flowers. *Ceanothus* 'Concha' is denser, with deep blue flowers.

FOR EXTRA COLOUR

Wildlife can introduce colour as well as flowers. Here *Lavandula angustifolia* 'Bowles' Early' is shown with painted lady butterflies. Many of the herbs grown in this garden, amongst which are lovage, angelica, marjoram, mints, lemon balm, fennel, rosemary, borage, thyme and sage, will also attract butterflies.

To attract a particular species of butterfly include plants the larvae need, as well as those that attract the adult.

Special effect

Grouping pots is an ideal way of providing a bank of colour at any point in the garden where it is temporarily lacking. In most cases pots in a range of sizes and shapes, but all of the same material, look most effective. Natural materials like pebbles, driftwood, shells and cones provide interesting detail.

Shady spot

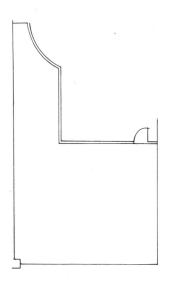

The existing small front garden in this shady spot had been destroyed when the house, suffering from subsidence, had to be underpinned so designer Sally Court had an almost free hand in its design.

Tall fences on either side, as well as trees that line the roadside, add to the shady aspect of this small space so this was an important factor that had to be considered in the new design. The owners also wanted to keep a snake-bark maple, *Acer capillipes*, that was already there and to retain the crazy-paving car parking space at the side of the house. This meant that the ground surface chosen for the garden had to blend with this. Sally opted for bricks, in tones to complement those of the house as well as the crazy paving, and used them to create a hexagonal terrace featuring an ornamental urn as its centrepoint.

▲ **Before conversion** *the garden had been all but removed while necessary remedial work was done on the house*

▼ **The planting scheme** *was designed to provide interest around the year and to create a colourful spring garden*

THE GARDEN'S PROBLEMS

The owners are away from home a lot of the time so they required a low-maintenance garden.

The garden is shady and dry because nearby large trees draw up almost all the moisture.

The design needed to blend in with the present car-parking area.

The area is tiny, with a very narrow planting space.

HOW THEY WERE SOLVED

Sally recommended the use of paving instead of grass and used mainly shrubs and bulbs for the planting. She also suggested they include an automatic irrigation system that could be programmed to come on and go off at regular times at the end of each day. Bark mulch is used on the beds to help retain moisture.

Both the irrigation system and the bark mulch help to alleviate this problem. Plants were chosen that could cope with the lack of sunlight and dry conditions.

Warmly coloured bricks were chosen and laid in a herringbone pattern, based on an Arran knitwear design to complement the owner's hobby. The colour of the bricks blends with the crazy-paving and marries house and garden.

By forming the design around a hexagon, space was created for deeper beds near to the house and opposite, to provide a view from within the house. The use of small-sized paving units also creates a spacious feel for the area.

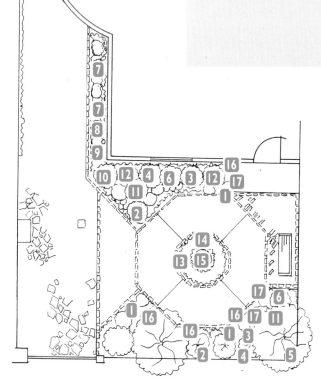

DESIGNER'S PLANTING SCHEME

Key plants

1 Rhododendron 'Everest'
2 Acer palmatum var. dissectum
3 Rhododendron 'Golden Sunset'
4 Rhododendron luteum
5 Cornus kousa var. chinensis
6 Rhododendron 'Gibraltar'
7 Euonymus fortunei 'Emerald Gaiety'
8 Scarlet trumpet honeysuckle, Lonicera x brownii 'Dropmore Scarlet'
9 Hydrangea petiolaris
10 Rhododendron 'Bluebird Group'
11 Rhododendron 'Narcissiflorum'
12 Yew, Taxus baccata 'Fastigiata'

Decorative detail

13 *Saxifraga paniculata* var. *baldensis* – in urn
14 *Sedum spathulifolium* 'Purpureum' – in urn
15 Houseleeks, *Sempervivums* – in urn
16 *Hosta* 'Royal Standard'
17 Evergreen fern, *Polypodium vulgare*

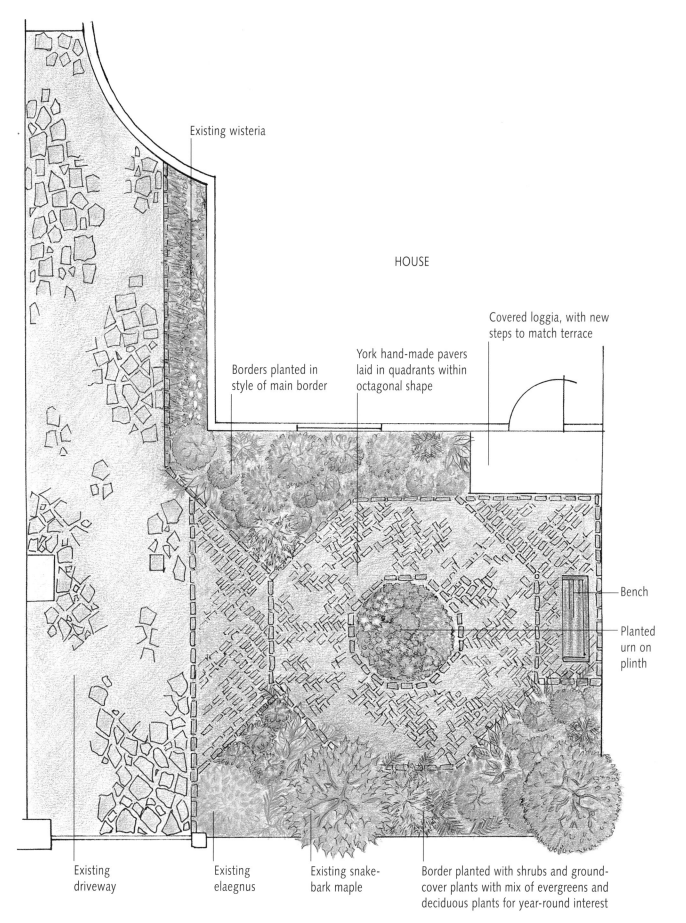

Existing wisteria

HOUSE

Covered loggia, with new
steps to match terrace

Borders planted in
style of main border

York hand-made pavers
laid in quadrants within
octagonal shape

Bench

Planted
urn on
plinth

Existing
driveway

Existing
elaegnus

Existing snake-
bark maple

Border planted with shrubs and ground-
cover plants with mix of evergreens and
deciduous plants for year-round interest

Shady spot
CONSTRUCTION

As this is a very small plot bricks were chosen for the main area of ground surface, the small-sized units being in scale with the setting. At the centre of the design stands a large ornamental stone urn and this in turn is placed in the centre of a brick hexagon that is divided into four separate sections of herring-bone laid bricks, each section outlined with a line of bricks laid straight.

A bench, that blends both in style and materials with the urn, looks into the garden and this is positioned outside the front door where it can take advantage of the small amount of sun that reaches this garden. On the opposite side of the hexagon the bricks continue as part of a further hexagon to meet the crazy paving of the car-parking area. The fences, which were already in place, provide some privacy.

▲ The centrepoint of the garden is a stone urn that also marks the centre of the hexagonal brick terrace. Planting in the urn is deliberately kept low so that the container itself forms the highlight

See also:
• Paved town garden, page 36
• Plants for dry shade, page 185

Shady spot
PLANTING

There are two main planting areas and the plants Sally has chosen are designed to reflect those found along a woodland edge. They include azaleas, rhododendrons, ferns and hostas. Both deciduous and evergreen azaleas are included and the deciduous species provide good autumn colour. Bulbs add a strong splash of extra colour in spring.

KEY PLANTS

▲ Sally created a low planting for the large urn in the centre of the garden. Here the cobweb houseleek, *Sempervivum arachnoideum* has been included with its rosettes of green and red leaves laced with a fine covering of white hairs that look as if covered by cobwebs.

◄ The hosta, 'Frosted Jade' is a good choice for a shady spot with its white-edged, strongly veined leaves. The almost white flowers tinged with a pinky lilac appear in early summer. Here a deep layer of mulch helps to conserve moisture.

◀ *Brick-like pavers divide up a large area of paving, adding extra interest to the expanse. They can also be laid to form a pattern in the centre, or to highlight the position of a sculpture, urn or bird bath*

1 Wavy-edge paving is used here and forms an alternative to bricks laid side-by-side. The blocks are laid in a simple side-by-side pattern so that each block fits snugly into the next

2 Herring-bone is the traditional method of laying bricks, or in this case pavers with an antiqued finish. Similar pavers are available that are suitable for a car parking area

3 This is an unusually shaped paver that mixes colours and tones and offers the chance to form a wide range of patterns

4 By mixing gravel and pavers a far wider range of patterns can be created, as here where a series of swirling circles is formed out of wedge-shaped pavers interspersed with gravel. These circles are duplicated again in the shapes of the pots which add a colourful display on the terrace

5 This tinted concrete material, impressed when wet with rubber mats to simulate cobbles, setts or paving, is tough enough to be used for a driveway and comes in a wide range of colours

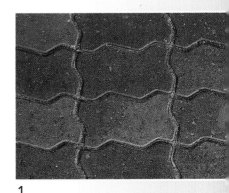

1

2

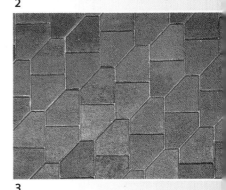

3

4

5

Special effect

Patterns with pavers and bricks This paving has many uses, from a patterned area in the centre of a terrace of larger paving, to a country look for a patio or car-parking area. By using different colours or laying the bricks in a range of patterns more effects can be created. Here five alternative ways of using small-sized paving units show some of the patterns possible.

FOR EXTRA COLOUR

For good ground cover include *Persicaria campanulata* which can grow to around 90cm/36in with a similar spread and tolerates light shade. This is a clump-forming semi-evergreen perennial that has hairy mid-green leaves which are lighter underneath. On the tall stems bell-shaped fragrant pink or white flowers (the variety 'Southcombe White' has white flowers) appear in clusters from mid-summer through to early autumn.

▲ This deciduous azalea, *Rhododendron luteum* has trusses of yellow funnel-shaped flowers that open in late spring to early summer and are strongly scented. Many deciduous azaleas provide colourful autumn hues before the leaves fall.

Windy location

This garden, on the side of a hill and not far from the sea, has good views of hills beyond but has two major disadvantages. It is exposed and windy and it is overlooked by a number of neighbouring houses.

Designer Jean Goldberry, whose garden it is, used an ingenious method of dealing with both these problems. By extending the fence with an uneven, undulating top edge she could hide views that were unattractive and highlight those she wanted to enjoy. Because the fence is not solid in its composition it also reduces the strength of the wind.

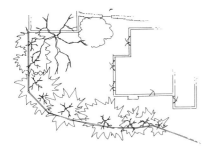

▲ **Before conversion** *the garden had as a boundary a picket fence and a row of Leylandii which had grown to 12m/40ft tall. Although these hid neighbouring houses the hedge in particular also obscured the attractive views*

THE GARDEN'S PROBLEMS

A view of a derelict garage on one side of the garden.

The garden was overlooked but also had a beautiful view of hills beyond the houses.

The garden had no surface of topsoil so was unsuitable for growing a wide range of plants.

HOW THEY WERE SOLVED

A large mirror was positioned at the end of the rectangular water feature. It not only helps to obscure the unattractive garage wall but doubles the apparent size of the pool.

By adding height to the fence and creating a wavy edge to the top, areas where the garden was overlooked could be hidden, while low scallops show off the views.

The first job was to obtain loads of well-rotted farmyard manure and recycled garden waste compost from the local authority and dig this in to entice worms and the necessary bacteria for plant growth to return.

Undulating line 'paddle' stone path edging

N, S, E and W symbols in Celtic script on metal plates screwed to tree sections. Circle of 'paddle' stones (water-worn flat rocks or slates) and timber block seats, each quarter section inlaid with a spiral of pebbles, marbles and glass 'dragon drops'

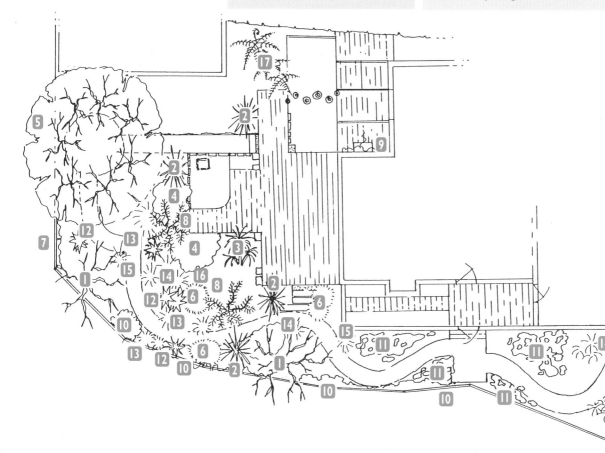

◄ **The planting scheme** *was designed to provide winter interest and was based on small-leaved plants that could withstand the wind*

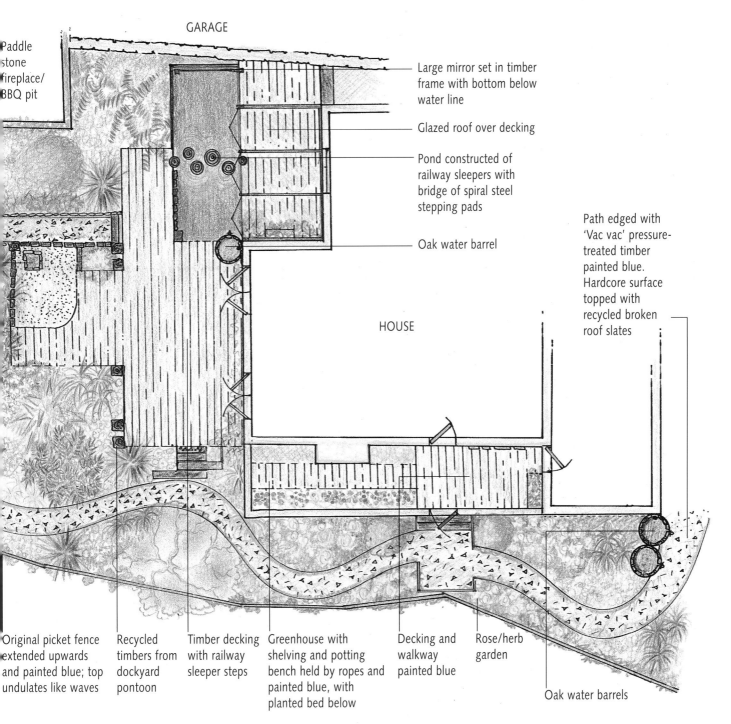

GARAGE

Paddle stone fireplace/ BBQ pit

Large mirror set in timber frame with bottom below water line

Glazed roof over decking

Pond constructed of railway sleepers with bridge of spiral steel stepping pads

Oak water barrel

Path edged with 'Vac vac' pressure-treated timber painted blue. Hardcore surface topped with recycled broken roof slates

HOUSE

Original picket fence extended upwards and painted blue; top undulates like waves

Recycled timbers from dockyard pontoon

Timber decking with railway sleeper steps

Greenhouse with shelving and potting bench held by ropes and painted blue, with planted bed below

Decking and walkway painted blue

Rose/herb garden

Oak water barrels

DESIGNER'S PLANTING SCHEME

Key plants

1 *Eucalyptus kybeanensis*
2 New Zealand Flax, *Phormium tenax*
3 Cabbage palm, *Cordyline australis*
4 Rock rose, *Cistus* x *corbariensis*
5 *Acer campestre* 'Schwerinii'
6 Cotton lavender, *Santolina chamaecyparissus*
7 Italian buckthorn, *Rhamnus alaternus* 'Argenteovariegata'
8 *Pinus mugo* var. *pumilio*
9 *Clematis* 'Venosa Violacea'

10 *Rosa* Molineux
11 Daisy bush, *Olearia traversii*
12 *Yucca filamentosa*

Decorative detail

13 Sedge, *Carex* 'Frosted Curls'
14 Sedge, *Carex flagellifera*
15 Pheasant's tail grass, *Stipa arundinacea*
16 Sundrops, *Oenothera fruticosa*
17 Soft tree fern, *Dicksonia antarctica*

Plants for added colour

California poppy, *Eschscholtzia*
Poppy, *Papaver rhoeas* Shirley Series
Mignonette, *Reseda odorata*
Livingstone daisy, *Dorotheanthus* 'Lunette' syn. 'Yellow Ice'
Alyssum 'Apricot Tapestry'
Statice, *Limonium* 'Pastel Mixed'

▼ *Brightly coloured barnacled buoys create a group sculpture on the veranda and help to give this garden a strong nautical theme*

▲ *Slipped in behind the steps that lead off the decking platform are slits containing broken roof slates randomly spattered with mussel shells and dotted with a range of magenta pink flowers*

See also:
- *Narrow front garden, page 40*
- *Plants for wind and poor soil, page 188*
- *Introducing water, page 126*

Windy location
CONSTRUCTION

Jean loves music-making and dancing and for this reason she chose to have a large area of decking in the centre of her garden with plenty of room to dance. She used southern yellow pine which had been 'Vac vac' pressure treated – a clear preservative, harmless to wildlife. The decking is non-slip when wet. Paths are edged with timber, painted blue to match the fence, or water-shaped flat stones and are made of compacted hardcore topped with re-cycled broken roof slate. Steps are constructed of railway sleepers covered with chicken wire to stop them from becoming slippery in wet weather.

A rectangular pool leads off a decking-floored veranda with a glazed roof just off the house. This is a box made of railway sleepers with a rubber liner. A mirror, cleverly positioned at one end from ceiling to below water level,

Windy location
PLANTING

The scheme was based on hot orange, brown and silver to complement the blues of the fence and pergola. Jean wanted a Mediterranean seaside look and a good winter structure. *Acer campestre* 'Schwerinii', with red-purple young leaves, were chosen to surround the Celtic circle; sedges, a tall soft tree fern, and pheasant's tail grass provide the exotic effect.

KEY PLANTS

▲ In late spring and early summer the decorative single creamy yellow flowers of X *Halimiocistus wintonensis* 'Merrist Wood Cream' open to display their beautiful bright yellow and maroon throat markings.

◀ The pale yellow-green curling evergreen leaves of the sedge *Carex* 'Frosted Curls' form waterfalls to tumble decoratively over the blue-painted timber-edged path. The sedge, *Carex flagellifera* is similar in appearance but has rusty orange leaves.

◀ *Steel spirals form stepping stones for the pond*

▼ *An undulating top to the fence obscures neighbouring houses and helps to break the wind*

doubles the apparent size. It is fixed to a backing of ply to protect the silvering and the glass is made water resistant by painting with glass fibre.

The picket fence, with its wavy top edge, cleverly reduces the velocity of the wind, unlike a solid wall or fence.

▲ *Pontoon timbers, rope and anchor continue the strong nautical theme*

FOR EXTRA COLOUR

A packet of seeds costs little to purchase and can provide a wonderful splash of colour when sown as a group display. Sow the seeds of poppies in spring in full sun and in fertile, well-drained soil and they will be in flower by summer. Flowers of many poppies then produce decorative large seed pods, allowing you to save the seeds for another year. This is the field poppy, *Papaver rhoeas* from the Shirley Series, the flowers of which come in single, semi-double and double flowers in yellow, pink, and orange, as well as red.

Special effect

Stepping across water For walking across the water stepping stones create a less obvious alternative to bridges. Here Jean has created spirals of steel to form the stepping stones, shown before being lowered into place. Paving slabs are another option. Using granite setts, with spaces between for the water to flow around them can create a similar effect.

▲ The strong, structural shape of this Adam's needle, *Yucca filamentosa*, provides a round-the year view from the house.

Overlooked garden

Designer Jean Goldberry uses a range of heights and clever divisions along the garden's length to break up the space in an interesting way, and to create the privacy that the owners longed for. She took advantage of a mature *Amelanchier canadensis* at the end of the garden to create a miniature woodland area with tree-trunk stepping stones and a seat of timber planks. A series of paved terraces breaks up the garden's length and groups of larger pebbles add a scuptural effect. There are raised timber-edged beds and two ponds.

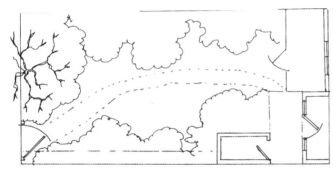

◄ **Before conversion** *the garden comprised very overgrown shrubs on either side with grass down the centre, over which a worn-away path led to the back gate*

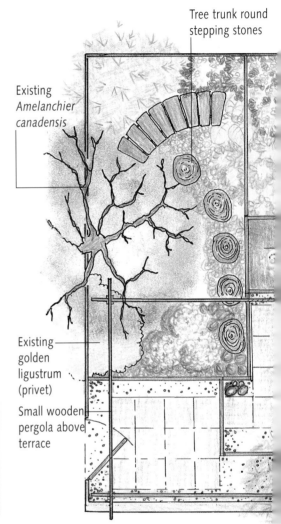

Tree trunk round stepping stones

Existing *Amelanchier canadensis*

Existing golden ligustrum (privet)

Small wooden pergola above terrace

THE GARDEN'S PROBLEMS

The original garden, with shrubs along the edge and a path down the centre, seemed very long and narrow.

Buildings on the right-hand side had a clear view of most of the garden, allowing those in the garden very little privacy.

A plain, rectangular space which was all on one level meant the garden lacked interest.

HOW THEY WERE SOLVED

Paving laid in squares and rectangles of different sizes breaks up the length by providing a series of garden rooms.

Pergolas are used to hide the garden from overlooking windows and create interest and views from the house.

The level was dropped in the centre, with steps down. Raised beds of different heights provide a series of tiers.

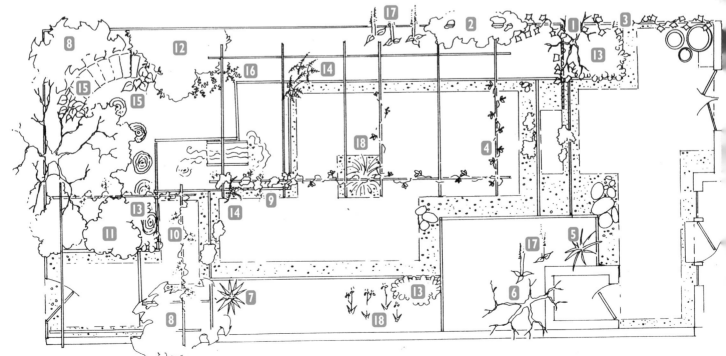

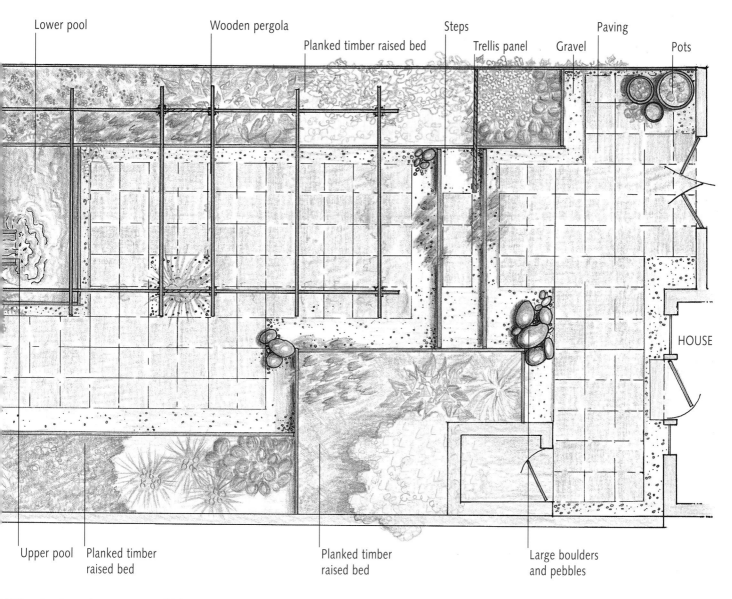

Lower pool

Wooden pergola

Planked timber raised bed

Steps

Trellis panel

Gravel

Paving

Pots

HOUSE

Upper pool

Planked timber raised bed

Planked timber raised bed

Large boulders and pebbles

◄ **The planting scheme** *uses cool blues
and white in the main, with some rose pink
to provide definition and some golden and
cream-variegated foliage*

DESIGNER'S PLANTING SCHEME

Key plants

Eucryphia milliganii

Rhamnus alaternus 'Argenteovariegata'

Vine, Vitis coignetiae

Golden hop, Humulus lupulus 'Aureus'

Mountain flax, Phormium cookianum ssp.
hookeri 'Cream Delight'

Cytisus battandieri

Yucca gloriosa

Phyllostachys aureosulcata 'Aureocaulis'

Clematis armandii

10 Jasminum officinalis 'Aureomarginata'

11 Daphne odora 'Aureomarginata'

12 Rhododendron 'Cilpinense'

Decorative detail

13 Bergenia cordifolia

14 Lady fern, Athyrium filix-femina

15 Hosta 'Sum and Substance'

16 Euphorbia robbiae

17 Foxglove, Digitalis grandiflora

18 Iris sibirica 'Flight of Blue Butterflies'

Plants for added colour

Morning Glory, Ipomoea tricolor 'Heavenly Blue'

Busy lizzies and balsams, Impatiens – in white
where spaces available

Wishbone flower, Torenia fournieri

Bells of Ireland, Molluccella laevis

Tobacco plant, Nicotiana Nicki Series – in white in
sunny patches

CONSTRUCTION

A certain amount of initial work was needed to transform this garden and produce the privacy required by the owners. First of all a range of levels was created along the length of the garden. Once these were constructed, paving was laid, with shallow steps edged in timber leading from one level to the next. Although the change of levels is only slight, this divides the garden into three separate sections and immediately makes it appear much more interesting.

Matching timber was used to frame the raised beds, with those in the central sunken area being three planks high and the one nearest to the house, on the left, slightly higher.

The pools are also on different levels so that water from the back pool cascades into the lower front pool then recirculates. Positioned directly opposite

▲ *The view from the central section of the garden, looking up the steps towards the back gate with the pergola posts just in the picture and the water feature out of sight on the right*

PLANTING

S ummer colour abounds in this garden but winter interest is not ignored. This appears in variegated foliage and in the exotic golden stemmed bamboo, *Phyllostachys aureosculcata* 'Aureocaulis'. Pink is introduced in late winter with the pale pink rhododendron 'Cilpinense' and in spring with the variegated *Daphne odora* 'Aureomarginata'.

See also:
• Introducing water, page 126

KEY PLANTS

▲ The decorative lemon yellow and pineapple-scented flowers of pineapple broom, *Cytisus battandieri*, which appear in mid- and late summer. Silvery green leaves form a sparkling background to the cone-shaped flowers.

◄ *Euonymus fortunei* provides winter colour in both its gold- and silver-variegated leaf varieties. *E. fortunei* 'Silver Queen' has bold white margins to the leaves and can also be grown as a climber. *E. fortunei* 'Emerald'n'Gold is bushy with sunny, yellow-margined leaves.

the steps that lead down from the terrace next to the house, the water feature creates a decorative picture from indoors, whatever the time of year. The long pergola that runs most of the length of the central section of the garden also provides interest from the house.

At the end of the garden a soft path of wood chippings is interspersed with stepping-stones made of sliced tree-trunks. These have been covered with wire netting to ensure they remain non-slip, an important consideration.

▲ *Looking from the terrace near to the house down the steps into the sunken garden. A vine (deciduous) and evergreen plants cover the roof of the larger pergola and create a green and private space*

▶ *Together with the fountain in the front pond the cascading water from the higher pool adds the soothing sound of moving water*

▲ *The water feature has a channel that takes the water down from the higher pool into the larger, lower one*

FOR EXTRA COLOUR

Flowering plants in pots add colour to any area in the garden where it is temporarily lacking. The plants can remain in a secluded spot until they reach their peak, and can then be moved into position when they can take pride of place. Most plants will cope with less than ideal conditions for a short time.

Conservatories can be too hot and dry for many plants in summer, but at this time the plants flourish outdoors to be brought back indoors when the cooler weather returns. In most areas this hydrangea could be wintered outside.

▲ The large leaves of this vine, *Vitis coignetiae* 'Incana' soon cover the expanse of pergola and provide dappled green shade and privacy during the months of summer.

Special effects

Natural sculpture In this garden groups of pebbles form simple but striking natural sculptures very much in keeping with the gravel edging that divides one area of paving from the next. Many other natural materials can be used equally successfully in this way. Shells or driftwood can be used to add character to a seaside garden. Tree stumps, cones and logs enhance a woodland area.

Concrete yard

F̶ew outdoor areas are less inspiring to look at, and more daunting to transform, than a concrete backyard. Rather than removing the surface designer Jean Goldberry has built on top of it, using a series of beds stepped up away from the house. A pergola and trellis allow for vertical planting and a raised pond adds a calming influence.

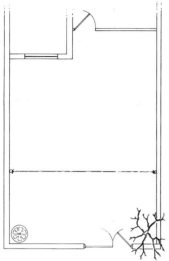

◀ **Before conversion** *the yard contained little more than its solid grey base, with a narrow bed down one side and a lilac tree at the end*

▼ **The planting scheme** *includes evergreens with leaves tinted in cream, gold and red, as well as other plants in striking shapes for round-the-year interest*

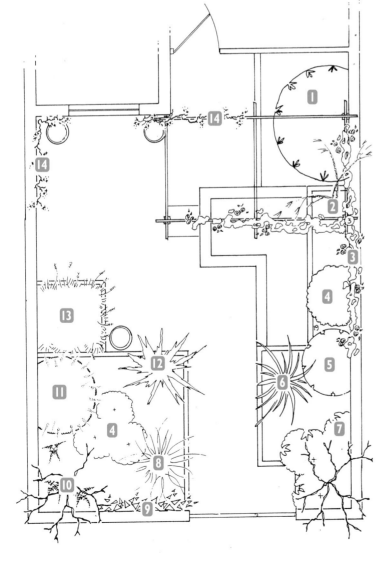

THE GARDEN'S PROBLEMS	HOW THEY WERE SOLVED
The garden's problems included its small size – just 7.7m/25ft long by 5m/16.5ft wide.	A range of levels is created by the pergola, trellis, raised beds and pond. This takes the eye away in many directions, and gives a feeling of space.
A concrete surface that would take time and a great deal of effort to remove.	Raised beds make removal of the concrete unnecessary, although the surface under the beds must be broken up to allow drainage.
A garden that is overlooked from the neighbours' upstairs windows.	The pergola, when plants clothe and cover the roof and uprights, will create privacy on all sides, as well as from above.
An uninteresting view from the kitchen window.	Vertical planting over the pergola, the raised bed at the end of the garden, and pots of herbs beneath the window create a view that changes with the seasons but remains interesting throughout the year.
An owner who has little time to spend on upkeep of the garden and wants to spend what time she has relaxing in it.	The raised beds are easy to maintain and, well mulched, require little weeding. Plants are chosen that are easy to care for and the wall around the pond provides relaxing sitting space.

DESIGNER'S PLANTING SCHEME

Key plants

1 *Choisya* 'Aztec Pearl'
2 *Fargesia murieliae* 'Simba'
3 Climbing rose, *Rosa* 'Félicité et Perpétue' – along trellis
4 Rosemary-leaved cotton lavender, *Santolina rosmarinifolia*
5 *Daphne odora* 'Aureomarginata'
6 Flax, *Phormium* 'Cream Delight'
7 *Helleborus argutifolius*
8 Grass, *Cortaderia* 'Gold Band'
9 Ivy, *Hedera canariensis* 'Canary Island'
10 June berry, *Amelanchier lamarckii*
11 Veronica, *Hebe* 'Red Edge'
12 *Romarinus prostratus*
13 Lavender, *Lavandula* 'Hidcote'
14 *Trachelospermum asiaticum*

Plants for added colour

Smilacina racemosa
Hosta 'Sum and Substance'
Schisandra grandiflora
Alchemilla mollis
Viola, *Viola cornuta*
Sweet pea, *Lathyrus* 'Old Spice'
Wallflower, *Erysimum linifolium* 'Variegatum'
Trailing petunia in shades of purple, petunias, in shades of deep purple
Nasturtiums, apricot and pale yellow
Fuchsia 'Tom Thumb'
Lady fern, *Athyrium filix-felina*
Lenten rose, *Helleborus orientalis*
Herbs, sage, chives, thyme, oregano
Pink, *Dianthus* 'Mrs Sinkins'
Madonna lily, *Lilium candidum*

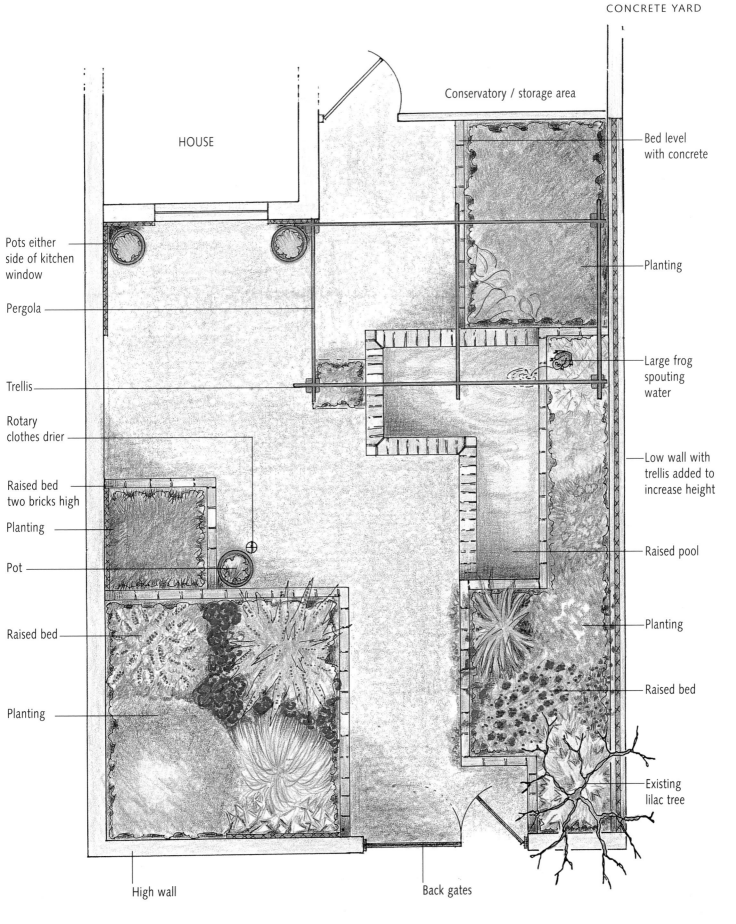

HOUSE

Conservatory / storage area

Pots either side of kitchen window

Bed level with concrete

Pergola

Planting

Trellis

Large frog spouting water

Rotary clothes drier

Low wall with trellis added to increase height

Raised bed two bricks high

Planting

Pot

Raised pool

Raised bed

Planting

Planting

Raised bed

Existing lilac tree

High wall

Back gates

BACK ALLEY

Concrete yard
CONSTRUCTION

The garden's design involved making three basic changes. These were the building of raised beds over the concrete, the erection of a pergola and trellis, and the addition of a pool. Areas of path between the beds are covered with softly shaded slabs, the lines of which help to give an illusion of spaciousness.

The raised beds start from the lowest level near the house, gradually increasing in height towards the end of the garden. As the original bed ran along the right-hand side of the garden it is possible to plant large deep-rooting shrubs like the Mexican orange blossom, *Choisya*, here.

The pergola and the trellis, fixed to rise above the low wall on the right-hand side of the garden, provide support for colourful climbers as well as giving privacy to this small space. More rampant, leafy plants are ideal for areas where shade is required, while plants with

▲ Looking towards the house through the archway of the pergola. Later, the burgeoning plants will turn this into a comfortable and shady sitting-out area

Concrete yard
PLANTING

Jean chose the plants for this small garden with special care so that they would create a verdant look and maintain privacy around the year. The secret of success was to pick key plants for their stunning shape (ensuring that this is well displayed) and to choose as neighbours those plants that best show off each other's colours and leaf shapes.

See also:
- Raised beds, page 108, 120
- Arches, pergolas and arbours, page 132
- Introducing water, page 126

KEY PLANTS

▲ For ground cover Jean chose lady's mantle, *Alchemilla mollis*. The tight frills of unopened leaves soon spread out to show off the hairy surface that holds the water in place after rain so that the leaves are speckled with jewel-like droplets of water.

◄ By the house, the scented white flowers of *Choisya* 'Aztec Pearl' can be seen in late spring, followed in late summer to autumn by a second lot of blooms, so providing a decorative view through most of the year.

slimmer, neater growth allow filtered sunlight where this is preferred.

The L-shaped pool creates a soothing, reflective spot and the supporting wall is designed to form a comfortable seat for those enjoying its calming influence.

◢ The view from the house looking towards the original lilac tree, included in the new design

▶ The L-shaped bed at the end of the garden echoes the shape of the pond and its plants are in view from the kitchen window

◢ A dense, low evergreen shrub with bright green aromatic leaves, *Santolina rosmarinifolia* is positioned partway down the garden in full sun. In mid-summer it produces round heads of bright yellow flowers.

FOR EXTRA COLOUR

For a natural effect, in comparison to the bolder pansy cultivars, Jean introduced the smaller, but scented, pale lilac, pink and white flowers of violas, *Viola cornuta*, which appear early, in spring, and flower through to summer.

Grow these, like pansies, in fertile, moist but well-drained soil in sun or partial shade and divide clumps in spring or early autumn to increase numbers.

Special effect

Shaped pergolas A pergola can be designed to fit into almost any shape or space in the garden. Once they are covered in climbers, they soon provide a shady spot for relaxing out of the direct sunlight.

For some alternative pergola materials and designs to the one shown here, see those on pages 16-27, 40-43, 58-61, 70-73, 76-79, 90, 94-95.

Steeply sloping land

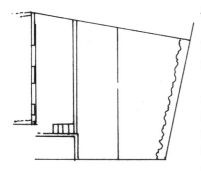

▲ **Before conversion** *the garden contained a lawn that sloped steeply towards the house, making it difficult to mow, and a flower bed that also sloped. There was a narrow slip of concrete beside the house from which steps went up to the garden*

This garden, on the side of a hill, with a high bank at the end of the garden and concrete retaining wall near to the house, was difficult and dangerous to manage before designer Jean Goldberry stepped in to terrace it, forming three flat areas, one above the other, linked by wide, shallow steps.

Jean took advantage of the steep slope, once it was terraced, in a variety of ways. First of all she placed the sitting area at the top of the garden to get the benefit of the stunning views and positioned a pergola to obscure the view of the town behind it. She added a water feature in the centre of the garden and included a steep waterfall, where the water splashed down from one garden level to the next to spread out into a shallow natural-looking pool. She also simulated the waterfall in a series of beds of cascading plants to provide colour that could be enjoyed from the house below.

▼ **The planting scheme** *Part of the brief was to produce a garden which placed special emphasis on autumn colour. Jean also used the steep slope to create a waterfall of blues, reds and oranges*

THE GARDEN'S PROBLEMS	HOW THEY WERE SOLVED
The very steep, sloping land.	This had the advantage of providing good views over the local countryside from the top and end of the garden so this spot was chosen for the sitting area, which was deliberately positioned to look towards the view rather than to the town, which was situated in the opposite direction.
The steep slope made the garden difficult to work in. No flat areas were wide enough to do so in safety.	Railway sleepers were used to form the edging for wide and shallow steps and to terrace the space into a series of flat beds and paved areas.
Old bank on the top boundary.	Jean used this as inspiration for the planting which she designed to mimic the effect of the roadside banks covered in wild flowers that were a natural feature of the local countryside.
The steep slope made it difficult to use a mower.	The design deliberately avoided any grass as even after the area was terraced it would have been difficult to get a mower into position to cut it.

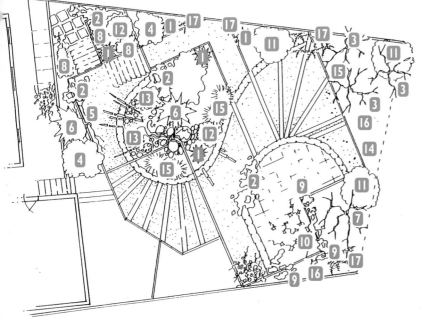

DESIGNER'S PLANTING SCHEME

Key plants

1. Juniper, *Juniperus communis* 'Sentinel' – vertical trees to balance the slope
2. *Rosa* 'Rushing Stream'
3. *Sorbus aucuparia* 'Sheerwater'
4. *Fothergilla major*
5. Cedar of Lebanon, *Cedrus libani* 'Sargentii'
6. *Buddleja davidii* 'Nanho Blue'
7. *Prunus* 'Okumiyako'
8. Ceratostigma plumbagnoides
9. *Rosa* 'Danse de Feu' up pergola posts
10. Vine, *Vitis coignetiae*
11. *Euonymus alatus*
12. *Berberis* 'Rubrostilla'

Decorative detail

13. *Juncus inflexus* 'Afro'
14. Sweet woodruff, *Galium odoratum*
15. *Nepeta* 'Six Hills Giant'
16. *Farfugium japonicum* 'Argenteum'
17. *Dryopteris filix-mas*

Plants for added colour

Pelargonium 'Lila Mini Cascade'

Lobelia in dark and sky blue to fill spaces

Nasturtium, *Tropaeolum majus*

Zinnia haageana 'Persian Carpet'

Pansy, *Viola* hybrids

Salvia farinacea 'Victoria'

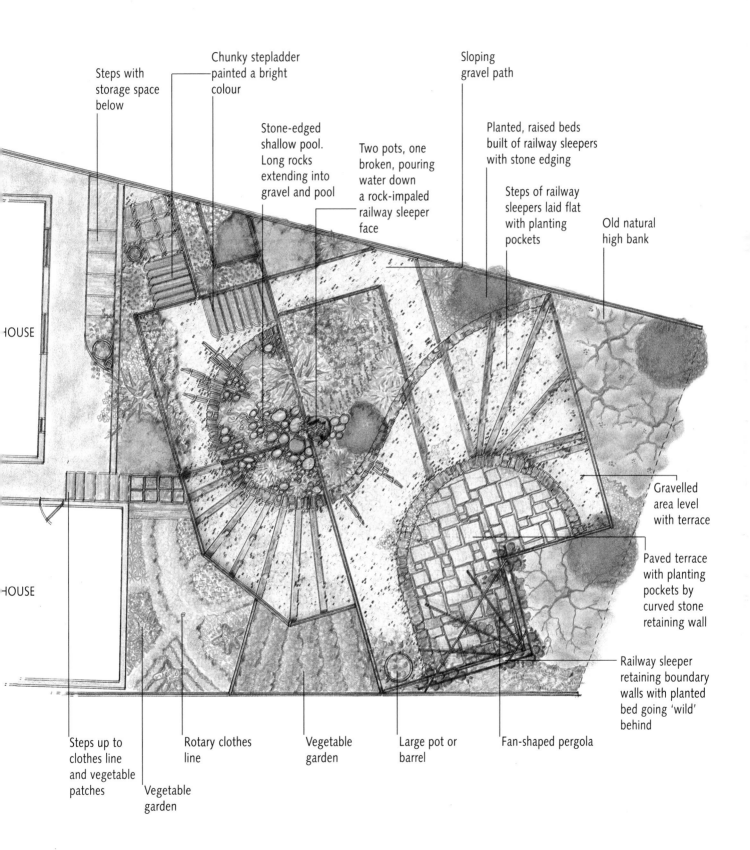

Steps with
storage space
below

Chunky stepladder
painted a bright
colour

Stone-edged
shallow pool.
Long rocks
extending into
gravel and pool

Two pots, one
broken, pouring
water down
a rock-impaled
railway sleeper
face

Sloping
gravel path

Planted, raised beds
built of railway sleepers
with stone edging

Steps of railway
sleepers laid flat
with planting
pockets

Old natural
high bank

HOUSE

HOUSE

Gravelled
area level
with terrace

Paved terrace
with planting
pockets by
curved stone
retaining wall

Railway sleeper
retaining boundary
walls with planted
bed going 'wild'
behind

Steps up to
clothes line
and vegetable
patches

Rotary clothes
line

Vegetable
garden

Large pot or
barrel

Fan-shaped pergola

Vegetable
garden

CONSTRUCTION

Terracing involves a lot of initial construction work but it is almost always the best method of dealing with a steep slope if the garden is to be easy to care for and able to be enjoyed on all its levels. Being thick, wide and tough, railway sleepers make ideal edging supports for this sort of terraced construction but any treated timber of similar strength would be equally suitable. Jean also included stone, a readily available local material, to form a low retaining wall alongside the steps and around the top terrace.

The centrally placed water feature uses the same materials. Here the water tumbles down the height of the retaining wall to end up in a shallow pebble and rock-lined pool on the terrace below.

The sun terrace, at the top of the garden, is constructed with a surface of

▲ *The view of the house looking down from the end of the garden and showing the series of wide and shallow timber-edged steps that are lined with gravel*

See also:
- Arches, pergolas and arbours, page 132
- Windy location, page 58
- Plants for dry soil, page 186

Steeply sloping land
PLANTING

This is a garden full of glowing autumn colour with *Fothergilla major*, *Ceratostigma plumbaginoides*, the vine *Vitis coignetiae* and *Euonymus alatus* all displaying brilliant orange and scarlet leaves in autumn, highlighted by the coral red fruit of the berberis 'Rubrostilla' and splashes of red, orange and yellow in the flowers of the nasturtiums.

KEY PLANTS

▲ The deep purple flowers of lavender, *Lavandula angustifolia* 'Twickel Purple' edge a raised bed that runs alongside the path joining one terrace with another to provide scent for passers by on sunny summer days.

◀ Thyme 'Pink Chintz' forms tight mats between the paving slabs. It is also used in the gravel, where it likes the free-draining conditions. The tiny pale pink flowers appear in summer. Mat-forming thymes need cutting back hard if they are to remain compact.

◀ A view, not long after construction, shows the steep path that leads up to the paved seating area at the top of the garden

paving and is retained by a stone wall. Spaces left at the edge of the paving provide planting areas for cascading plants and the pergola forms a framework for climbers such as a vine and the wonderful scarlet and orange rose 'Danse du Feu'.

▲ By using a range of climbing plants growing up a post of the pergola Jean has rung the changes and provided blooms through much of the year. A large early flowering clematis intermingles with the rose 'Danse du Feu' which has scarlet flowers later in the year.

FOR EXTRA COLOUR

Nasturtiums, *Tropaeolum* hybrids are easy to grow from seed in moderately fertile, well-drained soil and in full sun. They provide a colourful mass of red, orange and yellow flowers. *T.* 'Alaska' series, shown, have specially decorative leaves speckled and blotched in creamy white. These form good ground cover colour. *T. majus* is a climber, and *T.* 'Peach Melba' has pale creamy yellow flowers with streaked orange-red centres.

▲ A natural effect is emphasized by the timber and stone used to form the waterfall and the shallow pond lined with pebbles and rocks below it

Special effect

Waterfalls provide interest visually, and the sound of falling water helps to bring a sense of harmony with nature, a restful experience after a stressful day.

In this case the water appears, just as it might on a rocky hillside, from between boulders. Vertical sleepers provide the backing to the fall and strategically placed slivers of stone act as natural breaks to the tumbling water before it enters the pool below. The water is then pumped back up to the top of the fall, to follow the same procedure again and again.

This circulating water could be powered by a submersible pump if the height is not more than 1.2m/4ft. Otherwise a surface pump, which is more powerful, would be needed and this requires a separate electricity supply.

CHAPTER 4

DESIGNS WITH SPECIAL FEATURES IN MIND

A garden that is planned to have a central theme, a particular use, or one with a distinct advantage or specific requirements needs special thought in its design and in its choice of planting.

In this chapter we show how our garden designers have dealt with six gardens, each planned around a specific requirement.

Low-maintenance garden

With a garage and a lane at one end of this very long garden (and the house itself the other side of the lane), it was important to draw people into and through the garden to the opposite end. Designer Jean Goldberry created the main areas of interest at the far end and these include a pond, decking terrace for eating and a pergola above the extended original patio. Along the side of the garage she created a zig-zag pergola to follow the lines of the ground surface of gravel, grass and planting.

▲ **Before conversion** *the garden was surrounded with a conifer hedge on one side, with a high wall and timber fence on the other and was mainly weed-covered soil*

THE GARDEN'S PROBLEMS

The owners are busy people, both working full time, and they prefer to enjoy the garden rather than spend time working in it.

The space is very long and thin with a garage and the lane at one end.

A space to eat which could provide room for a range of numbers of people depending on the occasion.

HOW THEY WERE SOLVED

With easy care as a priority the garden contains mainly hard surfaces of decking, gravel and paving. Terracotta pots hold geraniums, which need little watering even in dry weather, and the planting is mainly of evergreens with beds mulched well with bark chippings to suppress weed growth.

Using heavy timber railway sleepers in a diagonal design helps to break up the length. The end furthest from the lane is deliberately made most interesting to draw visitors into the garden and to tempt them to follow it through to the end.

The eating area is formed of decking. Raised beds and paving at a higher level around the area create a well. The surrounding surfaces can then be used as seats.

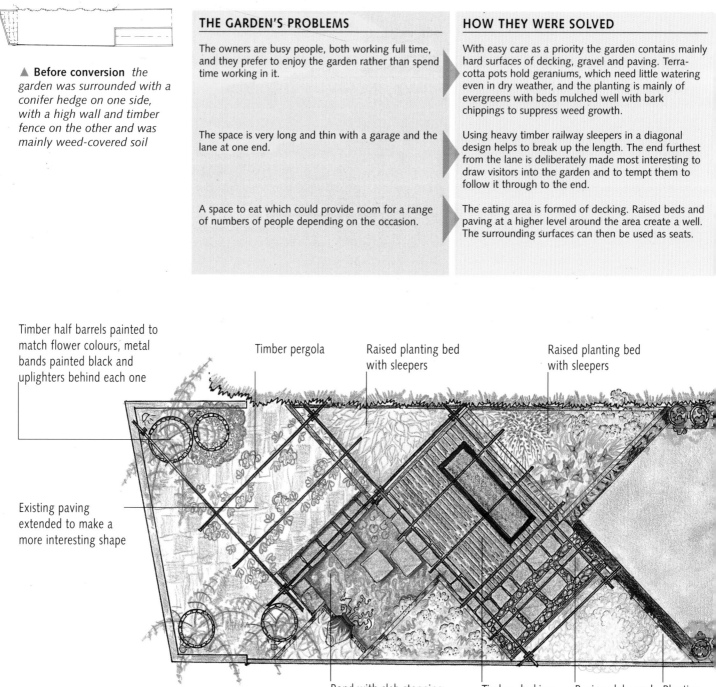

Timber half barrels painted to match flower colours, metal bands painted black and uplighters behind each one

Timber pergola

Raised planting bed with sleepers

Raised planting bed with sleepers

Existing paving extended to make a more interesting shape

Pond with slab stepping stones supported by brick pillars. Pump outflow in pot

Timber decking set down from terrace

Paving slabs and large pebbles on hardcore base

Planting bed

DESIGNER'S PLANTING SCHEME

Key plants

1. Japanese angelica tree, *Aralia elata*
2. Common myrtle, *Myrtus communis*
3. *Sophora tetraptera*
4. *Leptospermum scoparium* 'Red Damask'
5. Spotted laurel, *Aucuba japonica* 'Crotonifolia'
6. Spurge, *Euphorbia characias* ssp. *wulfenii*
7. *Cytisus* 'Killiney Red'
8. *Holboellia latifolia* – climbing
9. *Lonicera* x *tellmanniana* – climbing
10. *Rosa* 'Etoile de Hollande'- climbing
11. *Vitis vinifera* 'Purpurea'
12. Black bamboo, *Phyllostachys nigra*

Decorative Detail

13. Aquatic grass, *Glyceria maxima* 'Variegata'
14. *Rudbeckia fulgida* var. *sullivantii* 'Goldsturm'
15. *Nymphaea tetragona* 'Helvola'
16. *Doronicum carpetanum*
17. Daylily, *Hemerocallis* 'Frans Hals'

Plants for added colour

Pelargonium 'Mme Fournier'
Nasturtium Jewel Series
Pot marigold, *Calendula* 'Geisha Girl'
Antirrhinum majus Coronette Series
California poppy, *Eschscholtzia californica*
Bells of Ireland, *Moluccella laevis*

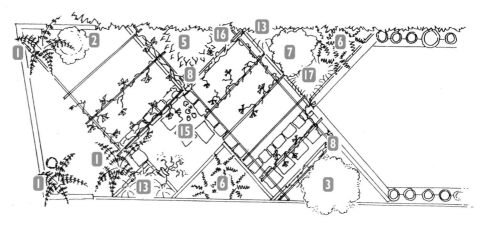

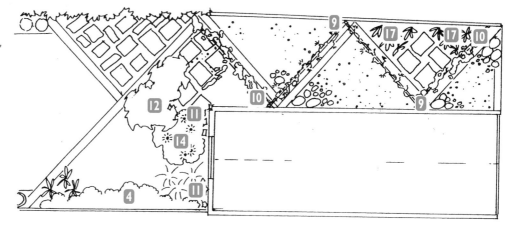

▲ **The planting scheme** *uses low-maintenance evergreens that need little pruning and bright yellows, oranges and reds which stand out against the dark blue-green pergola and decking*

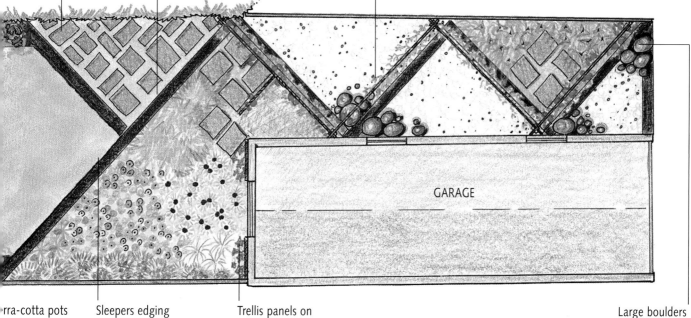

Slabs with herbs between

Sleepers covered in wire netting laid flat over free-draining base

Zig-zag pergola

Terra-cotta pots with bright red geraniums

Sleepers edging lawn

Trellis panels on either side of garage window

GARAGE

Large boulders and pebbbles

CONSTRUCTION

Strong diagonal lines and a range of heights divide up the length of this narrow garden into a number of interesting areas. The original paved terrace at the far end was extended to form a diamond-edged pattern which allows more space and a pergola was added to create interest at a higher level.

The square pond, set at an angle along one side of the terrace, is edged with paving, placed below the level of the terrace but at the same height as the decking that follows it. The decking is constructed of southern yellow pine which is pressure-treated to make it rot-proof and non-slip when wet. The higher sides provide seating and a low table completes the eating area.

The lawn that follows is edged with sleepers to retain the neat shape. These are set just below lawn level for easy

▲ The strong shape of the paved patio at the far end of the garden is repeated in the decking and pond, and the materials used contrast yet complement each other, highlighting the clean design

PLANTING

Jean uses plants in pots and raised beds to highlight the planting and this helps to keep trees and shrubs small. Three triangular raised beds border the sitting areas. Climbers – *Holboellia latifolia*, a copper-orange honeysuckle, *Lonicera* x *tellmanniana*, and the crimson rose 'Etoile de Hollande' are grown against the garage and over the pergola.

KEY PLANTS

◄ Runner beans and sweet peas intermingle and grow up a neat wigwam of canes in a half barrel container. These provide both height and colour, and the fresh young beans are easy to pick for use in the kitchen.

► The aquatic grass, *Glyceria maxima* 'Variegata' grows in a corner of the pond where the striking strap-like leaves, striped cream, yellow and green, contrast well with the shorter foliage that surrounds it. This grass can grow to 80cm/32in.

◀ *A zig-zag pergola leads visitors alongside the garage and into the main area of the garden. Paving slabs, set in grass, provide a practical short cut*

▼ *The square pond, set at an angle, has a raised bed behind it with planting that softens the straight lines. The brick edging contrasts with the other materials used*

See also:
• *Raised beds, pages 108, 120*
• *Containers, page 134*
• *Introducing water, page 126*

...owing. Beyond this, just before the ...arage, are slabs set on compacted soil ...ith herbs growing in the spaces.

Because running cables for electricity ...ould have been expensive, floating ...andles are used on the pond and jam-...rs of night lights hang from the pergola.

...Meadow rue, *Thalictrum* species, are lovers of ...amp and shady places and are at home in a ...mi-wild area by a water feature. They thrive in ...imates where summers are fairly cool.

FOR EXTRA COLOUR

Pelargoniums prefer a situation in full sun but require less regular watering than most container plants, which makes them easier to look after. Flowers continue through most of the summer if they are regularly deadheaded.

In frost-prone areas move container-grown pelargoniums indoors in winter, and cut back by about one-third. Repot in spring when the plants begin to grow.

Special effect

Easy-care plants in pots
Evergreens and pelargoniums make a good choice if you are looking for pot plants that need minimum care. By adding water-retaining crystals in the potting mix, you can ensure that soil will also retain moisture for longer. Plants that are grown in containers need to be fed regularly if they are to flourish but slow-release fertilizers can be used to help with regular feeding.

Pot-grown plants also need repotting, or at least to have some of the compost replaced, every year or two.

Terra cotta dries out quickly in hot weather so it is not necessarily the best material to use in a low-maintenance garden. In areas that are subject to frost check that the terra cotta is frost-proof as it can flake or crack when the water in the compost expands on freezing.

Lining a wooden container with plastic will help it to retain water and also lengthen the life of the timber.

Children's garden

The instructions to designer Jean Goldberry for this garden were clearly specified by the children of the house. It must have a sandpit, a football pitch with goal posts, a climbing frame, a home for the much-loved family tortoise, and an element of magic and mystery.

Jean came up with a whale-shaped lawn which doubles as a football pitch, space was found for the frame and sandpit near the house and the tortoise was provided with its own house and garden by the bicycle shed at the end of the lawn. A secret area was created within a ring of amelanchiers, and adults were not forgotten with seats and a hammock to relax on and a paved area for outdoor meals.

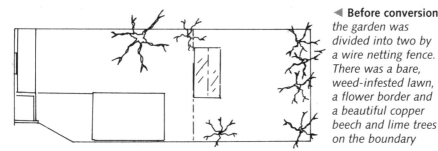

◀ **Before conversion** *the garden was divided into two by a wire netting fence. There was a bare, weed-infested lawn, a flower border and a beautiful copper beech and lime trees on the boundary*

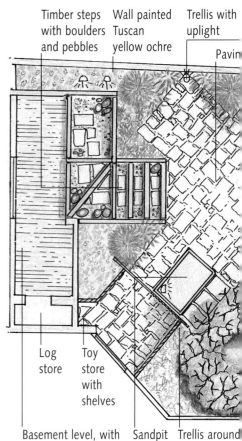

Timber steps with boulders and pebbles | Wall painted Tuscan yellow ochre | Trellis with uplight

Pavin

Log store | Toy store with shelves

Basement level, with decking and timber painted yellow ochre | Sandpit with light | Trellis around paved area w arch over gap

THE GARDEN'S PROBLEMS

For the boys the inclusion of a football pitch with space for goal posts at each end was very important.

The pet tortoise required a home and this had to be included in the design.

Space was needed for the climbing frame already in existence.

A strip of paving outside the basement kitchen and main living area which was too narrow for use.

HOW THEY WERE SOLVED

A long whale-shaped lawn provides the pitch and introduces an angle which avoids balls being aimed towards the house.

A pen at the end of the garden leads into adjoining space inside the bike shed. This forms night and winter quarters with easy access for cleaning out.

Jean sited this behind the 'magic' tree circle and painted the equipment a deep blue, introducing a blue slide and climbing rope.

This area was widened, and floored with decking which is painted yellow to match the colour scheme of the adjoining room, so extending the living area outdoors.

▼ **The planting scheme** *uses very bright colours and includes plants that are easy to grow such as sunflowers and nasturtiums, as well as trees picked for autumn colour*

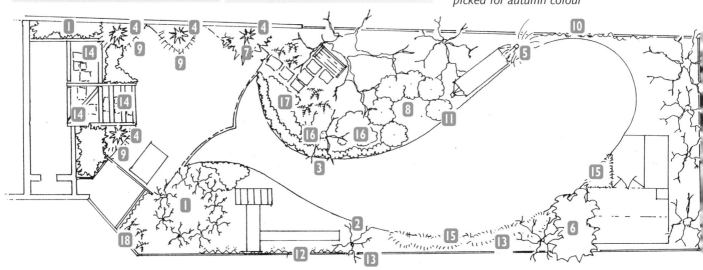

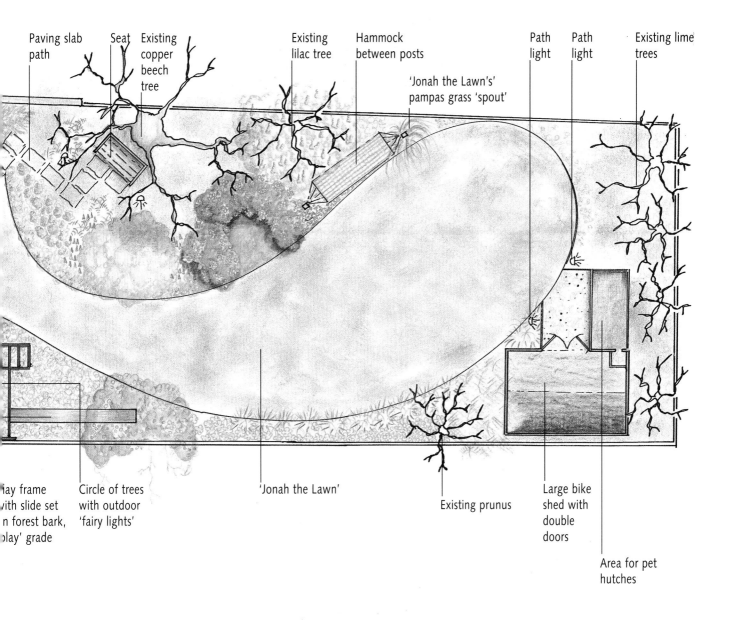

Paving slab path

Seat

Existing copper beech tree

Existing lilac tree

Hammock between posts

'Jonah the Lawn's' pampas grass 'spout'

Path light

Path light

Existing lime trees

…lay frame …ith slide set …n forest bark, …lay' grade

Circle of trees with outdoor 'fairy lights'

'Jonah the Lawn'

Existing prunus

Large bike shed with double doors

Area for pet hutches

DESIGNER'S PLANTING SCHEME

Key plants

1 *Amelanchier lamarkii* – to create a circle of trees

2 Crab apple, *Malus* 'John Downie'

3 *Sorbus* 'Joseph Rock'

4 Juniper, *Juniperus communis* 'Hibernica'

5 Pampas grass, *Cortaderia selloana* 'Albolineata'

6 Yellow-groove bamboo, *Phyllostachys aureosulcata* var. *aureocaulis*

7 Rosemary, *Rosmarinus* 'Prostratus'

8 Redcurrant, *Ribes rubrum*

9 Lavender, *Lavandula angustifolia* 'Hidcote'

10 Vine, *Vitis coignetiae*

11 *Tropaeolum speciosum* – growing over currant bushes

12 Thornless blackberry, *Rubus lacinatus*

Decorative detail

13 Black-eyed Susan, *Rudbeckia fulgida* var. *sullivantii* 'Goldsturm'

14 Daisy, *Bellis perennis* Roggli Series

15 Sedge, *Carex* 'Frosted Curls'

16 Catmint, *Nepeta* 'Souvenir d'André Chaudron'

17 Male fern, *Dryopteris filix-mas*

Plants for added colour

Sunflower, *Helianthus annus* 'Russian Giant'

Nasturtium, *Tropaeolum majus*

Love-in-the-mist, *Nigella damascena* Persian Jewel Series

Lettuce, green and red 'Salad Bowl', *Lactuca sativa*

Livingstone daisy, *Dorotheanthus bellidiformis*

China aster, *Callistephus* 'Kyoto Pompon'

Children's garden
CONSTRUCTION

Once the area outside the house basement had been laid with decking and the wall and floor surface painted a sunny yellow to match the colour scheme of the room behind, the timber-edged steps were constructed up to the terrace. This was laid with an integrated sandpit. The patio paving also extends as a short path to a seat beneath the copper beech which looks towards the house and the children's play area.

The giant whale-shaped lawn, created from tough perennial rye grass to withstand hard wear, extends almost to the end of the garden and the shape allows the goal posts to be positioned at an angle to the house, to avoid accidents with balls. The lawn's shape also creates curved edges for the beds around it.

At the far end of the garden a shed takes the bikes and in front, to one side,

▲ *The play space is provided with a 'carpet' of a thick layer of bark chippings for a soft fall*

▶ The brilliant yellow, dark-centred flowers of the black-eyed Susan, *Rudbeckia fulgida* var. *sullivantii* 'Goldstrum' grow alongside the whale and provide patches of bright colour behind the lettuce border.

Children's garden
PLANTING

Plants for this garden were chosen for a range of different but important reasons. The whale lawn was decoratively edged with cut-and-come-again red and green salad bowl lettuces to provide the tortoise, as well as the family, with a constant supply of food, and a neatly placed pampas grass provides the whale's water spout.

The circle of amelanchiers creates a magic fairy-ring when hung with lights, and these together with the sorbus 'Joseph Rock' and the vine, *Vitis coignetia,* provide rich highlights of red and gold as winter approaches.

KEY PLANTS

◀ The seat that overlooks the play area and the house is backed by euphorbia. The scented *Choisya ternata* is deliberately allowed to grow over it on one side.

◄ *Looking down the curving whale lawn towards the bicycle shed and tortoise house. The patio provides ample space for eating outdoors*

▼ *The sandpit, which is set into the patio, can be watched over from the seat under the beech tree opposite and the sand is kept clean by the use of a cover, lower right*

is the tortoise pen with sleeping quarters in the shed itself. This would work equally well for a rabbit or guinea pig.

The climbing frame and slide are tucked away neatly behind the circle of amelanchiers and the hammock provides a viewing point for games of football.

▲ The timber-sided paved steps that lead from the basement are lined with pebbles and overhung with evergreen shrubs, including a bushy hebe, the silver-grey lavender, *Lavendula* 'Hidcote' and an artemisia, all benefiting from the good drainage and sunny position.

FOR EXTRA COLOUR

Brilliant orange French marigolds, *Tagetes* 'Safari Tangerine' can be easily grown from seed by youngsters. The large seeds are easy to handle and can be sown *in situ*. They provide a patch of long-lasting bright colour.

Another great favourite with children is the sunflower, *Helianthus annuus* 'Russian Giant' which grows to a towering height.

Special effect

A sandpit soon falls out of use as the family grow up and take up new interests. However, it is not difficult to turn the dug-out area to new use as an ornamental pond when all danger of water in the garden is past. Alternatively, with the sand removed and the space filled with good topsoil, a bed can be created for ground-hugging plants.

Garden with a view

The owners of this garden surrounding a new house wanted an informal effect to tie in with the countryside behind the garden. The garden was sited on steep land emphasizing the view beyond.

Designer Sally Court divided it into two and gave each area a different feel. The top section, near the house, became a traditional country garden and the lower area was more wild to tie in with the landscape, with small waterfalls and rocky streams, but it also includes plants that were chosen to create a jungle-like luxuriance.

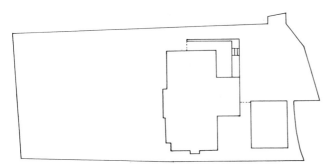

◄ **Before conversion** *As the house was newly built there was no garden, just a lot of builder's rubble*

THE GARDEN'S PROBLEMS	HOW THEY WERE SOLVED
A steep slope facing away from the house.	The area was flattened near to the house and a slate terrace built to catch the early morning sun. Large shrubs made this into an enclosed area with a view onto the opposite side of the garden.
Wonderful views.	The view was accentuated by planting tall trees and shrubs on the sides, but ensuring that the central area would remain low.
A new house with a garden full of builder's rubble and lacking any topsoil.	Rubble was removed and the land contoured, then quantities of topsoil were brought in. The soil condition was improved with compost and manure.
A cold garden that has very little sun.	Sally created a wet woodland feature with paths and tumbling streams running through it in the lowest part of the garden.

Utility area   Gazebo   Railway sleepers act as steps and paving

'Tree benches'

Sloping terraces with a series of small pools spilling into the bottom pool. Dramatic planting scheme creates a 'jungle' effect

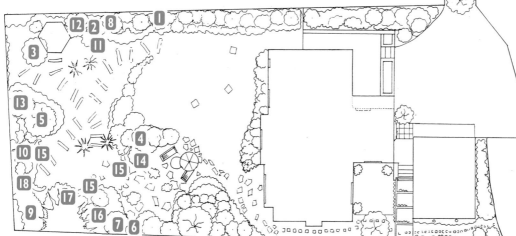

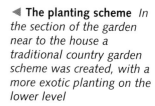

◄ **The planting scheme** *In the section of the garden near to the house a traditional country garden scheme was created, with a more exotic planting on the lower level*

Acid-loving border

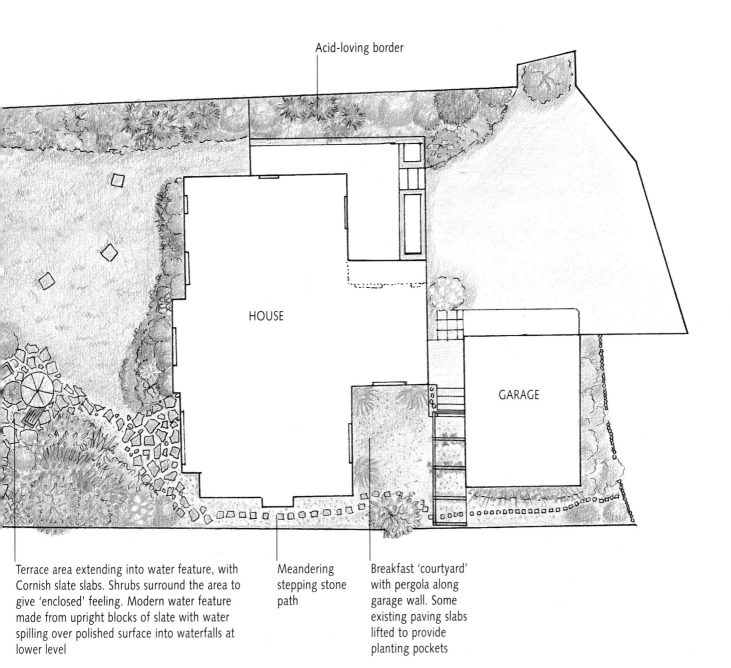

HOUSE

GARAGE

Terrace area extending into water feature, with Cornish slate slabs. Shrubs surround the area to give 'enclosed' feeling. Modern water feature made from upright blocks of slate with water spilling over polished surface into waterfalls at lower level

Meandering stepping stone path

Breakfast 'courtyard' with pergola along garage wall. Some existing paving slabs lifted to provide planting pockets

DESIGNER'S PLANTING SCHEME

Key plants

1 *Phillyrea latifolia*
2 Hawthorn, *Crataegus laevigata* 'Crimson Cloud'
3 Ornamental cherry, *Prunus avium* 'Plena'
4 *Elaeagnus* x *ebbingei* 'Limelight'
5 Paper bark maple, *Acer griseum*
6 Chusan palm, *Trachycarpus fortunei*
7 Strawberry tree, *Arbutus* x *andrachnoides*

8 *Osmanthus decorus*
9 *Robinia pseudoacacia* 'Frisia'
10 *Eucryphia* x *nymansensis*

Decorative detail

11 Lenten rose, *Helleborus orientalis*
12 Spindle tree, *Euonymus europaeus* 'Red Cascade'
13 Spindle, *Euonymus* f. *albus* var. *intermedius*

14 Maple, *Acer griseum*
15 Hostas, ferns and *Iris sibirica*
16 *Gunnera manicata*
17 Spurge, *Euphorbia characias* ssp. *wulfenii*
18 Foxglove tree, *Paulownia tomentosa*

▲ *Steps of railway sleepers in the gravel in the lower section of the garden lead down the slope and link one small flat terrace with another*

Garden with a view
CONSTRUCTION

Once the builder's rubble had been removed the garden was landscaped, with a level section created near to the house which dropped to sloping land below. From the house the lower section of the garden is not in view until the edge of the top terrace is reached and so forms a secret garden waiting to be discovered.

Small flat terraces were dug out at points on the slope of the lower area as places to sit. Here water forms in small pools before running down the slope again finally to end up in a larger pool at the bottom end of the garden, where a utility area is kept well out of sight. Terraces are linked by timber steps and gravel pathways that pass close to waterfalls and fast streams of tumbling water and end up at a gazebo hidden from sight until it is reached.

Garden with a view
PLANTING

The garden near to the house contains a long, wide herbaceous border along one side, and shrubs and trees opposite this provide shelter for the terrace. In the lower section of the garden a jungle-like effect is created with plants of dramatic shapes or colours, including the foxglove tree, *Paulownia tomentosa* with its fragrant lilac-pink flowers.

KEY PLANTS

▲ *Elaeagnus* x *ebbingei* 'Limelight' planted centrally in the border between the top and lower sections of the garden helps to form a link between the more traditional upper section of the garden and the more exotically planted lower section.

◀ The seat on the lower terrace looks down the timber-edged steps. Cranesbill geraniums provide foreground colour and a newly planted *Robinia pseudoacacia* 'Frisia' adds golden colour beside the seat.

The water feature starts from close to the top terrace in a pool, the position of which is highlighted by giant standing stones (right). The water then runs between rough-edged slabs of slate, some of which act as stepping stones, to spill over from the top terrace. It continues its run through the sloping section of the garden to the end of the garden below.

▲ The top terrace of gravel and sunken railway sleepers, and the timber bench, which catches the early morning sun, are enclosed by planting to create a sheltered nook and a place from which to enjoy the view of the countryside beyond

► Water tumbles down from the top garden in miniature waterfalls and along natural-looking streams lined and edged by large craggy rocks

Special effect

Running water Beautiful effects can be created by moving water. In this garden slabs of slate are used for areas of paving and spaces are left between the slates at intervals to form crevices for running water while other slates form stepping stones for crossing the water.

A similar effect for a more formal area can be created with granite setts, with spaces left between them for the water to flow around.

FOR EXTRA COLOUR

Eucryphia x *nymansensis* bears its cup-shaped white flowers through from late summer to autumn and provides colour at a time of the year when flowers are often in short supply. It is a tall evergreen shrub that can grow to as much as 15m/50ft, so is only suitable for a garden, like this, that backs onto open countryside. Here it acts as a frame to the view behind.

▲ Shown here in summer, the decorative peeling bark of the paper-bark maple, *Acer griseum* creates a focus even in winter.

With the elderly in mind

This garden, devised by Barbara Hunt in conjunction with the charity Age Concern was created for a garden exhibition at Hampton Court, London and was intended for the enjoyment of elderly people. It seeks to help to compensate for some of the problems that arrive as we get older, from lack of energy and mobility, to failing eyesight. With wide paved areas, the garden uses a range of materials, and has a pergola, raised beds and a raised pool. Many of the beds and the pond are edged with seating so that they can be enjoyed from close at hand. A bird bath, bird table and the inclusion of plants to attract bees and butterflies bring nature to the garden, which can be enjoyed from both inside and outside the house.

POINTS TO CONSIDER	SOLUTIONS
Mobility – a problem for some of those for whom the garden was designed.	Wide paths provide access for wheel chairs and allow for people walking side by side. Gentle slopes are easier to manage than steps, both for those who have walking problems and for those whose sight is poor. Lots of seating areas make the garden especially enjoyable, with a choice of sun or shade.
Eyesight may be poor for some garden users.	In age colours seem less strong and moving from light to shade becomes more difficult for the eyes to adjust to. Using strong and contrasting colours next to each other helps to combat this. Certain colours, in particular yellow and orange, are the easiest to see.
Scent is particularly important for older people.	Where eyesight or hearing becomes less good then flowers that give pleasure through scent are particularly valuable.

▶ **The planting scheme** uses bright colours and positions plants of contrasting colours side by side. It also includes a number of plants with either aromatic foliage or fragrant flowers and others to attract bees and butterflies

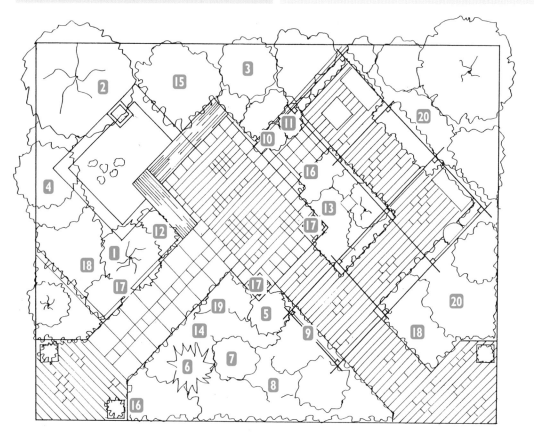

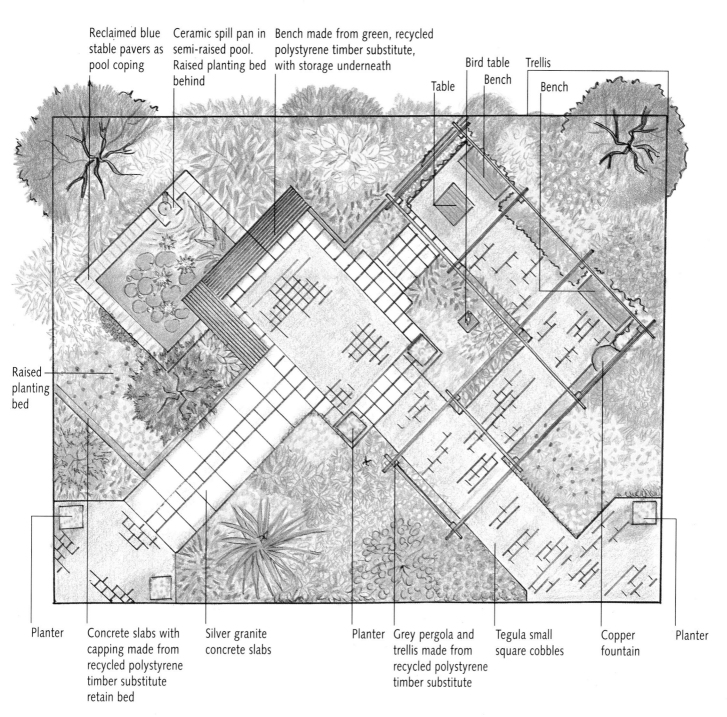

Reclaimed blue stable pavers as pool coping

Ceramic spill pan in semi-raised pool. Raised planting bed behind

Bench made from green, recycled polystyrene timber substitute, with storage underneath

Bird table

Trellis

Table

Bench

Bench

Raised planting bed

Planter

Concrete slabs with capping made from recycled polystyrene timber substitute retain bed

Silver granite concrete slabs

Planter

Grey pergola and trellis made from recycled polystyrene timber substitute

Tegula small square cobbles

Copper fountain

Planter

DESIGNER'S PLANTING SCHEME

Key plants
1 Japanese maple, *Acer palmatum* f. *atropurpureum*
2 Rock maple, *Acer saccharinum* 'Wieri'
3 Indian bean tree, *Catalpa bignonioides* 'Aurea'
4 Golden bamboo, *Phyllostachys aurea*
5 Dwarf mountain pine, *Pinus mugo*
6 New Zealand flax, *Phormium tenax*

Plants with aromatic foliage
7 *Artemisia* 'Powis Castle'
8 *Eucalyptus gunnii*

9 Mint, *Mentha rotundifolia* 'Variegata'
10 Jerusalem sage, *Phlomis fruticosa*
11 Rosemary, *Rosmarinus officinalis*
12 *Salvia officinalis* 'Icterina'
13 *Santolina virens*

Decorative detail
14 *Achillea* 'Moonshine'
15 *Buddleja fallowiana*
16 Lavender, *Lavandula vera*
17 *Argyranthemum* 'Jamaica Primrose'

18 *Rudbeckia* 'Marmalade'
19 *Salvia officinalis* 'Purpurascens'
20 *Lilium* 'Connecticut King'

Plants with fragrant flowers
Jasmine, *Jasminum officinale*
Lavender, *Lavandula angustifolia* 'Hidcote'
Japanese honeysuckle, *Lonicera japonica* 'Halliana'
Philadelphus 'Virginal'
Rose, *Rosa* 'Dreaming Spires'
Viburnum x *bodnantense* 'Charles Lamont'

With the elderly in mind
CONSTRUCTION

For safety the paving was picked for its non-slip and non-reflective properties and changes in colour and materials are used to herald clearly for the less well sighted that they are entering a new pathway or section of the garden. Seating surfaces in dark green over light, rough-surfaced concrete paving are made from a recycled polystyrene waste material which is warm to the touch, tough and relatively maintenance free. It does not absorb water so can be quickly dried after rain.

The pergola, constructed from the same materials as the seats, provides a frame for climbers, and shade for the seating area below, from which the scent of the climbers can be enjoyed.

Raised beds and the raised pond bring the pleasures of plants and water up to a more accessible level to those walking, sitting or in wheel chairs.

▲ The pond has a wide raised edge that provides comfortable seating and a chance to view plants and water close to

With the elderly in mind
PLANTING

Apart from providing a number of specimen plants with decorative leaf shapes and autumn colour, Barbara picked plants for their aromatic leaves or fragrant flowers. She chose bright colours that could be seen clearly by those with less good sight. Orange and yellow have been used extensively, often side-by-side for vivid contrast.

KEY PLANTS

▲A carefully selected mix of leaf and flower shapes and colours ensures that each plant is strongly defined against the other. The silver-grey new leaves of a *Eucalyptus gunnii* overhang the pale yellow flowers of *Achillea* 'Moonshine'.

◄ Sunshine colours show up strongly against a green background in the brilliant yellow flowers of the lily 'Connecticut King', the golden flowers of black-eyed Susan, *Rudbeckia fulgida* and an edging of bright orange marigolds.

▲ A bird table is ideally placed if it is close to buildings so that it is possible to view the feeding birds whatever the weather. Here the pond, planting and seating behind create a restful background

▶ The saucer-shaped water feature tumbles water into the pond below and doubles up as a bird bath. The water is recycled from the pond back up to the top saucer again

▲ In these raised beds Barbara has used the two colours most easily seen by older eyes. The bright orange flowers of *Rudbeckia* 'Marmalade' are elevated to eye-level creating a strong contrast against the paler yellow daisy-like heads of the *Argyranthemum* 'Jamaica Primrose'.

FOR EXTRA COLOUR

Flowers in tones of a single colour work well in a container. Here the small, soft pink flowers of *Nemesia* Carnival Series rise above the rim while the pendent deep pink flowers of the climbing *Rhodochiton* appear around the edges and trail down to the ground.

Special effect

Attracting the birds Bird baths and bird tables not only bring wildlife close to home where they can be more easily studied and enjoyed but they create attractive garden sculptures. Provided the situation is suitable and safe for birds, hidden from circling birds of prey and protected from marauding cats, bird baths and tables can be used as a focal point on a small terrace, at the crossroads of paths or the end of a pathway, and in many other situations.

Here potter and designer, Denis Fairweather has created a bird bath that is also a water spill from which water pours into the pond, adding sound to the enjoyment of the other senses.

The table and water spill are made from the same recycled polystyrene waste material as the pergola and seat tops, which can be sawn, drilled, nailed, glued and jointed in the same way as timber. He has formed a pair of pecking birds on the rim of each to attract the feathered variety to enjoy the facilities also.

Integrating a swimming pool

When the owners of this garden resolved to include a swimming pool, choosing its site was the first consideration. They wanted it to be out of sight of the house so that it would be a surprise feature and so that when the children invited their friends for a swim the noise of their enjoyment would not be too close to the house. The spot had to be free of trees, must not interfere with the line of the house drains, and should be in the sun for most of the day and in a sheltered situation. They chose a spot at the end of the garden with access through the flower garden and a pergola arch. As the garden is on a slope this meant digging out to create a flat terrace for the pool.

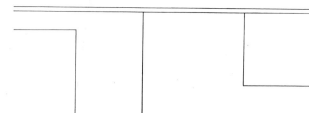

◀ **Before conversion** *the area used for the pool had been a lawn adjacent to the fruit garden*

Long border with climbing plants on wall

Paved area with stone bench

LAWN AREA

THE GARDEN'S PROBLEMS	HOW THEY WERE SOLVED
The line of the house drains was an important consideration.	Experts were brought in to check the route of the drains before the exact position for the pool was chosen, so that these would not have to be re-routed.
It was important that the pool would receive sun for the longest possible period every day.	The final site was chosen because the sun was on this area from first thing in the morning until evening.
It was important to choose a position that was sheltered from wind but at the same time lacked trees.	As the area chosen was originally lawn, trees were not a problem. A wall which runs down the garden on the windward side gives shelter. Digging out the sloping land to create a flat pool terrace also gave extra shelter.
The large expanse of water and overpowering nature of a swimming pool had to be considered.	Siting the pool out of view of the house, and sinking rather than raising the terrace which surrounds it.

▼ **The planting scheme** *Little extra planting was necessary. A retaining wall on one side backed onto a mature bed and these plants could then be enjoyed from both sides. A second narrow bed, with a low fence behind it, was newly planted and pots were arranged by the pool for additional colour*

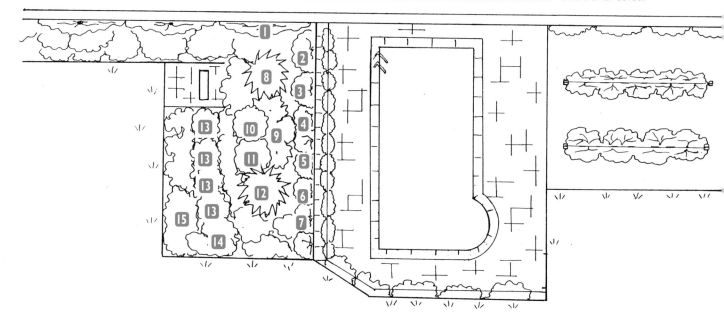

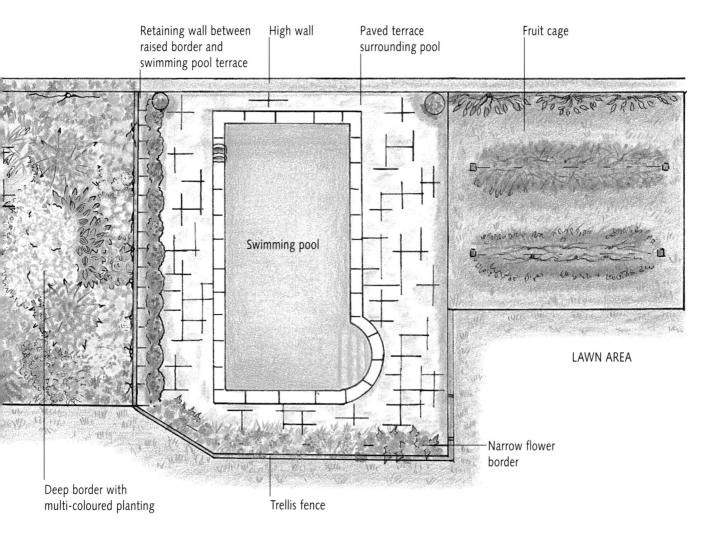

Retaining wall between raised border and swimming pool terrace

High wall

Paved terrace surrounding pool

Fruit cage

Swimming pool

LAWN AREA

Narrow flower border

Deep border with multi-coloured planting

Trellis fence

OWNER'S PLANTING SCHEME

Key plants
1 Climbing rose, *Rosa* 'Compassion'
2 Shrub rose, *Rosa* Graham Thomas
3 Shrub rose, *Rosa* Troilus
4 Shrub rose, *Rosa* Fair Bianca – a group of 3
5 Shrub rosa *Rosa* The Prince – group of 3
6 Shrub rose, *Rosa* Chaucer
7 *Rosa* x *xanthia* 'Canary Bird'
8 *Mahonia* x *media* 'Charity'
9 *Viburnum davidii* – a group of 3
10 Mock orange, *Philadelphus* 'Belle Etoile'

11 Mock orange, *Philadelphus* 'Manteau d'Hermine'
12 *Mahonia* x *media* 'Lionel Fortescue'

Decorative detail
13 Peonies, *Paeonia* – mixed species and varieties
14 Lavenders, *Lavandula* species
15 Cranesbill, *Geranium sanguineum* var. *striatum*

Flowers for added colour
Cosmos bipinnatus
Lavatera assurgentiflora
Phlox species

▲ *The sunken terrace in which the pool has been sited is sheltered from the wind in all directions and has the added advantage of mature planting along one side, with climbing roses tumbling over trellis to add colour to the pool area as well as the flower garden*

CONSTRUCTION

Having decided on a position for the pool, the owners set out to design the surrounding area themselves, with assistance from the pool construction company. A digger was used to dig out the pool and landscape the surrounding area to form a flat, partially sunken terrace, with the excavated soil being used elsewhere in the garden. Carting away the soil is expensive, so it is worth considering an alternative use for it, for example, as a rockery, or in raised beds.

The water is heated by electricity with all the necessary equipment well hidden. It is possible to use solar energy in many areas, even those without regular sunshine, if the panels are sited well. The pool is kept covered when it is not in use to maintain the water temperature, allowing it to be used for long periods throughout the year.

PLANTING

Climbing roses cover trellis that divides off the main flower garden from the sheltered pool terrace. These provide wonderful summer colour on one side of the pool. Along an adjoining side a new low trellis fence, built to keep out a young puppy, has been made almost instantly colourful with the addition of cosmos and lavatera species.

KEY PLANTS

▲ A vigorous, deep magenta pink cranesbill, *Geranium* x *oxonianum* forms clumps and flowers right through from spring to early autumn.

◄ The brick-built pergola, with a pathway leading through to the pool, is surrounded by deep beds with mixed planting giving colour and interest throughout the year. The brilliant scarlet flowers of *Crocosmia* 'Lucifer' stand out startlingly against the soft pink of the lavatera in the background and campanula to one side.

▲ A view-point from the flower garden close to the house pinpoints the pool's position on a lower terrace. It also shows the advantage of adding a pool where plants are well established

► A stone seat on the route from the house to the pool shows how well hidden the pool is. It also highlights the garden's mature and colourful summer planting

▲ Surrounding the ground around the trunk of a tree the cranesbill *Geranium nodosum* 'Whiteleaf' adds colour in what is usually a difficult spot to get plants to flower. This is an ideal plant for use in just such a situation as it flourishes in shade and dry conditions.

FOR EXTRA COLOUR

The exotic-looking flowers of clematis species and hybrids come in a wide range of colours. If they are carefully selected it should be possible to have one in flower from spring to autumn.

Clematis armandii, an evergreen with small, scented white flowers, is one of the earliest. *C.*'Nelly Moser' with its pale pink flowers, each petal decorated with a deep pink stripe, appears later, in spring to early summer. In mid-summer the brilliant magenta to scarlet flowers of *C.* 'Ville de Lyon' arrive, followed by the pinky purple flowers *C.* 'Comtesse de Bouchaud' (below) which continue until late summer.

Special effect

Brick structures are expensive to erect but bricks are one of the most durable materials for use in the garden. Here bricks have been used to build a series of pillars to hold up the timber beams for a pergola. The pergola itself extends from one side of the garden to the other and also divides the garden into a series of rooms. In addition it also helps to screen off the pool area from the house itself.

Wildlife garden

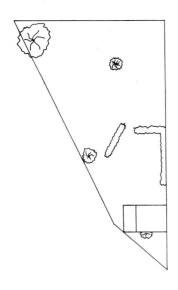

When garden designers Claire and Robin Roper came to design their own garden they had a lot of problems to contend with. Although it is situated in fairly wild countryside, the house is on an estate and surrounded by other houses and the site is windy. The garden previously had elderly owners who had been unable to keep it up and it had returned mainly to weeds and rough grass. More bio-diversity was required in the garden if it was to attract a wide range of local wildlife as they hoped it would.

◀ **Before conversion** the site was open, windy and bounded by the gardens of other houses on three sides

▼ **The planting scheme** uses a wide range of plants to attract wildlife, together with species that are also decorative in shape or colour

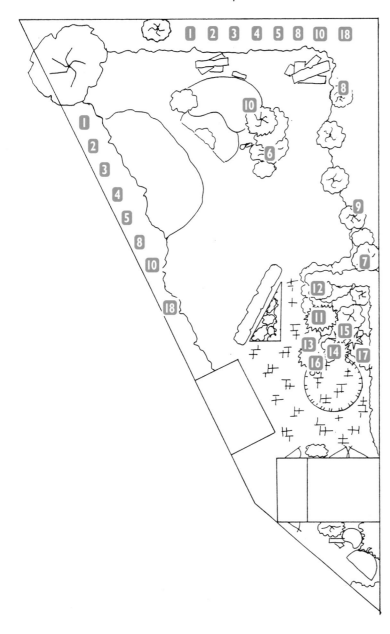

THE GARDEN'S PROBLEMS

The site is very windy.

The garden was open and overlooked and Claire particularly wanted immediate seclusion for a small eating area near to the house.

Natural drainage from surrounding gardens ended up in a lower area in this garden.

The soil is poor.

HOW THEY WERE SOLVED

Robin is a hedge layer and wanted to create a thick and wide boundary of mixed native hedge plants. Once they grow, the hedges will provide the best protection from wind there is and act as a mini-woodland area for wildlife.

Instant screening with bamboos and hazel wattle hurdles was arranged to partition this area off. A belt of small trees was planted behind these to create extra seclusion for the future.

Claire and Robin took advantage of this low, wet spot to form a pond and bog garden.

This is an advantage in a wildlife garden as, like that of ancient meadows and downland that abound in wild flowers, the soil is most suited to delicate species that might otherwise be smothered out by tougher, coarse plants which are also of less benefit to insects.

DESIGNER'S PLANTING SCHEME

Key plants
1 Hazel, *Corylus avellana*
2 Hawthorn, *Crataegus monogyna*
3 Holly, *Ilex aquifolium*
4 Blackthorn, *Prunus spinosa*
5 Dog rose, *Rosa canina*
6 Elder, *Sambucus nigra*
7 Ornamental crab apple, *Malus* 'Golden Hornet'
8 Guelder rose, *Viburnum opulus*
9 Alder buckthorn, *Rhamnus frangula*
10 Wild privet, *Ligustrum vulgare*
11 Japanese aralia, *Fatsia japonica*

Decorative detail
12 Tall bamboo, *Pseudosasa japonica*
13 Angelica, *Angelica archangelica*

14 Ladies mantle, *Alchemilla mollis*
15 Cardoon, *Cynara cardunculus*
16 Yellow foxgove, *Digitalis grandiflora*
17 Hart's tongue fern, *Asplenium scolopendrium*
18 Honeysuckle, *Lonicera periclymenum*

Plants to attract valuable insects
White rosebay willowherb, *Epilobium angustifolium* f. *album*

Jack-by-the-hedge, *Alliaria petiolata*

Thymes, *Thymus citriodorus* 'Aureus', *T. vulgaris*, *T. serpyllum* 'Snowdrift', *T.* 'Doone Valley'

Large-leaved ivy, *Hedera helix* 'Montgomery'

Mint, *Mentha spicata*

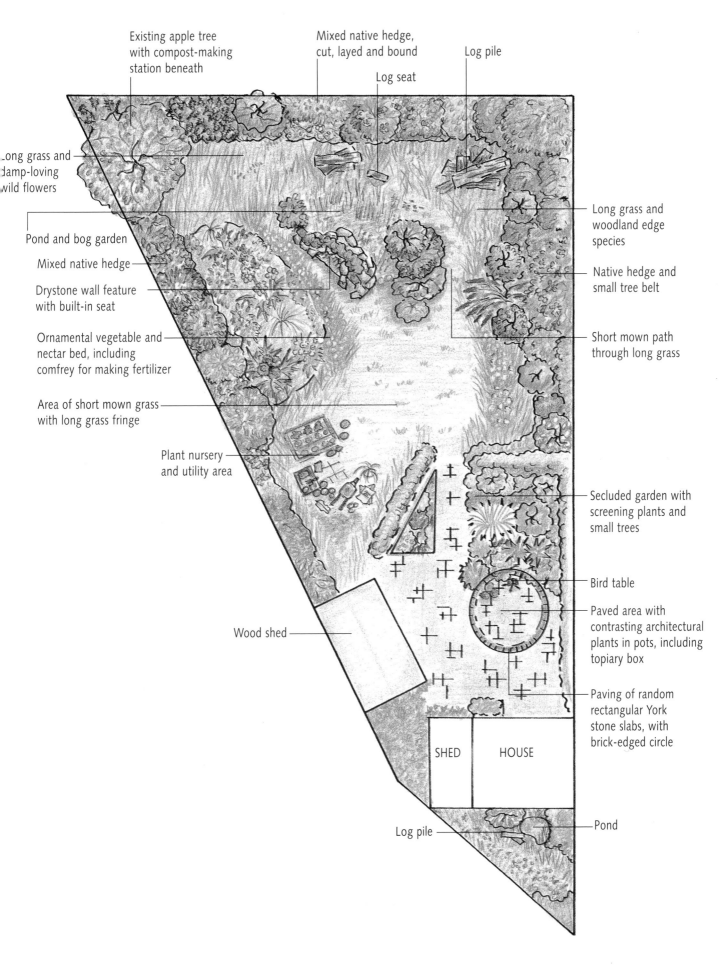

Existing apple tree
with compost-making
station beneath

Mixed native hedge,
cut, layed and bound

Log seat

Log pile

Long grass and
damp-loving
wild flowers

Pond and bog garden

Mixed native hedge

Drystone wall feature
with built-in seat

Ornamental vegetable and
nectar bed, including
comfrey for making fertilizer

Area of short mown grass
with long grass fringe

Plant nursery
and utility area

Wood shed

Long grass and
woodland edge
species

Native hedge and
small tree belt

Short mown path
through long grass

Secluded garden with
screening plants and
small trees

Bird table

Paved area with
contrasting architectural
plants in pots, including
topiary box

Paving of random
rectangular York
stone slabs, with
brick-edged circle

SHED   HOUSE

Log pile

Pond

Wildlife garden
CONSTRUCTION

Claire and Robin wanted the garden to provide a variety of habitats to attract a wide range of wildlife. They introduced hedges, two ponds and a marshy area, a wet meadow, a drystone wall, log piles, and fringes of long grass and wildflowers.

The shelved pond has a range of levels, from a shallow margin to a deep area. The liner was taken out horizontally from the edge of the pond to create an adjacent small wet meadow. On the pond's cold and windy side a drystone wall with a maze of overhangs, cracks, tunnels and chambers provides habitats for reptiles, amphibians and invertebrates. It also acts as a suntrap.

At the opposite side of the pond is a log pile which is topped up from time to time with extra dead wood. This attracts fungi and a wide range of animals and insects.

The mixed native hedge is already a useful shelterbelt and roosting, nesting and

▲ The terrace next to the house, backed by bamboos, hurdles and small trees for privacy, has an arrangement of deer antlers and lucky stones found locally, plus a topiary box, Buxus sempervirens *in a pot*

Wildlife garden
PLANTING

Plants were chosen for both their wildlife value and their ornamental shape. Dramatically shaped plants are included, such as angelica and cardoon. Most species are natural to the area of southern England where the Ropers live, and so are best suited to attracting local wildlife. It is always important to go for local native plants for this reason.

KEY PLANTS

▲ The herb bed contains an old favourite of England's King Henry VIII, good King Henry, *Chenopodium bonus-henricus*, as well as chives, thymes, bronze fennel, sage, and perennial onion.

◀ Looking across the pond from the 'wet meadow' which is created by extending the pool liner horizontally out from the pond edge. Plants include marsh marigold, cowslip, fritillary, lady's smock, meadowsweet, hemp agrimony, and water mint, all characteristic inhabitants of old wet meadows and damp pastures.

◀ *A pond is one of the most important wildlife attractions. This one is created to look as natural as possible with large rocks and gravel around the margin and contains locally native plants*

foraging site for birds. There is also a bird feeding station near to the house.

Insecticides, herbicides or fungicides are not allowed in this garden and as much as

possible is recycled. A worm bin makes nutrient-rich compost and there is also a compost bin, a bin for making comfrey fertilizer and water-harvesting barrels.

▲ *One of Robin's newly laid hedges with stakes and binders holding in place the live laid trees and cut brush-wood used to fill it out*

▼ A very architectural plant, angelica, *Angelica archangelica,* has large, divided leaves, bronze stems and greenish yellow flowerheads. Here it grows with an allium, far left and Jack-by-the-hedge, upper left, the larvae food plant of the orange tip butterfly.

FOR EXTRA COLOUR

You can sow even a small area of poor soil as a wildflower meadow using a mixture of grass and wildflower seed recommended for your type of soil and area. In the first year cut this at two-monthly intervals so that the grass does not smother out the wild flowers. After this, cut only early in spring and in autumn once the seeds have been shed. Here an area of regularly trimmed grass forms a pathway through the long grass in which oxeye daisies, *Leucanthemum vulgare*, predominate.

Special effect

Woven wigwams are created from supple hazel or willow rods that bend without breaking.

Make a wooden 'former', a shape with an odd number of evenly spaced holes in a circle. Sharpen the end of each upright rod and push one rod into each hole. Weave thinner rods in layers and finish the top by pulling the uprights together, weaving tightly. Pull out of the 'former', and fix by pushing the rods into the ground.

CHAPTER 5

GROUNDWORK

Recognizing the type of soil you have, and knowing how to improve it and what plants will thrive in it, ensures that the plants you grow will flourish. This chapter describes how to identify your soil type, how to enrich what you have and how to keep it in good condition. It also tells you when and how to water your newly planted plants to give them a good start and a strong and self-reliant root system. How to set about installing power in the garden is also covered, as this allows you to highlight decorative plantings and create wonderful effects with water. Lighting also extends the period you can sit outdoors and enjoy the garden, as well as making it safer to walk around in at night, and more secure from unwanted intruders.

Identifying your soil

Clearing the site

A new garden may appear to be little more than a heap of rubble with little or no topsoil. However, it can be radically improved if you take the following steps:

• Dig out and heap up bricks and larger stones if you think you can use them in the design. Otherwise dispose of them.

• Fork over or dig the soil to let in air and water. In the autumn cover with a thick layer of organic matter, then leave until the following spring.

• In the spring dig, then rake the surface smooth. Allow weeds to germinate and remove.

• After planting mulch well to suppress further weed growth.

Soil is rock which over thousands of years has been crushed and mixed with decayed organic matter, known as humus. The three main types of soil are light, sandy soil which is made up of large particles that do not adhere to each other and through which water and plant food pass easily; medium silt, which is made up of medium-sized smoother particles; and heavy clay, which is made up of minute particles which pack together, retain moisture and form sticky lumps that dry solid. Most garden soil is mixture, with one of the above predominating.

Topsoil is the name given to the relatively thin, darker top layer of soil which has built up over the years as it has been enriched with humus through the natural decay of organic matter such as dead leaves, animals and plants, and through cultivation. The subsoil lying below this gives the soil its general character and to a large extent determines whether it is rich or poor in nutrients, and whether it is warm or cold and has good or poor drainage, as well as whether it is acid or alkaline. Sometimes, especially where the garden hasn't been well cultivated or over poor subsoil, the fertile topsoil can be very shallow, with the infertile subsoil close to the surface. In a new house and garden there may be no topsoil at all, but subsoil can be converted into topsoil by good cultivation.

Fertile soil, loam, is an approximately equal mix of sand, silt, clay and humus. Humus is a vital, organic, ingredient which introduces a wide range of chemicals and bacteria into the soil. It improves soil texture in its own right, and encourages the activity of earthworms, whose work not only breaks it down and releases its vital ingredients as food for plants, but also aerates the soil.

SOIL TEST

To check what type of soil you have do the following test:

Pick up a handful of damp soil. (It should not be too wet.) Rub it between fingers and thumb.

It is sandy if it feels gritty, the grains do not stick together and it is difficult to roll your sample into a ball.

It is a sandy loam if it is gritty but can be rolled into a ball.

It is silt if it feels silky and can be rolled into a ball.

It is a sandy clay loam or a clay loam if it is gritty or sticky and can be rolled into a cylinder.

It is clay if it feels sticky and will form a cylinder which can be curved to form a ring.

See also:
• *Checking acid or alkaline levels, page 108*
• *Digging, page 107*
• *Mulching, pages 104, 111*

SOIL TYPE	ADVANTAGES	DISADVANTAGES
Sandy soil	Light, so easy to work Warms up quickly in spring	Free draining so quick to dry out Nutrients easily lost
Silty soil	Retains moisture well Often very fertile; improves well	Dries into hard clods
Clay soil	Retains nutrients well Improves well Good for growing a wide range of plants	Hard to work Retains water, so sticky when wet and compacted when dry Slow to warm up in spring

OTHER SOIL TYPES

Chalk soil, which is pale in colour, has many of the disadvantages of clay. It may form only a shallow layer and often contains a lot of stones. It is also usually very alkaline, see page 108.

Peaty soil is dark in colour and spongy in texture. It may be waterlogged and need draining but is often very fertile, being rich in organic matter.

Creating a sump

When installing drainage, even in a small garden, you need to provide somewhere for the drained water to collect and disperse from. You may be lucky enough to have a natural drain or ditch that you can use, but you will generally need to dig out a pit into which your water pipes can drain. This is known as a sump or soakaway. The sump should be situated at the lowest part of the garden, and needs to be at least 60cm/2ft deep and square. When you have chosen the site and dug the hole, fill it with building rubble or gravel (or a rubble topped with a gravel layer). Then place inverted turves over the drainage material and cover with more turves or soil.

LAYING LAND DRAINS

Poorly drained soils are cold and inhospitable, and their compacted structure deprives the plants' roots of the air they need. Very wet soils cause roots to rot and plants to die. If rain does not drain away but continues to lie in your garden, if only moisture-loving plants thrive, and if the lawn is full of moss, it may be that you need to install drainage.

Dig trenches in the garden for the drains leading into a soakaway (see above, right). Make these at least 30cm/1ft deep, with a slight fall towards the soakaway (following any natural slope). Place a layer of coarse grit or fine gravel along the bottom.

Lay the drains (which may be clay or perforated plastic) on the bed of gravel. Use a T-shaped connector if you are adding side drains.

To finish off pack more grit or gravel around and over the drains to improve drainage and to help to prevent the holes in the pipes from becoming clogged. Cover with inverted turves or perforated polythene sheet, then replace the soil or re-lay grass turves.

Improving soil condition

Testing for nutrient deficiency

To check if your soil is deficient in nutrients use a soil-testing kit. However, if you think you have a serious nutrient deficiency it is wise to send off soil samples for a professional laboratory test.

To take soil samples use a trowel and take soil from about 6cm/ 2 ½in below the surface. Take several samples from around the garden and test individually.

Measure into a jar 1 part soil to 5 parts water. The lid makes a good measure. Shake well then leave to settle and become reasonably clear. This can take from half an hour to a whole day.

(continued opposite)

To improve the structure of the soil on all soil types dig in lots of bulky organic matter each year, see page 107. In a good loam the soil is made up of crumb-sized pieces that can be seen by the naked eye. The spaces between the crumbs provide channels for aeration and drainage. This structure at the same time helps to maintain water and nutrients within the soil. On sandy and silty soil the addition of humus coats the soil particles to form crumbs. On clay soil it works conversely and helps to break down the solid clods into a crumb-like structure.

The benefit of worms to the soil

A good worm population is a sign of a good soil. Worms consume fresh organic matter like animal manure and part-rotted compost, breaking it down and providing nutrients which are immediately available to plants. At the same time their burrows through the soil create aeration and drainage channels.

▲ *Added organic mulches improve soil condition*

In planted areas

To keep the soil in good condition once you have put in your plants, add compost, manure and other organic matter as a thick layer of surface mulch. It will gradually be worked down to continue to improve the structure. Mulch also helps to prevent the soil from drying out, and suppresses weeds. Mulch when the soil is damp, or the material will draw water out of the soil.

▲ *Add coarse sand or grit to improve clay soil*

On heavy, clay soil

Apply lime to improve the structure (not suitable for alkaline clay, or for acid-loving plants, see page 109). Also dig in a good supply of coarse sand or grit as well as plenty of compost and manure. Do not be sparing with quantities, rather deal with one smaller area at a time.

SOURCES OF ORGANIC MATTER

- Horse, cow or pig manure
- Garden compost
- Compost from municipal waste
- Treated sewage sludge
- Spent mushroom compost
- Fresh, dried or composted seaweed
- Composted straw
- Spent hops

Quantities to use annually

- Manure: 5.5kg per sq m/10lb per sq yd
- Good compost: 2.5kg per sq m/5lb per sq yd or 1 barrow load per sq m/sq yd

Checking for nutrients

For healthy growth plants require a wide range of nutrients to be present in the soil. A consistently fertile soil should be obtained by annually digging in bulky organic matter. Mulching the soil throughout the growing season, using the conditioners mentioned, also helps to improve the soil's fertility. However, at the beginning of a soil improvement plan the soil may be deficient in some nutrients and quantities take some time to build up using this method. Also, to obtain a luxuriant look in a small garden planting has to be concentrated, and additional supplies of nutrients may therefore be necessary.

The most important nutrients are nitrogen, a component of chlorophyll, which aids healthy growth and gives leaves their green colour, phosphorus, which provides strong root growth, and potassium (potash), which is essential for synthesis of protein and carbohydrates, and which affects the size and quality of flowers and fruit. Nitrogen is the one most likely to be in short supply. It is washed out of the soil and not replenished in cold, wet weather. By digging in bulky organic matter supplies of phosphorus and potassium should remain high. Potassium deficiency is more likely to occur in light, sandy soil or chalk, and phosphorus deficiency in heavy clay soil or peat.

Even though they are required in only very small quantities trace elements such as iron, zinc, copper manganese and boron are also vital to plant growth. A very alkaline or limy soil can inhibit take-up of these important elements.

Applying fertilizers

Fertilizers are available dry, as powders or granules, or as a concentrated liquid to be diluted. Once diluted, the liquid form is watered onto the ground around plants. If the soil is dry, water it first. Liquid fertilizer can also be used as a foliar feed. Apply in the evening or in dull weather, spraying the plant's leaves thoroughly.

On bare soil apply dry fertilizer by first dividing the ground into 90cm/3ft squares. Spread the recommended quantity of fertilizer as evenly as possible.

On established plants scatter the fertilizer around each plant to feed the roots. Keep it away from the stem.

Lightly hoe the fertilizer in and water the area, unless rain is forecast. This makes it available more quickly.

(continued from opposite)

Draw off clear liquid from the top using a pipette and transfer this to the test and reference chambers of the kit container.

Pour the powder from the capsule provided into the test chamber. Shake well until the powder is dispersed.

Allow a short time for the colour to develop then check this against the comparison chart.

See also:
- *Checking acid or alkaline levels, page 108*
- *Digging page 107*

FERTILIZERS TO USE

General fertilizers that contain the three main nutrients
Organic Blood, fish and bone, seaweed meal, liquid animal manure
Inorganic Growmore formula and slow-release fertilizers that are released over a period of time, plus controlled-fertilizers that are regulated by the soil's temperature

For nitrogen deficiency
Organic Rock potash, dried blood, liquid seaweed, hoof and horn, fish meal
Inorganic Nitro-chalk, Ammonium sulphate (but makes soil more acid)

For potassium deficiency
Organic Liquid seaweed, wood ash
Inorganic Potassium sulphate

For phosphorus deficiency
Organic Bone meal, fish meal
Inorganic Superphosphate of lime

Trace elements
Organic Seaweed meal
Inorganic Chelated iron compound, proprietary tonics, and trace element granules

Garden compost

Compost bins

You can make compost by simply piling the materials up in a corner but using a bin is a neater and more efficient alternative. Compost bins are readily available. Buy the largest you can fit in. It should be at least lm/3-4ft square to produce more heat and help the contents to rot down quickly. Ideally you need two, one to take fresh material and one for partially broken-down compost, which can be forked over and left covered to go through the final stages of decomposition.

Plastic compost bin with lid, that comes in three slot-in sections.

A timber bin that is simple to construct as it comes as a kit. The timber is pre-cut and the bin is sold ready to assemble. Simply slot or nail the sections together, following the instructions.

Homemade compost provides on-the-spot organic matter to improve your garden soil. Compost is decomposed kitchen and garden waste, including grass clippings. Making it in a container not only looks neater than an open heap but aids the process of decomposition. The bacteria which break down the vegetable matter need air, warmth, moisture and nitrogen to decompose successfully.

Making compost

Decide on the position for your compost bin. It is best to stand it on bare soil. Fork over the soil in the base area to aid drainage. Then place an 8-10cm/3-4in layer of twiggy material or straw at the bottom to help provide good aeration. Follow the stages below to add the materials to be composted. Bulky material soon shrinks down. Continue to fill the bin until you reach the top. Contents should be forked over occasionally, if possible, to bring in the material around the edge to the centre, where the heap is warmer, and so even out decomposition. Finally, cover the heap to keep in the warmth: a piece of old carpet, which allows ventilation, makes an excellent cover. In summer your compost should be ready for use in three to four months. Winter cold slows down decomposition and it will probably take until the spring for it to be ready.

Pile on kitchen and garden refuse

that will rot easily. If you want to add stems and twigs they will need shredding first. It is best to add compost materials in larger, mixed quantities if possible. A good way of doing this is to keep two plastic bags beside the bin, one for kitchen waste and the other for garden waste, then mix together before adding.

Include a layer of manure when a thickness of about 15cm/6in has been reached. If this is not available use garden soil and add an activator such as seaweed meal, blood, fish and bonemeal or a proprietary compost activator to introduce more bacteria into the heap. Keep the material in the heap moist – you may need to water it in dry weather. Continue to add in layers as above.

Once the bin is full, lift it away and place it by the side of the rotting heap. Cover the heap and start a new one.

◄ With two heaps side by side, one pile can rot down while the other is being built up

WHAT TO COMPOST

- Kitchen vegetable waste, such as peelings
- Teabags, tea leaves, coffee grains
- Eggshells
- Vacuum cleaner waste
- Old potting soil
- Lawn mowings
- Thin prunings
- Bonfire ash
- Straw
- Animal manure
- Seaweed
- Autumn leaves
  It is best to rot down autumn leaves on their own in a wire basket. These take longer to decompose – up to two years – but the resulting leafmould is ideal for use as potting or seed compost.

WHAT NOT TO COMPOST

- Animal waste such as meat scraps, which could attract rats
- Diseased plant material
- Perennial weeds
- Evergreen leaves like holly or ivy (you can include conifer needles)
- Woody material
- Any man-made waste (such as plastic)

EXTRA COMPOSTING MATERIALS

You can never have too much compost. For extra supplies visit market stalls and green-grocers' shops at the end of the working day. Use seaweed, straw or green bracken (check first with local regulations that gathering them is legal), or manure from riding stables.

Quick compost tips

- When you use eggshells on your compost heap, crush them before adding them to the waste. This will speed up the rate at which they break down.
- If your garden produces a lot of thick, tough plant material such as woody stems and shrub and tree prunings, consider investing in a shredder.
- The bigger the pile, the more heat builds up inside it and the faster it will break down.
- Forking the heap as it rots, to turn the drier outside material to the middle, helps it to rot evenly.

DIGGING

Digging not only allows you to introduce soil-improving conditioners but also aerates the soil and exposes pests to be gobbled up by enthusiastic predators. To incorporate manure or compost put a layer in the bottom of the trench, then half-fill it with soil. Add more manure and finally fill the trench with soil.

First mark out size and position of the trenches, using tough garden string. Dig out a square of soil the width and depth of the spade, starting at the end of the first trench. Pile up the soil at the end of the bed.

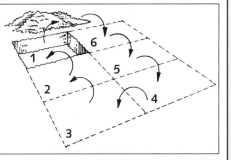

Drive the spade into the soil at right angles to the surface, and a spade's width away from the first opening, then pull back on the handle to lever and loosen the bite of soil.

Lift the spadeful of soil and twist it over, with a flick of your wrist, to invert the clod of soil into the first space. Keep your back straight while doing this, and lift with your knees.

At the end of the row remove the first bite in the next row by driving the spade in at right angles to the first row, then insert the spade between these cuts and parallel to the first trench.

Checking acid or alkaline levels

Growing plants unsuited to your soil

If you long to include plants unsuited to your soil, build a raised bed and import soil to suit the plants you have chosen.

Raised beds

The construction tips on page 120-121 can be used for building a raised bed, but omit mortar from some joints in the first line of bricks. These gaps provide spaces for excess water to escape. When building a raised bed, lay the complete rectangle of bricks that form the bed sides at each level, so that the sides are tied in with the front and back. To fill the bed, first put in rubble to one-third of its depth, then complete by adding soil to the top.

▲ A raised bed or a planting area can be made with wooden boards. Pressure-treated timber should be used.

See also:
• Digging, page 107

Another important aspect of the soil which influences its fertility and what you can grow is the pH level, or the amount of lime in the soil. This has an effect on the availability of nutrients to plants. The pH is measured on a scale of 1 to 14. The low numbers indicate an acid soil, a neutral soil has a pH of 7 and the higher numbers highlight that the soil is alkaline or limey. Most soil is slightly acid and a pH of 6.5 is ideal for a wide range of plants, including vegetables. A drop of only one point on the scale shows a soil ten times more acid (and increasingly 'sour') and a rise of one point shows it to be ten times more alkaline.

In a garden that has been cultivated for a long time, the soil often tends to become slightly more acid, whereas an alkaline soil is less likely to be affected long-term by the treatment it gets. Sometimes a limey soil has been made even more alkaline by the over-use of garden lime, which is used for improving the soil condition for vegetable growing especially for brassicas (cabbage family).

If the the pH falls below 5.0 nutrients are affected. Below this phosphate can become unavailable to plants and as the pH drops and the soil becomes more acid calcium, potassium and magnesium can be washed away, while other nutrients can appear in such large quantities that they become poisonous to some plants. The vital micro-organisms also become gradually less active. However, a very alkaline soil is equally hostile to many plants, and can cause nutrients to be 'locked' into the soil. Some plants only survive in acid conditions while others thrive if the soil is alkaline. It helps therefore to know the pH level of your soil and so which plants suit it and will thrive, see page 109 for examples.

If your soil is acid you can raise the pH level fairly simply by adding lime. It is important to do this at a different time from using manure, compost or fertilizer. If these are mixed there is a harmful reaction. If you dig in or mulch with manure in the autumn then leave liming until the early spring, about six weeks before planting. Add only a little lime at a time, then test again later and add more if necessary as it can quickly build up.

Measuring the pH level Use a pH kit (right) or a probe meter to check this. Take samples from around the garden. Follow the instructions for whichever method you use.

▲ A sprinkling of lime improves acid soil

Raising the pH on sandy and other acid soils Divide the area to be limed into 1m/1yd squares, using pegs and string and weigh out enough lime for each square. Use gloves or a spade to apply the lime one square at a time, sprinkling it as evenly as possible over the surface.

▲ *Adding garden compost and manure will help to make the soil more acid*

Raising the pH on clay soil Follow the instructions for sandy soil; left, but thoroughly dig the lime into the soil, see digging page 107.

Lowering the pH It is more difficult to make an alkaline soil more acid, although digging in garden compost and manure helps. Use liquid seaweed foliar spray to provide a quicker method of correcting deficiencies. The most successful answer is to choose plants that prefer the natural conditions you have.

LIME

Ground limestone and calcified seaweed are expensive but last longer in the soil. ·
Alternatively use slaked or garden lime. Hydrated or builders' lime can also be used, but in smaller quantities – approximately three-quarters of the quantities given below. It needs to be replaced annually as it is quickly lost.

Quantities to use
Use the following quantities of ground limestone to raise the pH by 1pH.
- On sandy soil 225g per sq m/8oz per sq yd
- On loamy soil 450g per sq m/16oz per sq yd
- On clay soil 680g per sq m/1lb 8oz per sq yd

Some plants for acid soil

If you have an acid soil you are lucky, as most garden plants thrive in a fairly acid soil, and over-acidity can be easily corrected by the use of lime. A few plants, including most heathers and lilies, must have acid soil and refuse to grow without it. Camellias (*right*), azaleas (*below, right*) and rhododendrons (*below*) are among the species that will not tolerate lime.

Some plants for alkaline soil

Alkaline soils can demand a more selective approach to choosing your plants. Many species fail to thrive when too much lime in the soil prevents them taking up all the nutrients they require. However, there are also many chalk and lime lovers, including lilacs (*right*), all the clematis (*below, right*), and buddleia (*below*).

Watering

Installing an automatic watering system

These systems include a huge range of sprinkler, spray and drip-feed heads as well as pop-up nozzles for watering the lawn that sink below the surface when they are not in use.

Connect the master unit to a hose from the garden tap. This reduces the water pressure and contains a filter that can be removed for cleaning. An electronic timer can also be screwed to the tap to turn the system on and off automatically.

Lay out the main supply tube. Position this where it will not be too visible: beneath a hedge, alongside a path or just beneath the soil surface.

Connect smaller diameter branch tubes. Position these, using the special connectors, where you need to take water to another part of the garden.

In tubs and baskets or for individual plants fit drip-feed heads to the pipe. These are held in place with special pegs.

For general localized watering use a spray head (see below).

Conserving water is important now in most areas of the world. For this reason we need to water wisely. This is also important for the production of strong, healthy plants. Plants that are watered sparingly but often produce a root system close to the soil surface and these roots soon suffer in dry periods. The healthiest plants are those that develop a strong, deep root system which is able to tap into more reliable reserves well below ground level.

Watering systems

▲ *Micro-adjustable dripper*

Automatic systems work from a garden tap. A main pipe is laid around the garden then smaller branch tubes are added which lead from it to areas where water is required. Spike fittings are positioned alongside plants to be watered, then tiny spray or sprinkler units are screwed into these. The system can be used to water containers and hanging baskets as well as beds and lawns. It is estimated that in most gardens the system needs to be turned on for only ten minutes twice a day, early in the morning and again in the evening in dry weather to provide sufficient water. A timer is also available which, fitted to the tap, automatically turns the water on and off for you.

Seep hoses can be part of the above system or laid separately along the

ground. Tiny perforations allow the water to seep out slowly and sink well into the soil. Seepage hoses are similar but can also be buried just below the soil's surface. This minimizes water loss through evaporation.

Sprinklers can be difficult to train accurately and are easy to forget, so they can be very water wasteful. Oscillating sprinklers can be adjusted to cover areas of different sizes, static and rotating sprinklers water in a circle, and pulse-jet sprinklers rotate to eject the water in a series of pulses.

Hand watering, using a watering can or a garden hose with a spray attachment, is accurate but time consuming. However, it does give you a chance for checking the health of your plants as you water each in turn, and the method is ideal for watering containers and baskets. Allow at least a full can for each large container.

▼ *A soaker hose in use*

What and when to water

▲ *Adjustable lawn sprinkler in use*

Lawns A lawn of newly sown grass-seed or newly laid turves needs regular watering in dry weather if it is to become established. However an established lawn can survive a period of drought and soon greens up again when rain arrives. If consistently green grass is particularly important to you give the lawn a good soaking once a week. In dry periods mow frequently but adjust the height of the blades to a longer 4cm/1½in. This encourages dense growth and helps to trap any dew.

▼ *A hose extension is a help for watering borders*

Large shrubs and trees need regular watering when first planted to create a healthy root system. Once deep roots are established they are able to find water for themselves and rarely need watering, even in dry periods.

Small shrubs and hardy perennials start to droop as a sign that they require water. Give the plants a good soaking in the evening when the sun is off the area.

Bedding plants and vegetables need regular watering in dry weather if they are to flourish. Water these plants either first thing in the morning or during the evening (never when they are in strong sun). The closer together plants are positioned the more water they need.

▼ *Compost in containers can dry out quickly*

Tubs, window boxes and hanging baskets should be treated as for bedding plants and vegetables. They can dry out very quickly in hot weather, and may need to be watered every morning and evening. Revive hanging baskets by soaking them in a bucket of water.

Saving water

Fix water butts to downpipes to store as much waste rainwater as you can. It is also possible to divert bath and shower water into storage tanks where it can cool prior to being used on the garden.

Watering tips

- Never water plants when the sun is on them. This not only causes leaf burn but wastes water in evaporation. Instead water in the evening.

- A good layer of mulch, about 8cm/3in, spread over the soil surface will prevent evaporation and so help to keep the soil below moist. Mulch when the soil is wet. Never add mulch to dry soil or the mulch will draw water away from the soil instead of holding it in.

- Use ground-cover plants to fill any spaces of bare soil. Once established they look decorative and help to shade the soil and prevent it from drying out.

See also:
- *Ground-cover plants, page 174*

Electricity in the garden

Safety pointers

The often damp conditions outdoors, and direct contact with the earth, make safety considerations vital. A fault could easily lead to a fatal accident.

- Ensure that installation work is carried out by a fully qualified professional electrician.

- Never service or work on equipment without first switching off and disconnecting from the power.

- Use only fittings and cables designed specifically for outdoor use.

- Check on the condition of cables and equipment and service them regularly.

- Use a residual-current circuit breaker on all sockets used for garden tools so that power is cut off if anything goes wrong.

If you wish to include garden lighting or install a pump to power a fountain or waterfall in a garden pool it is best to organize this early on, once the garden has been planned, so that you avoid the disruption of having to dig up the garden after it has been planted. Security lighting, if it is fixed to the house walls, can be run off the house supply. Some low-voltage garden lighting does not need installing, but uses cables that can be run above the ground. From a safety point of view, consider installing an outdoor socket or fitting one under cover in a garage or porch. This helps to obviate the need for long lengths of cable running from within the house: a hazard for all when you are working with electrical equipment outdoors.

Hidden power The best way to provide permanent power in the garden is to run it underground. Either special cable must be used or the cable must run through a galvanized steel or rigid plastic conduit. Both run in a channel well below ground level. An installation of this type needs to be fitted by a professional electrician as there are strict regulations which must be met and cables and connectors must be weatherproof.

▼ Electricity in the garden enables you to install pumps for water features, and garden lighting

Above-ground cables Low-voltage lighting, which uses a low-voltage transformer sited under cover in a garage or shed, can be installed, in most cases, with the cables running along the ground. In this case lay the cable in a position which is hidden from the house but easily seen when you are working in the garden to avoid accidentally cutting through it. Avoid taking the cable over sharp edges like steps or paving which could damage it. If you need to join cable use a special outdoor cable connector and for extra protection wrap this in plastic.

Circuit breakers

Outdoor socket A weatherproof socket outlet is useful, and safer, for use with power tools (such as those shown below). It must be protected by a residual-current circuit breaker (RCCB). This reacts almost instantly to break the current circuit when a fault occurs or a cable is accidentally cut.

Where to use power

Garden lighting This falls into two main categories. Lighting which is installed for safety, to enable you to find your way around the garden in the dark, or for security, to highlight and deter interlopers, may be run off the mains supply if the lights are fixed to the house walls. Cable that runs along the wall outdoors must be protected by a length of metal or plastic conduit and all fittings must be weatherproof.

On the other hand, if you wish to highlight the garden's decorative features, such as a shapely or colourful tree or shrub, you have the option of using underground cable or a kit that connects to a low-voltage transformer. Follow the manufacturer's instructions for connecting the light fittings to the flex.

Fountains and waterfalls An electric pump can be sited in a garden pool to provide the power for a waterfall or fountain, both of which continually recycle the same water. Pumps may be designed to be run from the mains supply or they may use a low-voltage transformer. Hire an electrician to install a mains-supply pump.

▲ *This contemporary free-standing lantern illuminates both the path and patio area. Night-time lighting can be activated just when the area is in use and is also ideal as a security measure*

▼ *An elaborate and unusual water feature, powered by an simple pump, in which little frogs spurt jets of water into the lowest fountain tier*

CHAPTER 6

FORM AND SHAPE

With a strong skeleton the garden will look interesting at all times of the year, even if there is the odd planting disaster. This chapter covers the materials that, together with the way they are used, make up the nuts and bolts of a garden's design.

The colour, texture and size of the paving or other materials you choose for paths and sitting areas, the way you define the boundary – whether you outline it with walls, fences or hedges, or a mixture of these – all these choices create quite different final effects. The way the space within the garden is broken up by special water features or given height with arches and pergolas contributes to its form, as does the arrangement of highlights such as containers and ornaments. Children as well as adults need to be able to enjoy the garden. And, finally, once the garden design is in place you will want to be able to sit back on comfortable and complementary furniture, with the addition of a barbecue and garden lighting, to enjoy it in all its moods, both during the day and in the evening.

Ground surfaces

Working out quantities

Paving, bricks and timber
Multiply width by length to work out the number of square metres/square yards of material that will be needed.

Gravel or shingle Multiply width by length, then by depth. One cu m/35cu ft will cover an area of 20sq m/215sq ft to a depth of 5cm/2in.

Hard surface choices
- Concrete paving slabs
- Setts and pavers
- Stone and reconstituted stone
- Timber
- Bricks
- Cobbles
- Shingle and gravel

Soft surface choices
- Grass seed
- Turf
- Wildflower meadow
- Chamomile
- Creeping thyme
- Clover

▲ *Brick is traditional looking and hard-wearing*

▲ *Timber decking gives a warmer, softer look*

The materials used for paved or hard-surfaced areas and lawns, together with the shape of these key areas, are extremely important in forming both the style and the bold background outline of a garden. Paving or other hard materials provide hard surfaces, in the same way as vinyl, tiles or timber do this in a house, while the lawn creates the softer, gentler effect of a carpet.

Planning paved areas

When planning the positions of areas to sit in, balance the practical use of the garden with aesthetic effect. Important points to consider are the position of the sun, the need for shade, shelter from wind, a good view, and privacy.

If you plan to have more than one paved area, each situated in a different part of the garden, this can provide the choice at any one time of relaxing in the sun or sitting in the shade.

Once you have decided on the position, size and shape of a paved area use hosepipe or rope to outline it on the ground. Allow plenty of space for chairs and tables and, possibly, plant containers. Arrange the furniture within the outlined area to check that it will all fit in the space comfortably. You may need to adjust the area size to take into account the paving material you choose so that you avoid having to cut slabs.

Leaving spaces for planting can look effective but it does restrict the use, so work out positions for these areas carefully. Containers, which can be moved around, are a less rigid alternative.

◀ *Paving is both durable and pleasing to the eye*

Choosing the materials

Consider both the style of the garden and the materials used in the construction of the house; this is most important if the paved area adjoins the house. A paved area next to the house should have a slight fall away from the house so that rain drains away from the building rather than towards it.

Pre-cast concrete paving slabs are reasonably priced and easy to lay. They also come in a wide range of colours, shapes and finishes. Avoid a highly textured finish where you intend to use furniture. Check the change of colour when slabs are wet and how slip resistant they are.

Bricks blend well with a traditional brick-built house and provide a natural, country effect. They can also be laid in a range of patterns. House bricks are too soft to be suitable and flake if exposed to winter weather. Choose frostproof, hard-

▼ *Pebbles or other materials can be mixed with paving slabs to vary the effect*

▲ *Natural stone is perfect next to an old house*

wearing bricks such as engineering bricks or brick pavers.

Setts are another small-sized and decorative alternative. Granite setts are exceptionally hard-wearing, and look particularly at home in areas where granite is the local building material. Concrete setts give a similar effect, and are cheaper.

Timber decking is a popular surface, sympathetic to the surroundings in most gardens. With the use of paint or stain you can add colour if you want to. Old railway sleepers are sometimes available as a very strong, and cheaper, alternative. If timber becomes dangerously slippery when wet or in frost staple fine chicken wire over the surface.

Stone Sandstone, limestone, ironstone, York stone, and slate all blend beautifully with most garden styles but these materials are expensive and difficult to lay. Reconstituted stone is cheaper. Both come as straight-sided slabs or with uneven edges to be laid as crazy paving. Alternatively you can use broken stone or concrete slabs for this.

Cobbles are uncomfortable to walk on but ideal for forming smaller patterned areas in plain paving.

Gravel and shingle are both cheap, easy to use and give a softer finish. But they provide some problems too. They

▼ *Gravel is more suitable for pots than furniture*

are best retained by an edging as they tend to 'walk' with you into the house and onto the lawn, where they can create a danger when mowing. Although some plants look very effective growing through the surface, regular weeding will be necessary if you don't want the area to be overtaken by seedlings. Laying plastic sheeting underneath the gravel helps to avoid this but holes will need to be made in the plastic for drainage.

Gravel and shingle both provide a measure of security in a front garden as any visitor's arrival is very audible.

SOFT SURFACES

A lawn from turf gives you an instant result, once the ground is prepared, and turf can be laid at most times of the year, but it is cheaper to sow a lawn. The best time to create a lawn, whichever method you use, is spring or early autumn. In both cases there are two widely available alternative grass mixes you can use. Those that include ryegrass are hard-wearing and easy to care for. Garden owners who want an exceptional-looking finish and are prepared to spend time on looking after a lawn should go for a fine, dense grass.

Alternatives to grasses are clover, camomile and creeping thyme but these are suitable only for small areas. You can also sew an area as a wildflower meadow using a mixture of recommended grass and wildflower seeds. In the first year this should be cut at two-monthly intervals so that the grass does not smother the wild flowers. After this cut only early in spring and in autumn once the seeds have been shed.

Mixing materials

By combining materials you can create decorative effects. For instance use larger quantities of cheaper paving and provide character, pattern and design detail with small-sized, more expensive alternatives such as granite setts or cobbles to create an uneven surface. This makes a paved area or a path more interesting. Below, pebbles are introduced between areas of paving slabs on a pathway.

Lay the pebbles in spaces left between paving slabs. Fit them as closely together as you can on a bed of mortar.

Lay a stout piece of wood across the pebbles from one slab to the next to check that the pabbles are flush with the paving. If necessary tap the wood with a hammer to bed them in and ensure the surface is completely even.

Paths, steps and edgings

Laying stepping stones

Stepping stones that meander across a lawn are less intrusive than a path. They also provide a way of moving across gravelled areas without taking the tiny chippings with you.

Work out the positions of the stones by walking along the route the path will take. Take normal strides and mark the position of each step as you go.

Place the stones in the positions marked and check the effect visually. Walk over the stones to double-check the spacing.

Cut around each stone with a spade, to a depth slightly more than that of the stepping stone.

Cut beneath the slice to be removed and lift the turf out.

Level the base of the cut-out space with sand. Position the stone, check that it is level and just below surrounding grass to avoid damage to the mower.

Path and step choices
• Concrete paving slabs
• Setts and pavers
• Stone and reconstituted stone
• Timber and bark chippings
• Bricks
• Cobbles
• Shingle and gravel
• Grass

Edging choices
• Bricks
• Tiles
• Terra-cotta strips
• Timber, logs, railway sleepers
• Rocks or giant pebbles
• Low-growing plants
• Low hedges or fences
• Shells

Paths, like paved areas, highlight the design of the garden, providing definition, while the materials you use to create them enhance (or detract from) the character. Steps which lead from one level in a garden to another work in the same way, and can follow the form and materials used for the linking path or add new and interesting textures by introducing different materials. Most of the options covered in ground surfaces – not forgetting grass, if the area will not get much wear – are also suitable for paths and steps. Edgings add definition and act as a practical divide to keep soil off paths and lawns and to contain softer path materials.

◀ *The contrast of bricks with stone is used effectively for steps and raised beds*

Providing links

Paths provide a convenient link with each section of the garden from the house, allowing you to wander and admire as well as to work without damaging soil structure. They can be straight or meandering, according to the garden's design, but need to lead to a specific point of interest, which may be as mundane as the garage or garden shed, a place to sit and relax or a closer view of a point of special interest such as a statue, pond or group of pots. Where paths meet there is an opportunity to create a central pattern using the same or a different material. Pebbles or bricks are ideal for this. If there is space this area can then be used to show off a sculpture, an ornamental urn or a container holding a topiary bush or a shapely shrub or tree.

The width you choose will be governed by both the garden's size and some practical factors. The narrowest width advisable for a path is 30cm/12in. This will be wide enough for just one person to use the path. If you need to use the path for a wheelbarrow just over twice this width will be more suitable.

If a path will create too hard a line and make an over-strong impression on the space it needs to go through, breaking up the design of an area such as a lawn, consider using paving slabs as stepping stones instead. These can also define a route along a path made of softer materials such as grass or gravel.

Moving from one level to another

Garden steps, both for safety and for aesthetic reasons, are best if they are constructed as wide and shallow as possible. A flight of steps does not have

▼ *Steps should be wide, broad and shallow*

▲ *Terra-cotta edging finishes off a brick path*

▲ *Plants soften the edge of a straight path*

Laying timber edging

Timber edging comes as wood strips wired together. You can cut the wire to shorten the strip, or wire two lengths together.

Unwind the roll and use wirecutters to cut it to length.

Dig out a trench for the edging, having first worked out the height you want the edging top above the ground.

to be straight. Curving steps not only look good but provide a range of aspects as you pass up or down them. Angle steps slightly forwards to avoid the danger of standing water, and bear in mind that you will need an alternative route for wheelbarrows and lawnmowers.

Consider using a different material for the riser and step surfaces– for example bricks topped with stone slabs.

Edging paths, patios and beds

An edging not only defines the shape of a path, patio, flower bed or steps but it is a practical method of containing soft materials such as soil, chippings or gravel.

Apart from materials made specially for the role – for example, timber edging, corrugated plastic strip and coiled terra cotta – you can use hard materials such as bricks (either flat or set diagonally on edge), paving, tiles or logs, and even railway sleepers. For a purely decorative effect consider the use of large pebbles, shells or other suitable natural material.

Beds can take a softer edging with low hedges or a line of ground-hugging plants, which are ideal for showing off the shape, but to keep the soil and grass in place first fit a lawn edging strip. Make sure that the top of the strip sits just below lawn level to avoid damage to the mower.

Lay the edging in the trench, checking the height and that it is level along the length. Back-fill with soil and firm well. .

For a straight top place a length of timber over the edging strip. Use a club hammer to knock it firmly in place.

See also:
• *Ground surfaces, page 116*

▼ *An informal combination of materials*

▼ *An inventive but formal design*

Walls and screens

Building a low brick wall

Even a low wall needs to be built on a firm foundation, or footing, of hardcore and concrete.

Form the footing by excavating a 30cm-/12in-deep trench. Fill it to a 13cm/5in depth with consolidated hardcore. Drive in pegs as a guide for the top of the concrete and check that peg tops are level.

Complete the footings by pouring in concrete. Level it off with the peg tops. Use a piece of wood to tamp the concrete level and to remove large pockets of air. Leave to harden for a few days.

Lay the first course of bricks. Form a pier at each end by placing two bricks sideways. On a long wall you will also need to repeat piers at regular intervals.

(continued opposite)

A brick wall is the traditional way of outlining a boundary to a garden and providing it with privacy, and is both very long lasting and attractive to look at. It can also help to keep out intruders and animals, provide shelter, or screen an ugly view. A boundary wall, because it encloses the garden, highlights its size and shape. To give the shape less emphasis, to make the space appear larger, or to create more interest, vary the material used around the perimeter or vary the wall's height. When mixing walls and fences construct areas of fence on a low brick or stone wall to create a more integrated look. Where complete privacy is not required pierced concrete or open terra-cotta blocks provide another visual effect.

Walls are also used as retainers, to hold the soil in a series of stepped terraces in a sloping garden or to create a sunken area. High or retaining walls are not easy to construct and are best erected by a specialist. Materials used may be bricks, stone, reconstituted stone, flint or concrete blocks, which can be faced with stone if preferred. A wall needs capping to protect the construction. Some choices for capping are bricks, set side-by-side across the width, concrete slabs, or some other weatherproof material.

Walls as internal dividers

Within the garden, strategically placed openwork screens can divide the garden into a series of 'rooms' with an enticing

▲ *A dry-stone wall is a haven for plants*

view of something interesting beyond. Alternatively, with a covering of plants, they can hide necessary eyesores like the garden shed or dustbin, or provide

▼ *A low brick wall can make a screen or divider*

▼ *Raised beds can team with boundary walls*

(continued from opposite)

Lay subsequent courses after running a ribbon of mortar along the top of the previous row. As shown, 'butter' one end of each brick before you position it.

Frequently use a spirit level to ensure bricks are level. As you work strike off any surplus mortar from the wall sides.

Firm and adjust the level of each brick as you lay it, using the handle of the bricklaying trowel.

Finally fix coping and pier caps to complete the wall and protect the brickwork from excessive moisture.

▲ *Trellis-work breaks up an otherwise dull surface and filters the wind*

▲ *Combining painted trellis panels with traditional picket fencing creates an original look*

privacy for a paved sitting or eating area. Apart from openwork masonry walls, timber trellis, slatted wood, and even openwork wire mesh can be used to form slim dividers. Screens of this type also filter wind and sun very effectively. As they allow some air-flow they do not act as a total barrier creating eddies of wind in the way that a solid wall can do.

Low walls can edge a pond or patio, or act as a decorative divide between different areas and levels in the garden without supplying a feeling of enclosed spaces. To soften the hard lines of a wall use dry-stone walls with nooks and crannies for plants, or create a double-shell wall with a space in the centre to take soil for planting. A higher, flat-faced brick or stone wall can be used as a sheltering background for climbers and a wall that faces the sun makes a home for tender plants. Brick wall piers can act as plinths for containers of flowering plants, and wall baskets and similar containers can add the softness and colour of plants to an otherwise bleak wall.

Wall materials
• Reconstituted or natural stone
• Bricks
• Flint
• Concrete blocks
• Pierced concrete
• Pierced terra cotta

Screen materials
• Timber trellis, stained or painted
• Openwork terra-cotta or concrete walling
• Slatted wood

See also:
• *Fences,* page 122
• *Hedges,* page 124

GATES

An opening in the garden boundary wall, fence or hedge usually needs a gate to complete it and to keep children or pets inside the garden or livestock and wildlife out of it. Several factors help you decide what type of gate is best suited to your specific situation. The general surroundings, the purpose of the gate, and the materials used for the boundary are all involved in deciding on the best design and materials. High, close-boarded gates provide privacy and security, while low, openwork designs allow a sight of the house or a view from it. Timber or ironwork gates are the common choices. Both look best if they match the boundary in height, although the top may be shaped to form an inverted curve or an arch.

Fences

Erecting a panel fence

The simplest way to erect a fence is to set the posts in metal spikes.

Position the spike with the protective head inside the top and drive it in with a sledge-hammer. Make sure that the spike remains vertical. Check often with a spirit level.

With the post in position in the spike top, check that this is absolutely vertical.

Lay the first panel in position, next to the post, and mark the spot for the next post spike. Drive the spike in as before.

(continued opposite)

Fences are quick to construct and relatively cheap in comparison with walls. They act as windbreaks, hide an ugly view, keep out animals, and outline a boundary. There are advantages and disadvantages to erecting a high and solid barrier, however it is constructed. Height provides privacy but high walls or fences throw long shadows, keeping off sun and rain, which can prove a major problem in a small space. While hedges and trellis filter the wind and reduce its strength, wind is only diverted by a solid barrier, not stopped in its tracks, and this can cause turbulence on the opposite side. A lower fence, topped with trellis and covered in climbing plants, provides a better alternative and still gives privacy. A wall or fence that faces the sun can give protection for plants that grow against it on the sunny side.

◀ *A closeboard panelled fence*

Fences make an instant boundary, take little space, do not compete with garden plants for food and water, and provide immediate privacy. They are erected on posts which may be of wood, concrete or metal. These can be fixed into the ground directly, set into concrete, attached to a concrete spur or pushed into the top of a metal spike driven into the ground. In the two latter methods a timber post is not in contact with the soil and so is likely to last longer. Concrete posts are the longest-lasting but are visually less compatible with timber fencing.

Style options

Fences come in a wide range of materials and designs to suit every situation and type of garden.

Panel fencing is the simplest high fence to construct and it is cheap to buy and very popular. There are two designs, overlapped and interwoven. The overlapped panels provide more privacy. Panels of either design are fixed to posts but are not very strong and are almost impossible to repair.

Closeboard fencing is tougher and can be made to any height. It is constructed from overlapped boards held into position on horizontal, triangular-shaped rails. The best method of construction for both types includes a gravel board. This runs along the bottom to protect the board ends from damp, and is easy to replace. The top edge of a closeboard fence can be cut straight or shaped to form scallops between posts.

Woven hurdles are used in the classic cottage-garden fence. Hurdles come in a range of heights and are usually made from pliable stems of willow or hazel

▼ *Woven hazel hurdles for a country look*

▲ *Diagonally set timber for a contemporary look*

▲ *Picket fencing is a country classic*

(continued from opposite)

Nail panel brackets to the first post. Nail matching brackets to the second post, then remove the second post temporarily.

(which is coarser), which are woven in and out of stouter upright stems. Hurdles are not long-lasting but are easily portable and provide a good temporary barrier while shrubs or a hedge grow. They also form a decorative method of hiding an unattractive structure such as a garden shed, bin or compost heap.

Picket fencing, either stained or painted white, provides a good, low boundary for a front garden. It is constructed in a similar way to closeboard fencing but with spaces between the uprights. The top edge of each upright may be rounded, pointed or cut in any design.

Post and rail, baffle or ranch fencing is simpler in design, constructed from posts linked with two or three horizontal rails. Wire is often fixed between the rails in country areas to keep animals out.

Wire with concrete posts forms the simplest of utilitarian designs. To hide the basic structure plant fast-growing evergreen climbers along its length. Plastic-coated chain link or chicken wire provides additional plant supports.

Plastic fencing is an easy-maintenance option but is not as strong as most other materials. It is available in ranch style or as post and plastic-coated chain.

Trellis fencing comes in a wide range of widths, heights and thicknesses, in both timber and plastic and in square or diamond shapes. Expanding trellis is also available but is not very strong. Trellis makes an excellent internal divider. It can also form attractive open areas in a tall boundary fence and can be fixed to the top of a wall or fence to give extra height for climbing plants.

Position the panel and get someone to hold it while you position the second post. Check the panel is horizontal, then nail into it through the brackets.

Nail a post cap to the top of each post to complete the fence.

Materials choice
• Timber, metal or plastic

Style choices
• Woven panels
• Closeboard
• Wattle hurdles
• Picket fencing
• Post and rail fencing
• Trellis

See also:
• *Walls and screens, page 120*
• *Hedges, page 124*

▼ *Post and rail fencing is available in rural or more cultivated style (as shown here)*

▼ *Diamond-shaped trellis panels finish off this opening in a plain fence*

Hedges

Planting a hedge

Before you plant a hedge it is important to prepare the ground well. Dig a trench and, to improve the soil's structure, dig in plenty of garden compost or well-rotted manure. The prepared strip needs to be at least 60cm/2ft wide. Before planting break down large clumps of earth and sprinkle on a balanced garden fertilizer. If planting in autumn or winter use a slow-acting type.

Caring for bought plants Hedging plants are often sold in bundles of bare-rooted plants. Keep the roots moist, for example by placing them in a temporary planting hole. Separate them as you plant.

To ensure a straight hedge use a garden line and insert markers spaced as recommended for each plant. Do not place too close together, when there is a risk that individual plants may die. In a windy situation or on a boundary stagger the planting of the trees as shown here.

(continued opposite)

Hedges can mark a boundary, divide the garden into smaller, room-like spaces or form a low, neat outline to decorative patterns on formal beds. They can also protect plants from adverse weather conditions, deter burglars, help to lower noise levels and attract wildlife. Hedges have another advantage, they rarely collapse in a storm in the way that fences, or even walls, can do.

Formal hedges
A neat, clipped and compact evergreen hedge looks much the same throughout the year and is ideal for creating a formal outline in or around the garden. The plain colour and smooth lines also provide a good backdrop for flowers and plants within the garden. These hedges need clipping regularly to maintain their shape.

The traditionally grown plants for evergreen hedges are privet, yew, laurel, and box. Conifers are also commonly used. Avoid speedy-growing Leyland cypress and go for slower-growing alternatives such as *Chamaecyparis lawsoniana* 'Ellwoodii', which will, in the end, produce a more satisfactory hedge. For neat, low hedges there is the dwarf box, *Buxus sempervirens* 'Suffruticosa'.

▼ *A clipped yew hedge is always an attraction*

◄ *It takes several years for a hedge to thicken up*

Less formal effects
There is a wide range of flowering and fruiting shrubs that can be trained to form decorative but looser-growing hedges. For spring colour go for forsythia with its sunny yellow flowers that appear before the leaves. For a low hedge *Berberis thunbergii* 'Atropurpurea' has purple-bronze foliage turning a rich red

▲ *A low box hedge encloses a lavender bed*

in autumn. Hornbeam, *Carpinos betulus*, has yellow or green catkins in spring and turns a yellow-orange in autumn before the leaves fall. Beech, *Fagus sylvatica*, can provide a formal or informal outline depending on how tightly you trim it. Although it is deciduous, the autumn leaves often remain on the hedge all winter; the copper beech, *F. s. purpurea*, has purple leaves that turn a deep, rich copper colour in autumn.

Plant a mixed hedge for a traditional country look and to attract a wide range of birds who will appreciate the food, protection and nesting potential. Country hedges usually include some of the following: hawthorn and blackthorn,

▲ Rosa rugosa *is usually still in flower when the first hips ripen*

◀ *A proper country hedge is laid in the time-honoured way to become thick and impenetrable*

(continued from opposite)

hazel, beech, holly, spindle, privet, dogwood, dog roses, honeysuckle and guelder rose.

Hedges for security

Thick, prickly hedges form ideal deterrents to unwanted visitors if you plant them along road-sides or bordering a front garden. The common holly, *Ilex aquifolium*, and its varieties are excellent for this. For a variegated form choose 'Ferox Argentea' with cream-margined leaves or 'Golden Queen' with golden margins. *Berberis* x *stenophylla*, also dense and thorny, is a colourful alternative, with its gold flowers in spring and purple-red leaves.

A rose hedge can be both decorative and extremely prickly. Choose *Rosa rugosa* varieties for their closely prickled stems. Many also have flowers with a beautiful scent and large red hips in autumn. The flowers come in white, yellow, and many tones of pink through to deep crimson. *Berberis thunbergii* is also thorny but grows to only about

1m/3ft high. Its fresh green leaves above, blue green below, turn orange in autumn and it has red-tinged, pale yellow flowers and red fruit. Hawthorn, *Crataegus monogyna*, is also suitable and has white or pink-tinged flowers in spring followed by red fruit.

▲ *A bushy fuschia hedge, seen in full bloom, is an attractive alternative to a formal clipped hedge*

Dig a large hole for each plant and position it, spreading out the roots. Fill the hole with soil and firm it well.

Finally rake the soil level and water plants thoroughly. Keep well watered for the first season.

Some hedge plant choices
Evergreen hedges
• Box, *Buxus sempervirens*
• Holly, *Ilex aquifolium*
• Viburnum, *V. tinus*
• Cedar, *Thuja occidentalis*
• Laurel, *Prunus lusitanica*
• Yew, *Taxus baccata*
• Privet, *Ligustrum ovalifolium*

Colourful hedges
• Rose, *Rosa rugosa*
• Hawthorn, *Crataegus monogyna*
• Cotoneaster species
• Hornbeam, *Carpinus betulus*
• Escallonia varieties
• Mexican orange blossom, *Choisya ternata*

Low herbal hedges
• Lavender, *Lavandula* species
• Sage, *Salvia* species
• Cotton lavender, *Santolina chamaecyparissus*
• Rosemary, such as *Rosmarinus officinalis* 'Severn Sea'
• Hyssop, *Hyssopus officinalis*

See also:
• *Digging*, page 107
• *Fertilizers, page 105*

FORMING A FEDGE

A fedge is a combination of fence and hedge and is a good way of creating the effect of a hedge in a narrow space. Plant ivies about 2.5-3m/8-10ft apart against a fence until they intermingle to form a dense cover over the framework, then clip to control growth. The traditional fedge is made by pushing in and weaving willow stems, which soon root and grow to form a narrow, green barrier.

BEWARE FAST-GROWING HEDGES

The fast-growing Leyland cypress, *Cupressocyparis leylandii*, is not really suitable for a small garden, particularly if you wish to remain on good terms with your neighbours. The advantage of its speedy growth is outweighed by the fact that it does not simply stop when it reaches the required height but continues on apace and so needs topping as well as trimming every year.

Introducing water

Creating a pond

A preformed shape enables you to install a pond very quickly, and little skill is required.

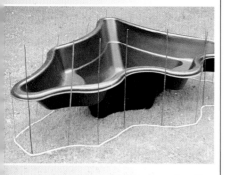

Place the pre-formed pond on the ground and mark out its outline with canes. Lay rope around the canes to mark the shape.

Dig out the the pond area, taking into account shelves and changes in depth. Make your hole slightly bigger than the shape.

To check depth measure down from a plank across the hole. Use a spirit level placed across the plank to check that the pond is also level.

(continued opposite)

There is room for a pond or pool in even the smallest garden. Although a larger pond creates a wonderful light-reflecting focal point, something as small as a waterproof tub can contain a miniature pond where space is at a premium.

Some thought needs to be given to the pond's position. It should be situated in an open, sunny spot. Overhanging trees not only cast shadows which prevent water plants from flourishing but their falling leaves create problems too.

The next decision is whether to go for a formal or informal effect. An informal pond is best sited where a natural pond would occur: that is in a low-lying area of the garden. If you wish to place it elsewhere, perhaps where it can be viewed more easily from the house, build up the background, using the excavated soil, to create a bank or rockery behind. On the other hand, a formal pond sits well in the centre of a paved area, or a lawn. There is no reason to stick to just one pond. A series of interlocking ponds creats a stunning water garden. Fountains and waterfalls, using a pumped recycling system, help to keep the water in good condition, whereas care needs to be taken to balance a still pond if the water is to remain crystal clear.

▼ *If you want a natural effect position the pond in the lowest part of the garden. Design its surroundings (including the approach and pond-side area) to form part of the whole feature*

▲ *A tub can be made into a small container pond*

Formal effect

In a symmetrically planned formal garden simple rectangular, square or round ponds look most in keeping, although a semi-circular pond placed against a wall or fence on the patio can also slot into the design neatly. Formal pools can be raised, with a surrounding wall providing a ring-side seat. This is ideal for a pond or a patio. Alternatively the pond can be sunk into the ground.

Use a pond to alter the apparent shape of a garden. A long, narrow pond placed across the width in a long, narrow garden will help to make the space appear wider. Or, more unusual but equally effective, take the pond almost from one side of the garden to the other at an angle. A walkway across the water can lead you from one area to the next.

MINIATURE PONDS

Any container that can hold water can be turned into a miniature pond. Wooden tubs, old sinks, plastic plant containers, fish tanks are all suitable. The pond can either be sunk into the ground or placed on top of it. If you add a 15cm/6in layer of compost to the base you can plant a small water lily and one – possibly two – aquatics. Cover the soil with a layer of gravel and add a few large pebbles, then fill with water.

The natural look

An informal pond needs to look as natural as possible, in both shape and surroundings. Squared-off sides are out, as are blue liners (choose black or brown instead). A natural pond looks smaller once it is planted, so allow for this in your choice of size. If you want the water to attract wildlife take grass right up to the edge and provide a shallow beach at one end to make it easy for animals to enter and leave the water. Birds will use this area for drinking and bathing.

Pond-making materials

The simplest method of constructing a sunken pond is to use either a preformed shape or a flexible liner. It is wise to buy the best quality material you can afford as once the pond is installed it becomes a major problem to fix a leak, should one

A stone surround finishes off the pond and keeps the lining anchored

▲ For a natural look you need to use a liner

occur. A flexible liner gives more freedom as you can make the pond any shape you like. If you wish to introduce fish or larger waterlilies you will need a depth, at least in part of the pond, of 45-60cm/18-24in. Shelves around the edge allow you to include marginal plants which thrive in shallow water.

A sunken formal pond can also be created using these materials. A raised pond is usually constructed using concrete for the base and tough external bricks or reinforced concrete blocks for the sides. A colourful effect can be created by lining it with mosaic tiles.

Pond edgings

With lined ponds it is important to cover the pond edge to avoid an unnatural finish. If you use paving, tuck the liner underneath the slabs and allow the paving to overlap above the water. If you run grass right up to the pond edge the flap of the liner should be turned down and buried so that the grass has soil to grow in. Allow the grass edge to meet the water and hide the liner. Pebbles also create a natural-looking outline.

POND SAFETY

Avoid ponds while you have small children. It is possible to drown in very shallow water. Instead, if you long for a water feature consider installing a wall-fixed recycling fountain. A mill stone or a low basin of pebbles, where water jets out then trickles over the surface, are also suitable.

(continued from opposite)

Place the pool in the hole and check that the edges are completely level from all angles, using the plank and spirit level.

When the pond is snugly in place run water into it, packing fine soil around the edges as the water level rises. Finally push soil firmly under the shelves, ramming it down with a piece of wood.

Material choices
- Pliable plastic or rubber liner
- Pre-formed rigid liner
- Concrete raised pool

Miniature pond containers
- Half-barrel
- Trough
- Saucer-shaped stone or concrete container
- Plastic or other waterproof container

See also:
- *Water plants, page 178*
- *Moving water, page 128*

Moving water

Choosing a pump

A pump is necessary to provide the power to circulate the water for a waterfall or fountain. Pumps can either be submersible, sited in the water, or surface-fixed nearby, in which case they need a housing to protect them.

Submersible pumps are less powerful but will deal adequately with most fountains up to about 1.2m/4ft high or a small waterfall. They work silently, and low-voltage models are available which can be connected to the house electricity supply.

Surface pumps are more powerful, and with a surface pump a range of fountains and waterfalls can be run from one system. The pump and its housing should be positioned as close to the pond as possible so that only short lengths of tube are necessary.

When buying materials for a water feature, discuss with the suppliers exactly what effect you want to create. They will then be in the best position to advise you on the pump most suited to the effect you wish to achieve.

Moving water features
- Fountain
- Waterfall
- Cascade
- Millstone
- Bridges, stepping stones, and walkways

Moving water provides exciting effects while at the same time creating a tranquil atmosphere: something most of us appreciate in today's fast-moving world. A fountain, tumbling stream, waterfall or gently falling droplets all provide the tinkling sound of moving water. More and more inspirational ideas on ways to use moving water are appearing all the time and these can be seen on display in water-garden centres, on television gardening programmes and in specialist water-garden books. Some novel ideas include vertical falls of water which stream down light-reflecting backdrops, and slow-drip bamboo pipes, as well as the more traditional tumbling streams and gullies. You will need to install a pump for moving water features.

▲ A multi-bowl fountain splashes and sparkles

There are innovative fountain heads using almost any material or shape through which a pipe can be threaded, as well as specially produced animals, heads, figures, shells and flowers. Much larger areas of even small gardens are being turned over to water with ambitious features such as a series of ponds or canals bridged by stepping stones and walkways to create their own effects.

Fountains These are the simplest moving-water structures to fit and usually suit a formal area or formal pond best. A fountain can be an independent feature of single or multi-storey bowls where water falls from a head at the top to ever-larger dishes set one below the other. In this case no extra work is needed except to site the fountain and set up the electricity required to power it and recirculate the water. A fountain added to a garden pond can be positioned centrally in the pond or placed at the edge. Bear in mind that it will look most effective if it is in scale with the pond. A large ornament and wide-spreading jet of water will look incongruous in a small pond and vice versa.

According to the head you choose, water from a fountain can appear in a wide number of shapes from a single spout to multi-tiered sprays, whirls, bells,

▼ Water spilling into a trough over wood arranged in tiers encourages contemplation

▲ *Water cascading over stone ledges needs a natural-looking setting to be effective*

fishtails and geysers. Fountain kits are available which include a fountain jet, a flow adjuster to alter the speed of the water, and a submersible pump. The pump should be positioned on a brick or other block to keep it raised above the bottom of the pond. The electricity to power the system can either be taken direct from the mains or make use of a low-voltage connector.

Waterfalls and cascades In most cases waterfalls look best in a natural setting. Here the soil excavated from the pond can be used to form the base for a rocky outcrop from which the water tumbles in tiers. A waterfall can be constructed from

the same materials used in making a pond. Additional rocks and stones embedded in the surface give a more natural finish. Pre-formed stream sections are also available. In most cases the distance from the pond surface to the top step of the waterfall should not be greater than 90cm/36in. Get advice on the most suitable pump for the job when working out the design and buying the materials.

Millstone and pebble fountains Water spouting out of the centre of a millstone or falling to run over a layer of pebbles in a shallow saucer creates an effective small-sized feature. These usually come as a kit and are simple to install. Wall-fixed fountains for use indoors or outside can enliven the end of a small terrace or pathway. For a stronger impression use a wall-fixed fountain that sprays the water into a larger semi-circular pond below.

Bridges, walkways and stepping stones A series of interlocking ponds creates a bold and stunning water feature. Ponds can be large enough to go from one side of the garden to the other, provided a safe method of crossing the water is included in the design. Ornamental timber bridges are the traditional method used but flatter concrete or timber walkways on a level with the pond edges, or stepping stones of slabs, provide a less obvious route.

▲ *A millstone fountain takes very little space. The gurgling sound of the water bubbling up from the centre is soothing and water brings a shine to the surrounding stones*

▲ *An arched timber bridge is the traditional way to cross a pond or garden stream although there are plenty of equally attractive alternatives*

POND LIFE AND MOVING WATER

Fish benefit from the introduction of a fountain or waterfall. The splashing increases the amount of oxygen in the water and the rate at which carbon dioxide is released, as well as helping to prevent ponds from freezing over. However, water lilies and other surface plants, plus some deep-water aquatics, are best kept away from splashes and turbulent water. Water lilies need warm, static water, and are damaged by constant splashing which submerges the flowers and rots pads.

Plant frameworks

Some simple plant supports

Lines of crossed canes set in pairs in a row give support to runner beans or sweet peas. Tie pairs together near the top, then slide a long horiizontal cane into the V and secure.

Wigwams of tall canes arranged in a circle are pulled together at the top and tied in place with string. You can also use a specially produced holder (above) through which the canes are pushed to hold them evenly spaced.

(continued opposite)

In small gardens where there is limited space for plants it makes sense to utilize vertical surfaces as frameworks and grow plants skywards. Walls and fences are obvious choices but free-standing structures covered in plants can considerably enhance the garden's design, providing colour at a higher level and helping to support and protect plant stems at the same time. Climbing plants may be trained up timber trellis, wire, plastic or twine to clothe walls or fences, and the use of cane wigwams, ornamental obelisks or metal corkscrews allows you to introduce extra height wherever you feel it is required, without the need of a wall. As well as climbers, tall plants with soft or brittle stems need supporting if they are to cope with windy conditions or heavy rain. Herbaceous plants form the best shapes and remain in place in windy weather if they are supported by wire frames or twig cages.

Unobtrusive or deliberately decorative

Frameworks may be unobtrusive, simply holding a plant in place, and can be home-made from bamboo canes, plant sticks or stems and twigs cut down in the garden. They can also be very decorative in their own right if they are woven in arched or wigwam shapes. Metal corkscrews, timber obelisks, metal or timber arches and pergolas all create strong features as part of a garden's design. Tall and decorative supports such as obelisks, wigwams and corkscrews add height attractively to an area of low-growing plants. Arches and pergolas can divide up a garden, forming a number of separate sections, each with a different theme or colour scheme. A strategically placed support densely planted with climbers can also hide an eyesore.

Home-made frames

Supports made from natural plant stems, saplings or twigs are less obtrusive than manufactured alternatives. Willow, hazel, birch or any other supple wood, can be bent and used to create a support as an alternative to more rigid vertical bamboo canes and pea sticks. A circle of canes is easily arranged to form a wigwam with the cane tops tied together. If string is wound around the poles in a spiral

▲ A wooden framework for climbing plants will provide a shady sitting area

▲ A climber trained around the front door gives height to this small front garden

An obelisk makes a delightful focal point

effect, plants are more easily trained and the result can be very decorative. Place the canes in a circle of at least 75cm/30in diameter. If extra strength is required for more robust climbers add a central stick and use canes of larger diameter. A double line of angled canes, the pairs crossed at the top with a horizontal pole placed in the V, forms a straight barrier and support for a row of climbers such as sweet peas or runner beans.

Shorter twiggy stems, pushed well into the soil in a circle or square and intertwined, make a cage shape which is a good support for herbaceous plants. Provided the cage is positioned early on in the growing season the plants will happily grow through the support to hide it as it keeps them in shape.

QUICK-GROWING COLOURFUL CLIMBERS

Clematis hybrids • Runner beans • Canary creeper • Ivy • Sweet peas • Nasturtiums Morning glory • Honeysuckle • Golden hop

▲ The framework for climbing plants can be an ornamental feature in itself

Supports to buy

A wide range of metal supports is available to suit many plant shapes, heights and arrangements. Most last longer than home-made alternatives. Some are designed to blend into the background as the plants grow. In others, such as obelisks and metal spirals, the frame itself forms an important part of the final effect and looks best if it is not completely obliterated by plant life.

▼ Climbing roses growing up the verandah posts enhance this timber structure

(continued from opposite)

Twiggy sticks can be pushed well into the ground to support plants. Insert them early on to allow the plants to grow up through them.

Metal supports come in a wide range of sizes and can be linked together to suit individual plants.

A sturdy stake, hammered well into the ground, is needed to support most trees. Use a special tree tie that holds the stem away from the stake, thus avoiding any damage to the stem.

Choice of plant supports
• Walls and fences
• Arches and pergolas
• Wigwams
• Crossed canes
• Herbaceous plant frames
• Metal corkscrews
• Obelisks
• Trellises or wires fixed to fences or walls

Arches, pergolas and arbours

Building a rustic arch

These tips on building an arch could also be followed to construct an arbour.

Sketch a design on paper. To suit your situation and the height and width you require.

When fixing a horizontal section to an upright use this basic joint.

Where two pieces cross, mark the position and cut halving joints in each one, using a saw and chisel.

Use wood glue and a rust-proof nail to hold each joint.

(continued opposite)

Taking the eye up and away from ground level, arches, pergolas and arbours add new dimension to a garden. They also provide a perfect opportunity to grow a wide range of climbing plants.

▲ *Tubular metal arches such as this can be bought as ready-made units and extended at will*

Arches come in a range of shapes which may be round-topped, pointed or square. An arch may be independently positioned to frame a view. It may lead the way from the house to the patio, or highlight the entrance to a pathway or the route beyond a fence or hedge. A row of arches may be lined up along a path.

A pergola is a larger structure made up of a series of joined arches. This may form a single divide between one area of the garden and another but it is also commonly made of a double row of uprights held together by roof struts and placed to span a path or form a covering for a patio. A pergola can also be attached along one side to a wall or fence, or to one end to the house or garage.

Depending on where it is sited, an arbour is a partially enclosed space that may be a garden hideaway, a place in which to sit in private, or a ring-side seat from which the whole garden can be viewed. An arbour or a pergola can be made more rainproof by adding a translucent roofing material to the top.

Construction materials

Arches, pergolas and arbours all form a striking part of a garden's design and look most in keeping if they suit the house and the garden's style. Stained or painted squared-off timber is popular for modern situations, while rustic poles are commonly used to recreate a country-garden style. These can have the bark removed to help prevent rot and insect infestation or left on to attract small insect-eating birds. Iron or tubular steel with a galvanized, painted or plastic-coated finish can also be used. For a long lasting, but more expensive, alternative

▼ *This timber pergola crowned with roses takes little ground room and adds a vertical element*

SCENTED CLIMBERS

Include some of these wonderfully scented plants amongst those you choose to clothe arches, pergolas and arbours:

Honeysuckle Common honeysuckle, *Lonicera periclymenum*, has white to yellow flowers in mid- to late summer, followed by bright red berries. *L. hildebrandiana* is evergreen or semi-evergreen with fragrant cream-white flowers in summer, also followed by red berries (which are poisonous).

Jasmine Common summer jasmine, *Jasminum officinale* has white flowers in mid- to late summer. *J. beesianum* is evergreen with fragrant pink-red flowers in early and mid-summer.

Rambler and climbing roses 'Etoile de Hollande' is a climbing rose with dark crimson, very fragrant flowers, 'Sutter's Gold' blooms early with yellow, pink-veined flowers, and 'Compassion' has salmon pink to apricot flowers in summer. 'Félicité et Perpétue' has small, double, pale pink to white flowers.

brick or stone uprights may be built and married up with timber roof struts. Garden seats with an arch incorporated in the design are available and these only need to be positioned against a solid background to form a simple arbour.

Arches, pergolas and arbours can be made on site from scratch to suit a particular situation or bought in a range of sizes already cut and in sections to be easily erected on site. In most cases you will need to allow for poles which are at least 60cm/24in longer than the height required, to provide a fixing into the ground. A span of about 1m/3-4ft is about the widest suitable for an arch.

Siting an arbour

An arbour is usually sited in a sunny spot, with the frame and plants providing shade as required. In a windy situation it is best to site an arbour with its back to a wall, fence or hedge to provide protection. The structure can be positioned parallel with a side or end boundary, run diagonally across a corner, or sited centrally within an open space.

As a seat is the central ingredient of an arbour decide on its size and shape first, then build the structure around it. The frame material and thickness will need to be strong enough not only to take the span required but also to support vigorous climbers. Draw up a rough sketch of the design you would like to produce. Include the measurements and take this with you when buying the materials so that you can obtain advice

▲ *A crisp white arbour with a built-in seat*

on the thicknesses required. The open frame will soon be transformed by clambering plants to make an enclosed space. Scented climbers will make sitting in the arbour a special pleasure.

QUICK COVER-UPS

Your chosen climbers may take some time to get established. While they are growing, sow seeds of annuals such as morning glory, *Ipomoea indica*, which has rich blue flowers; sweet peas, *Lathyrus odoratus*, especially 'Galaxy' group, which come in a wonderful range of colours; or the cup and saucer plant, *Cobaea scandens*, which has bell-shaped flowers that open creamy green and age to a deep purple, finally displaying large, decorative seed heads.

(continued from opposite)

Bird's mouth joints are useful for connecting horizontal or diagonal pieces to uprights. First mark the position carefully then cut out a V-shape about 2.5cm/1in deep in one piece and saw the second piece to fit. Drive a nail diagonally through the joint.

Assemble each arch side and the top separately on the ground first. Insert the uprights in already prepared holes, fix temporarily with wooden struts, then drill and screw the top in position. Secure the uprights firmly.

Materials choice
- Sawn timber
- Rustic poles
- Wrought iron
- Tubular steel – galvanized, painted or plastic-coated
- Posts of brick or stone

Containers

Container plant care

Plants grown in containers need a little extra care if they are to flourish and reward you with a constant show. In hot, dry weather water at least once, and if possible twice, a day.

Watering Water retaining granules in the compost can save on watering. A hosepipe makes watering a number of containers relatively quick and easy. For out-of-reach hanging baskets use a lance attachment, compression sprayer or special basket pump. Alternatively, attach a cane to the hose end to lengthen it and keep it rigidly upright.

Feeding To avoid having to feed regularly use a slow-release or controlled-release fertilizer and add it to the compost when you plant the container.

For shrubs and trees sprinkle either of the above fertilizers on the surface in spring, then fork lightly into the compost surface.

(continued opposite)

Plant-filled containers add an exciting extra dimension to almost all gardens and are a must for areas without soil such as roof gardens and balconies. They are very versatile, allowing you, amongst other things, to clothe an uninteresting wall in colour or transform an area of the garden when it is not looking its best.

Containers can create a welcoming doorway, highlight a paved sitting area, line a row of steps or lead the eye down a pathway. Hanging baskets and window boxes add colour and greenery at a higher level. By grouping containers in a range of sizes you can create a 'bed' of colour in any area or, conversely, you can use a beautifully shaped container-grown shrub or tree to form a focal point where space is at a premium. By under-planting a container-grown tree or shrub you can add a splash of temporary colour when this is needed.

Plants in smaller pots can be moved about, allowing you to show off decorative flowers such as lilies, which look stunning for a comparatively short time, and then hide them away in a less obvious spot when the flowering period is over. Tender plants grown in pots can be transferred to a more sheltered spot in colder weather. Pot-grown annuals can be

▲ *A rough-hewn stone trough adds rustic charm*

partially immersed in a flower bed when added colour is required, then easily removed and transferred elsewhere.

Choosing containers

Plastic and fibreglass containers are cheap and come in a wide range of shapes and sizes. They are lighter than most of the alternatives and therefore

▲ *Terra-cotta pots come in a huge range of shapes and sizes*

▲ *Plants grown in pots can be moved for protection against frost in winter*

▲ *Regular watering and feeding helps plant growth, which soon hides the container*

▲ *Window boxes can be used to make a mini garden but must be securely fixed*

(continued from opposite)

Routine care Once a week check containers, dead-head flowers, remove yellowing leaves and those that show signs of pests or disease. Control pests and disease as soon as you find them.

Container choices
- Plastic
- Fibreglass
- Timber
- Concrete
- Reconstituted stone
- Terra cotta
- Glazed pots
- Baskets
- Buckets
- Chimney pots and clay drains

See also:
- Ornamental extras, pages 136-137

▼ *A wooden half-barrel makes an ideal container for a small conifer and colourful pansies*

ideal for roof gardens and balconies. Fibreglass, often made to imitate lead, is the stronger and more durable of the two. With careful planting a plastic container can almost disappear behind the contents, or you can use paint to antique or decorate the outside. Check before buying that a plastic container is suitable for use outdoors.

Terra-cotta pots provide a popular country-garden look. They also come in a range of shapes and sizes, from plain-finished clay pots to those with ornate raised patterns, as well as urns with handles and those with side pockets for planting. Earth or compost in terra cotta dries out quickly in hot weather so plants need to be checked regularly. Ensure the terra cotta is frost-proof as it can flake or crack in freezing weather. In winter never stand pots in water-retaining saucers as the water may freeze and crack the pot.

Wooden tubs, half-barrels, and troughs can look rustic or classic depending on the shape and finish. Timber will rot in time but if treated with paint or a plant-friendly preservative its life can be extended. Lining a wooden container with plastic will also lengthen its life.

Large baskets, such as log baskets, have become popular because they make unusual, attractive and reasonably priced containers. Prolong a basket's comparatively short life by oiling it well before planting. Cover the bottom of the basket with cut-down plastic plant-pot bases to keep the soil off the basketware and line it with plastic in which drainage holes have been made.

Glazed pots in wonderful jewel-bright colours are now available. Not all are frost-proof, so check when buying if this is important. Choose a colour to complement the intended contents.

Concrete makes a cheaper alternative to reconstituted stone. To age a new-looking exterior smooth it with yoghurt which will encourage algae to grow.

Recycled containers Many decorative holders can be transformed into plant containers. They need to be deep enough and should have a base that can take drainage holes. Suitable plant containers are chimney pots, clay land drains, buckets, paint pots with all signs of paint removed, and wheelbarrows, which are also easy to move about.

Window boxes come in all the materials mentioned above and look most effective when plants cascade over the sides so that the container is almost invisible. Boxes filled with compost are very heavy and need to be securely fixed in position.

Hanging baskets and wall troughs may be made of plastic-coated or plain wire, of iron, basketwork or solid plastic. Liners are available in many materials. Baskets look best when young plants are inserted in the sides as well as the top so that the plants grow to form a flowering ball.

Ornamental extras

Tips on disguising an eyesore

- A carefully positioned upright tree can soon obscure a power pole. Stand in the viewing position with someone else holding the tree so that they can move it backwards and forwards and from side to side until the best planting position is found. Planted closer to you a shorter tree will hide more.

- Climbers grown up strategically positioned trellis will soon hide a fixture such as a garden shed, dustbin area or coal bunker.

- Grow climbing roses up a chicken-wire framework to hide drain pipes. The thorns deter burglars and other intruders.

- Stand a low pot containing trailing annuals on a manhole cover to hide it, or buy a specially designed bowl-shaped cover which can be planted but still removed if necessary.

- Use a pergola to hide an ugly overhead view, with a fast-growing climber forming a roof.

Ornamental choices
- Classic figures
- Birdbaths
- Wildlife and pet sculpture
- Water features
- Beach bounty
- Rocks and pebbles
- Logs and tree stumps

▲ *Large stone mushrooms – a fun feature on the lawn*

A well-positioned ornament or decorative feature will add the finishing touch to imprint your character on your garden. This kind of feature gives a small garden it final flourish, and can provide extra interest, an element of surprise or even amusement It may be something as stylish as a traditional stone figure, a decorative urn or a moder sculpture. It may be something entirely natural, such as a group of giant stones, a heap of logs in a wild area or the addition of sea-washed driftwood and shells to a wate feature. It may add a touch of humour that makes you smile – plastic decoy ducks on a pond, a concrete cat sitting amongst the catmint, ornate life-sized metal birds pecking a the lawn, or even a hard-working gnome or two.

▲ *A classical lead urn for timeless elegance*

Choosing the right site
Positioning is all-important. Drawing the eye, a focal feature can be placed where it is instantly seen centre stage in the garden or to catch the eye where two paths cross. Hidden around a corner, a light-coloured ornament set on a plinth amongst shrubs and adorned with ivy provides a surprise and brings life to a dull spot. At the end of a path, forming the view that draws you on, a figure can be set beneath an arch.

An ornament also needs to work with its surrounding. When choosing what to use, bear in mind both plants and surface materials used in the spot where you want to place it. Finally, don't be rigid about the positon but move around the object you have chosen until you are sure that you have found the best place for it. There is no need to choose a single item: a group of pots, natural materials, figures or gnomes will create an interesting focus. Take time to arrange the position of each until you are happy with the overall result. You could re-arrange the items periodically to keep other members of the family and friends on their toes!

Range of choices
Whatever you choose make sure that it will withstand being outside in all weather conditions.

Pots and urns Glazed pots are available in wonderful rich tones that are ideal for providing colour and texture to an over-shadowed part of the garden. Classic terra-cotta urns with handles, or narrow-necked tall, slim jars also make perfect focal points on their own or grouped, perhaps with one lying on its side.

Classic figures in traditional designs are produced in reconstituted stone or concrete, or in fibreglass with a finish that looks like lead.

Animals and birds specially made for outdoor displays come in concrete, metal

▲ A metal resin lizard wall fountain

▲ An armillary sphere that is also a sun-dial

▲ A garden elf water feature adds winsome humour in a green pond-side corner. Water features like this and the one shown top left are relatively simple to install.

and plastic. Arrange water birds around or in a pond, or position one or two birds or animals under a tree or amongst low plants in a bed.

Birdbaths, birdtables and sundials combine usefulness and decoration, proving that garden features do not have to be purely ornamental.

Water features A small moving-water feature immediately forms a focal point. Many pre-formed designs are available or you can construct your own. The only requirements are a drainage hole in the base and matching hole in the top

section so that the water can be circulated, and a position for the pump. Use an urn on its side to drip or pour water into a shallow saucer as part of a small water feature.

Garden gnomes Colourful, cheerful and eye-catching, gnomes make a strong and humorous focus wherever they are positioned, alone or in a group.

Natural materials Some of the most effective garden ornaments are designed by nature and available free to be picked up on the beach or in the woods. Smooth, colourful pebbles, big pieces of stone, a group of scallop or spiral shells and driftwood can be used to enhance a water feature. Tree stumps, cones and logs add interest to a woodland area.

'stone' birds are made of fibreglass and are completely frost-proof

▲ This inventive yet realistic bird is made from recycled pieces of metal welded together

▲ This wooden bird house provides a stiking feature whilst taking up little space

Children's play space

In a garden where there are small children their safety is paramount and the following points should always be considered.

- Position play features so that they are clearly visible from the house, so that you can easily keep a watchful eye on what goes on from indoors.

- Keep chemicals and garden tools locked away. Ensure that the garden shed is always kept locked, or erect a special lock-up cupboard in the garage.

- When in use make sure that electric cables on garden tools are easily seen, and use a residual-current circuit breaker on all sockets used for garden tools. Ensure that power tools are never left unattended.

- Check gates and fences regularly to make sure that they remain child-proof.

- Never leave small children playing unattended near a pond or water.

- Ensure that the garden contains no poisonous plants. Foxglove, deadly nightshade, laburnum, ivy, caster oil plant, lily of the valley, rhododendron, oleander are just a few to be avoided. Most fungi are best eradicated.

- For a safe landing under swings and climbing frames use a thick layer (10-15cm/4-6in) of pulverized bark.

Play structures
- Sandpit
- Swing
- Climbing frame
- Playhouse
- Personal garden

Fine weather draws children, like a magnet, outdoors to enjoy the freedom of space. If you provide a range of exciting play choices to stimulate the imagination they will be happily occupied for hours. In a small garden there is rarely room for a completely separate area for children's play projects. If you don't want play structures to overpower the design of a small garden consider position and materials at the design stage, along with the requirements of all members of the family, so that sandpits, swings, climbing frames or playhouses can be built to blend in with the rest, using materials that appear elsewhere in the garden.

▲ This all-in-one play structure, with its sandpit floor, would keep any child happy for hours

Lawns need to be tough if they are to stand up to energetic play so use seed or turf with a high percentage of perennial ryegrass, which can better survive the rigours of pounding feet.

The garden provides a wonderful first insight for small children into the world of nature. Take time to explain how wildlife and plants of the garden live and grow. Involve children in the siting and fixing of bird tables and nesting boxes, as well as feeding the birds. This provides a useful introduction to looking after pets responsibly. With the help of the child involved choose an area of the garden specially put aside for him where he can grow his own plants from seed. Quick-result plants such as sunflowers and sweet peas are a good choice, as are beans, carrots, lettuces and spinach which can later be picked, cooked and eaten.

Structures that adapt
Flexibility is important as children's requirements change quickly and play structures soon fall out of use. However, with some forethought equipment can be erected with the future in mind, so that a play space can take up a new role when the children lose interest in using it.

Swing A well-constructed archway can form a sturdy frame for a swing. Provide a

surface of grass or bark chippings for safety. When the swing is no longer in use the arch can form a frame for a selection of climbers and soon become a decorative feature.

Sandpit Dig out an area large enough to make exciting sand construction projects of buildings, boats, automobiles or whatever catches the imagination. A sturdy surround will help to keep the sand in place, but avoid sharp-edged materials and instead use sawn logs with the bark removed. If you form the sandpit in an interesting shape the framework can be used to edge a flower bed or pond when the sand is removed.

Climbing frame If you need to fell a tree at any time this could easily become part of an exciting natural frame. Add platform, steps and swings to create extra stimulus. A mature tree in the garden

begs to become a climbing frame and will undoubtedly be used, so it pays to add rope ladders and platforms that make it a safer spot to play. Alternatively construct a climbing frame as part of a pergola or build it with a future use as a pergola in mind. A thick layer of bark chippings, extending well beyond the frame, provides the safest ground surface. It will blend in well if you also use bark chippings as a mulch on beds.

Playhouses Playhouses provide hours of fun and form the inspiration for all sorts of fantasy situations. Specialists provide a range of imaginative designs. Alternatively adapt a small garden shed by painting it and adding special decorative features inside. Use only unbreakable glass, plastic or PVC for the windows. The house can go on to become a teenagers' retreat or revert to additional storage space. If you lack the space for a permanent playhouse make an instant one by using a wigwam frame as a base. When required simply cover the frame with blankets or a specially decorated old sheet. Later grow runner beans or peas up it or introduce scent with honeysuckle or roses.

◀ A little raised play house, with its own ladder access, makes a perfect secret hideaway

▲ When making a play area for your children, line the ground with a thick layer of bark chippings to soften their inevitable falls. This material also makes the area look more in keeping with a gardener's garden and will help to improve the soil

Including water

As a small child can quickly drown in water as shallow as 4cm/1.5in, it is not wise to include a pond at an early stage in a youngster's life. If you move to a house with a pond, drain it and use it for a sandpit instead. Water does not have to be completely excluded from the garden – instead add a wall fountain or a small running-water feature such as water flowing from an upturned pot into a shallow pebble-filled saucer.

See also:
- Ground surfaces, page 116
- Plant frameworks, page 130
- Arches, pergolas and arbours, page 134

Garden furniture

Well-chosen and well-sited garden furniture extends living into the garden in the most comfortable and relaxing way possible. For most people, with interior space at a premium, garden furniture either needs to be tough enough to stay outdoors all year or be fold-up or stackable so that it is easily stored away when not in use. There are two main types of garden furniture – that which is used for eating outdoors or for short periods when you want to relax with a cup of tea or coffee, and that for longer periods when you simply want to opt out and lounge in the sun or the shade.

▲ The ultimate in poolside luxury: loungers with drinks tables attached that can be wheeled back into store. The separate table and sunshade complete this relaxing scene

Caring for garden furniture

Timber needs checking out once a year. Sand down and stain or paint when signs of weathering appear. Some timber needs oiling.

Metal needs regular attention if it is not protected by a plastic coating. As soon as any rust appears, sand to remove, and repaint to seal the surface.

Plastic only needs wiping down with a damp, soapy cloth.

Stone and concrete benefit from a periodic wash down with soapy water and a soft brush. Rinse well to remove all soap traces.

Materials choices
- Timber
- Reconstituted stone or concrete
- Cane and wicker
- Metal
- Plastic
- Canvas
- Metal or plastic frame with padded cover

Furniture used for eating outside will usually double up as a temporary resting spot, but garden benches spaced strategically around the garden make a decorative addition and allow the opportunity of moving from sun to shade at any time. Place a single bench to create a visually attractive element as part of the garden design and in a position where it provides a new and different view of the garden from that of the main sitting area. This type of furniture needs to be robust enough to remain permanently in place. Additional comfort can be quickly provided with a few cushions.

The most popular chairs for sunbathing, or relaxing in the shade, usually have a light, fold-up plastic or plastic-coated metal frame that can be positioned at a range of angles on a ratchet system, and a long, padded, slip-

▼ Teak furniture suits most surroundings and simply needs oiling to keep it in good condition

▲ This well-designed and sturdily built garden furniture comes in ready-painted wood

over cushion. These chairs can be moved about with ease so that anyone can follow the sun or shade as required.

Material choices
Furniture can either be chosen to blend with its surroundings or to make a colourful statement. In most cases permanent furniture looks best if it blends with other materials used in the garden, for example natural timber for a brick patio, or a wooden bench to stand below a tree at the end of the garden. For painted furniture, choose colours to blend with those used in nearby rooms of the house or mimic the colours of nearby garden flowers. White furniture works well where white or bright colours are used and green blends attractively into a leafy background.

Timber furniture may be natural in colour, and in tough hardwood such as oak or teak or less robust stained

◀ Moulded plastic may not have a long life but it is cheap and light, the chairs stack easily and seat cushions will give added comfort

softwood, or it may be painted. Unless wooden furniture is fold-up, it is designed to stay in place around the year. However, wood takes a beating from rain, cold and frost in winter and hot, dry weather in summer, so it needs to be regularly maintained with oiling or painting if it is to last when kept outside.

Stone or concrete seats are tough and easy to maintain, requiring little more than a periodic scrub. They are perfect for an individual bench seat in a tranquil part of the garden or built-in as part of a sunken patio or low divider wall. Curved designs are available, that can be placed together to go round the trunk of a tree.

Cane and wicker, like timber, blend beautifully with the natural surroundings of a garden but they cannot be left outdoors as sun and rain soon damage them. Their light weight makes these chairs and tables easy to transport but they take up space indoors. Storage can be a problem, but if the patio leads off a conservatory then the furniture can double up for indoor and outdoor use.

Metal furniture may be traditional wrought iron, which is heavy and needs constant maintenance if it is not to rust, or a lighter aluminium copy. Plastic-coated metal is easier to maintain, only needing to be wiped, although a cheaper surface coating can deteriorate.

Moulded plastic furniture, usually in white or green, is now very popular as it is easy to look after, light to move, and weather resistant. Most table tops and legs come apart for storage and chairs stack to take up a minimum of space

over winter. Plastic furniture can be left outdoors throughout the summer. Buy good quality furniture if you want it to last. Cheaper alternatives can crack and discolour on exposure to sunlight.

Canvas-covered, perennially popular, deck chairs or director chairs are light to move and fold flat for storage. Director chairs are also smart enough to provide seating indoors when required. Canvas rots in time but is simple to replace.

Padded fabric loungers with metal or plastic frames can be adapted to lounging or upright position, are light to move around and fold up for storage.

Home-made seating adds an individual look to your garden. Concrete paving slabs can be built onto the top of a low wall, a plank screwed to a couple of tree stumps could make a temporary stop-over spot in a wild garden or, for something very different, use a special metal chair frame shape and plant it with box to make a topiary seat.

▲ A marble-topped metal bistro table and co-ordinating folding chair. This type of furniture is decorative and useful for summer drinks, and the table can be left out all year while the chair folds up for easy winter storage

▼ This wooden lounger seat comes with its own well-padded mattress, and with built-in wheels is easy to move around

Barbecues

Barbecue choices

- Built-in barbecues
- Kettle barbecues with domed lids
- Portable table-top designs
- Trolley barbecues
- Gas wheel-around barbecues

Safety points

- Always site barbecues well away from overhanging trees, and from shrubs and timber fences or buildings. A gust of wind can easily send sparks flying which could start a fire.

- Never try to light a barbecue with petrol or paraffin but use special barbecue lighters and begin about 45 minutes before you want to start cooking.

- Don't leave a barbecue unsupervised at any time while it is alight.

- Remember that charcoal takes a long time to cool down. Spray with water to speed up the process. This also saves the loss of any coals still burning, which can be stored for future use.

- Have a bucket of water or sand available to damp down flames in an emergency.

- Think of the neighbours and make sure you site the barbecue where the wind won't blow your smoke, and cooking smells, into their garden. This also applies if they have hung out their washing to dry on a line.

In good weather the garden provides a relaxed place to eat, whether it is daytime or evening, and whether it is a family mealtime or you are entertaining friends. Few people who enjoy eating outdoors would now consider being without a barbecue. If you regularly eat in the garden it is well worth building in a barbecue area as an integral part of the patio design. The best place to site a barbecue is a sheltered spot, well away from trees and large shrubs, and close to the kitchen so that it is easy to transport any food and equipment to and fro.

Choosing a barbecue

Choice of barbecue depends on how often you are likely to use it, how easily and quickly you want results, how many you want to be able to cook for, and whether you have easily accessible storage for the barbecue when it is not in use. For those who prefer heat at the turn of a switch there are wheel-around gas barbecues, or if you are only one or two, and you like the simple life and taking a barbecue with you on trips to the country or sea a small portable barbecue may be more appropriate.

Built-in designs A built-in barbecue that is incorporated in the patio design and uses the same materials is much the least obtrusive, can stay in position around the year and can be made to measure your needs exactly. Barbecue boxes that come in a range of sizes are widely available and these can be slotted into a brick- or stone-built frame allowing you to build the barbecue to a height and design that is individual and specifically suited to you. If you include weatherproof storage space for fuel to one side and a good-sized worktop area for utensils, plates and food, the barbecue will be ready for use whenever you want it – and you will have no storage problem.

Wheel-around gas barbecues Provided you have the space close by to store a barbecue run on bottled gas this is by far the quickest and simplest to use. Heat arrives almost instantly at the turn of a switch and the lava rocks used give food a similar taste to that of a charcoal barbecue. Another feature is that the heat is easy to control, with several types of

◄ *Brick-built patio barbecues are available commercially (as shown here), but if you are good at DIY you can design and build your own custom-made version*

adjustable flame. Gas barbecues come in a wide range of sizes, with a lid that keeps heat in and will also keep the food warm if you don't want to eat instantly. Many of the designs available provide worktops at either side and storage space below. Weatherproof covers allow you to keep the barbecue outdoors during the summer months, so that it only needs to be stored away through the winter. Gas-powered barbecue woks and griddles are also available, and wheel-around charcoal-burning barbecues are another option.

▲ *Gas barbecues, with wheels, and lids that close down over the cooking area, are availabe in a range of sizes and styles*

▲ *A simple portable barcecue is ideal for campers and picnic lovers, and can still be used in the garden. Winter storage is no problem with this type of equipment*

◀ *Portable gas-fired woks and griddles are a more unusual alternative to barbecues for outdoor eating*

Portable barbecues These are easy to store and transport if you also like to take the barbecue with you when you go out for the day. There is a huge range of sizes and designs available from small, brief-case slim styles to bigger and more robust pot-bellied shapes. If you want to use the barbecue regularly at home it is a good idea to build a platform to bring smaller and flatter portable barbecues up to a working height to avoid bending.

Lighting

Points to bear in mind

- Consider the neighbours when siting garden lighting. Avoid positioning lights that shine directly towards them. Position lights to point downwards.

- Use only lighting fitments designed specifically for outdoor use and use a professional electrician to fit stronger permanent lighting.

- Lights that play on moving water are specially effective. Follow any installation instructions that come with a fitting very carefully and conceal ground-level fitments among tall waterside plants.

- Show off stylishly shaped plants or striking garden features with hidden spotlights.

- Use difused, softer lights to highlight a specific area of the garden.

- Give a party feel to a special evening event with strings of hired coloured lights, garden flares and protected candles.

Materials choice
- Fixed buried lighting
- Low-voltage lights from a transformer
- Solar-powered lights
- Gas lights
- Lanterns
- Pond lights
- Garden flares
- Garden party lights

See also:
- Electricity in the garden page 112

Garden lighting considerably increases the enjoyment of the garden. In winter you can sit in the warmth and comfort of your home and view the magical effect of plants or decorative features transformed by frost or snow. On a balmy summer night you can eat outdoors or just sit on the patio and admire the surroundings. Lights can show off prize plants, a pond or statue or simply create a romantic ambience. Most important are carefully positioned lights which allow safe passage through the garden or provide good working light for barbecue chefs and helpers, and security lights to show up any uninvited visitors who try to slide in unseen.

Highlighting plants and special features In a small garden it is usually most effective to pick out only two, or perhaps three, features to spotlight. Whether you choose to show off a tree, shrub or special architectural feature, highlighting shape rather than colour usually provides the most effective result. This type of lighting should be professionally installed as there are strict rules governing outdoor cables, which need to be buried, plus the waterproof connectors and fittings that are necessary.

Angle the lights to shine away from the viewing position and avoid allowing the source itself to show. The fitting can be concealed behind a low shrub, wall or other fixture or use stones or logs. Before deciding on the final position for a light source move the fitting around, trying different heights for the best effect.

For a more muted light which softly shows up groups of smaller plants use low-wattage lights run off a transformer that brings down the power to a safe level. A lighting set of this type usually

▲ This outdoor dining area is lit by candle-light, with extra light coming from the house

▼ A set of garden flares is attractive for parties

includes the transformer and cable (which can be run above the ground), connectors that clip into the cable at any point you choose, and the light fittings, which push into the ground on spikes. This makes it comparatively easy to move the lights about, allowing you to temporarily highlight a different area when plants look their best.

Solar-powered lights that draw off energy from the sun in the daytime to give off a soft, diffused light at night conserve energy, cost nothing to run and require no wiring. Gas lighting also provides an attractive, gentle glow.

◀ *This garden displays almost every possible form of garden lighting, including underwater pool lights. Lights near the pool not only highlight the planting but make it possible to use the pool at night. Accent lighting and uplighters illuminate garden features and plants*

▼ *This flat-backed zinc wall lantern can be wired in to a power source*

▼ *These post lanterns have reflectors to keep the light focused on the patio and away from the neighbours*

Walking around with safety Eating and cooking areas need good lighting for safety reasons as well as decorative effect. If the patio is close to the house, simply leaving curtains undrawn may provide enough light. Alternatively fix lights to the exterior house walls. These are simple to fit as, being so close to the house, they can be connected to the internal mains power supply. Lighting up house names and numbers is an aid to newcomers to your home, and lighting beside the front door or in the porch allows you to identify callers before you open the door. Paths and routes around the garden also need to be well lit. Arrange fittings to show the route along paths and to point out any hazards such as steps or nearby water features.

An aid to security Lights that switch on when they are approached, sensing body heat, are not only an excellent security measure but can double up as safety lighting. The alternative is to use timed lighting which comes on and goes off at a pre-arranged time every evening, whether you are at home or not.

Temporary party lights Coloured garden party lights can be bought or hired to string around the patio. If you use oil-filled lamps and candles position them where they cannot be knocked over. Special garden candles and flares add atmosphere, and insect-repellent candles keep the bugs away. Candles need to be placed in open-topped containers such as jam jars to keep any breeze from fanning the flame and blowing them out. Safety is important: remember to keep a bucket of water close at hand. In dry weather plants can soon catch fire.

CHAPTER 7

KEY PLANTS

The background plants form the basis for the garden's living framework and create round-the-year interest and form. These are the plants to consider first when designing a garden, as they will look decorative whatever time of the year it is.

Shrubs and trees are the backbone of any garden planting and even the smallest garden can accommodate some of each. Their bold outlines, textures or leaf-shapes bring architectural plants to the fore wherever they are grown. Those plants with variegated leaves of green and silver, white or gold are a wonderful source of colour all year round, especially when flowers are in short supply, while distinctively shaped climbers bring the eye up to a new level, as well as providing privacy, breaking up wind flow and hiding an eyesore.

This chapter provides a taster of the huge and exciting range of these key plants.

SHRUBS

Moving an established shrub

If you decide a shrub has been planted in the wrong position it should be possible to move it to another part of the garden. However, before you start removing the shrub make sure that you have dug a hole large enough to take it and have prepared the soil by digging in well-rotted manure or compost.

Dig out a trench all around the shrub, having first tied up the branches to make it easier. Use a fork and gently loosen the soil around the deeper roots.

To reduce the size of the ball of soil, if it is too large to remove, use the fork – working carefully so as not to damage the roots – and remove more soil.

(continued opposite)

Shrubs provide the vital backcloth to the garden's planting. Foliage comes in many tints and there is a huge range of leaf shapes. Some shrubs have variegated leaves, others provide stunning autumn colour, while some keep their leaves throughout the year. Their flowers, some wonderfully scented, come in every shape and colour, and many produce decorative fruit. And the huge range of shrubs available means that there will always be some in flower whatever the time of year.

Although some of the shrubs described here can grow to quite a height and spread, most can be kept to the required size for a small garden by cutting out whole stems or pruning back regularly.

Arbutus unedo, Strawberry tree
Height and spread up to 8m/26ft ▉ *A. unedo 'Elfin King' is smaller, with height up to 2m/6ft, spread 1.5m/5ft* ▉ *Full sun* ▉ *Fertile, well-drained soil; suitable for alkaline soils*

Really a tree, but shrubby in growth, the strawberry tree provides lots of winter interest with white flowers in winter to early spring, strawberry-like autumn fruit and a rough, shredding red-brown bark.

Camellia, Camellias
Height and spread up to 4.5m/15ft, depending on variety ▉ *Good specimen plants* ▉ *Suitable for containers* ▉ *Partial shade; plant away from early morning sun* ▉ *Moist, well-drained, acid soil*

Camellias, with their deep green, glossy, round-the-year leaves, thrive in acid soil, although many will tolerate neutral soil. They provide wonderful winter or early spring colour with their exotic single and double flowers from deep red, through all shades of pink to white, plus yellow.

Cornus stolonifera, Dogwood
Height up to 2m/6ft, spread 4m/12ft ▉ *Full sun – partial shade* ▉ *Fertile, well-drained, neutral to acid soil; also tolerates wet soil*

A deciduous shrub that is grown for its decorative, dark red young winter stems. Some forms of dogwood have bright yellow, orange or green stems. The small, white, late spring flowers are followed by white, often blue-tinged fruit. Variegated leaf forms are available.

▲ *Camellia japonica*

Cotinus coggygria, Smoke bush
Height and spread up to 5m/16ft ▉ *Full sun – partial shade* ▉ *Moderately fertile, moist soil*

The fluffy festoons of purple flowers in mid-summer and autumn almost hide the small green leaves to give this decorative shrub its common name. Leaves turn yellow, orange and red in autumn.

Deutzia, Beauty bush
Height and spread 60cm/24in to 3m/10ft, depending on variety ▉ *Full sun* ▉ *Moderately fertile, moist soil*

In mid-summer, the pretty pink or white, small, star-shaped flowers, cover this deciduous bush to such an extent that they cause the branches to arch attractively.

Escallonia, Escallonia
Height and spread 2.5m/8ft ▉ *Full sun, with shelter from wind* ▉ *Fertile, well-drained soil*

A frost-hardy, evergreen shrub, especially good in coastal areas. E. 'Apple Blossom' has early and mid-summer flowers in the mixed tints of apple blossom, white, pink and red.

Euonymus alatus, Winged spindle
Height 2m/6ft, spread 3m/10ft. E. alatus 'Compactus' is smaller, with height and spread 1m/3ft ▉ *Full sun – partial shade* ▉ *Well-drained soil*

This is a dense, bushy, deciduous

▼ The Dogwood, *Cornus alba* 'Red Stems'

▲ Catkins of *Garrya elliptica*

shrub with dark green leaves that turn a brilliant scarlet in autumn, and purple and scarlet seeds.

Garrya elliptica, Silk tassel bush
Height up to 4m/12ft, spread 2-4m/6-12ft ▪ Full sun – partial shade, with shelter from wind and frost ▪ Moderately fertile, well-drained soil

An upright, evergreen shrub grown for its long, slim, silvery green catkins that, in the male form, can be up to 20cm/8in in length and cover the plant in late winter to look like silver rain. Female catkins are smaller but are followed by purple berries when male and female plants are grown together. Prune in spring to keep down in size.

Hamamelis x intermedia, Witch hazel
Height and spread up to 4m/12ft ▪ Sun –partial shade ▪ Moist, well-drained, acid to neutral soil

Witch hazel is grown for the fragrant yellow or dark red winter flowers. *Hamamelis x intermedia* 'Pallida' has clusters of large yellow flowers. (See also *H. x intermedia* 'Diane', page 169.)

Mahonia x media, Mahonia
Height up to 5m/15ft, spread 4m/12ft ▪ Shade ▪ Moderately fertile, well-drained soil

An ornate shrub throughout the year, with its sharply toothed, long, dark, evergreen leaves, and long streamers of bright to lemon-yellow, highly fragrant flowers from late autumn to late winter. This makes a good specimen plant.

Philadelphus, Mock orange
Height and spread 1.5m/5ft ▪ Full sun – partial shade ▪ Moderately fertile, well-drained soil

The white flowers that appear in mid-summer have a scent similar to orange blossom. *Philadelphus* x *lemoinei* has arching branches and very fragrant, pure white flowers. Makes a good specimen plant.

Potentilla fruticosa, Potentilla
Height up to 1.5m/5ft, spread 1m/3ft ▪ Full sun – partial shade, depending on type ▪ Poor, well-drained soil

This compact, bushy, deciduous shrub likes bright sun and produces flowers over a long period from late spring to mid-autumn. Colours vary from white, yellow and pale pink to deep red. *Potentilla fruticosa* 'Sunset' prefers light shade and has deep orange to rusty red flowers.

Pyracantha, Firethorn/ Pyrancantha
Height up to 3m/10ft, spread up to 2.5m/8ft ▪ Full sun – partial shade ▪ Fertile soil

A spiny, evergreen shrub pyracantha is usually chosen for its colourful yellow, orange or red autumn berries. *Pyracantha* 'Soleil d'Or', with its red-tinged shoots, has sunny golden yellow berries following on from white flowers in early summer.

Rhododendron, Rhododendrons
Height up to 3m/10ft, spread 4m/12ft or more ▪ Mostly shade, where colour is highlighted ▪ Most require moist, well-drained, acid soil

▲ *Rhododendron* 'Cynthia'

A huge range of species and cultivars provides us with the showy flowers of rhododendron from autumn through winter and, most commonly, in spring, in an enormous range of shapes and sizes. Flower colours can be almost anything: white, pink, apricot, red, yellow, purple, lilac; and sizes range from dwarf alpines and small shrubs to large trees. Some rhododendrons also have attractively coloured young growth. Some of these shrubs are suitable for containers.

Viburnum plicatum 'Mariesii', Japanese snowball tree
Height up to 3m/10ft, spread 4m/12ft ▪ Full sun – partial shade ▪ Moderately fertile soil

This deciduous shrub has a spreading, layered shape with white flowers held in swathes above the green leaves in late spring. In autumn the leaves turn red. It makes a good specimen plant.

▼ *Viburnum plicatum* 'Mariesii'

(continued from opposite)

Use a sharp spade to cut beneath the plant, once the root ball is of a manageable size. Work around the plant from each side.

Have ready a piece of hessian or tough plastic for carrying the shrub. Roll this up, tilt the plant and slip it underneath, then rock the root ball back over it and unroll the hessian around it.

Lift the shrub with assistance, move it to the new planting hole and gently lower it into position. Check that the soil height on shrub and surrounding earth is the same, and remove the wrapping. Fill in the hole, firm the soil, and water thoroughly. In dry weather water well for several months.

DECIDUOUS TREES

Planting a tree

To provide a new tree with the best start in life plant it with care, and in the right position.

First remove the soil to a depth of 30cm/12in. Fork over the rest well, working in plenty of garden compost or well-rotted manure.

Insert a stake, placing it on the side of the prevailing wind and leaving plenty of space for the root ball. Hammer it in well.

(continued opposite)

There is room for one or two carefully chosen trees in the smallest garden. Some can be kept small by growing them in a pot. They provide a focus, can hide unattractive surrounding structures and create interest at a higher level. A tree may be chosen for its decorative leaf shape or colour, for its spring or summer flowers or the fruit that follows, or for the colour or texture of its bark – and sometimes you can find all these features in one tree. The dimensions given here are for maximum growth, often reached only after many years.

Acer griseum, Paper-bark maple
Height and spread up to 9m/30ft ▪ *Full sun – partial shade* ▪ *Fertile, well-drained soil*

This slow-growing tree has a spreading canopy of dark green, hand-shaped leaves that turn a wonderful orange then crimson in the autumn. Yellow flowers hang from the branch ends in summer. In winter its beautiful orange-brown peeling bark shows up. This tree is suitable for containers.

Amelanchier lamarckii, Shadbush
Height up to 9m/30ft, spread up to 12m/40ft ▪ *Full sun – partial shade* ▪ *Acid, fertile, moist, well-drained soil*

Small tree or shrub which has white hair-covered young shoots and leaves. The new bronze leaves turn green, then orange and red in autumn. Small white flowers, in trailing festoons up to 12cm/5in long, appear in spring, followed by black fruit.

Betula pendula, Silver birch
Height up to 25m/80ft, spread up to 10m/33ft ▪ *Full sun – partial shade* ▪ *Moderately fertile, moist, well-drained soil*

Graceful garden tree, well known for its eye-catching silvery bark. Male catkins up to 6cm/2.5in long appear in spring and leaves turn from green to yellow in autumn. Bare branches show a deep purple haze of twigs in winter.

Cercis canadensis, Eastern redbud
Height and spread up to 10m/33ft ▪ *Full sun – partial shade* ▪ *Deep, fertile, moist, well-drained soil*

Often multi-stemmed, *Cercis canadensis* 'Forest Pansy' has crimson to pink flowers which appear in clusters before the leaves. The heart-shaped leaves are a deep red-purple when new, turning to orange in autumn before falling. In frost-prone areas they need protection in winter when young.

Cornus mas, Cornelian cherry
Height and spread 5m/15ft ▪ *Full sun – partial shade* ▪ *Fertile, well-drained, neutral to acid soil*

The dark green leaves of this small, spreading tree turn a wonderful red-purple in autumn.

▼*Petula pendula,* Silver birch

▲*Acer palmatum* 'Autumn colours'

Balls of yellow flowers appear in late winter, followed by the leaves, and bright red fruit are usually produced in late summer.

Crataegus monogyna, Common hawthorn
Height up to 9m/30ft, spread up to 8m/26ft ▪ *Full sun – partial shade*

▲ *Crataegus monogyna*, with haws

■ *Any soil, except very wet*

Thorny tree with small, dark green, glossy leaves and fragrant white flowers with pink central anthers in late spring. Glossy red fruit (haws) appear in autumn. Suitable for a hedge (kept trimmed) or specimen tree, and suitable for towns and coastal areas.

Crataegus laevigata 'Paul's Scarlet', May
Height and spread 8m/26ft ■ *Full sun – partial shade* ■ *Any soil, except very wet*

Similar to *Crataegus monogyna*, above, *C. laevigata* 'Paul's Scarlet' has abundant clusters of double, deep pink flowers in late spring. Like *C. monogyna*, it is suitable for towns and coastal areas.

Fagus sylvatica 'Dawyck Gold', Dawyck beech
Height 18m/60ft, spread 7m/22ft ■ *Partial shade* ■ *Almost any well-drained soil, including chalk*

This column-shaped but compact beech has bright yellow young foliage, later turning green and finally orange-brown in autumn.

Malus 'Royalty', Crab apple
Height and spread 8m/26ft ■ *Full sun – partial shade* ■ *Fertile, moist, well-drained soil*

A small, spreading tree with richly coloured, dark red-purple leaves that mostly remain this colour to turn red in autumn. Almost matching, crimson-purple flowers appear in mid- to late spring, followed by small, brightly coloured dark red fruit in autumn.

Prunus padus, Bird cherry
Height 15m/50ft, spread 10m/33ft ■ *Full sun* ■ *Moderately fertile, moist, well-drained soil*

A spreading tree that is more conical in shape when young and produces fragrant white flowers in pendulous streamers in spring, followed by small, glossy black fruit. The dark green leaves turn yellow or red in autumn.

Prunus serrula, Cherry
Height and spread 10m/33ft ■ *Full sun* ■ *Moderately fertile, moist, well-drained soil*

This is a rounded tree with richly coloured, peeling, glossy chestnut-brown bark. As the leaves emerge in spring, white, single flowers appear in small clusters, to be followed by edible, but unpalatable cherries.

Robinia pseudoacacia 'Frisia', Black locust / False acacia
Height 15m/50ft, spread 8m/25ft ■ *Full sun; needs shelter from strong winds* ■ *Tolerates poor, dry soil but prefers moderately fertile, moist, well-drained soil*

A fast-growing tree that is roughly columnar and has golden yellow foliage, which turns a more yellow-green in summer and orange-yellow in autumn.

Salix matsudana 'Tortuosa', Twisted willow
Height 9-25m/30-80ft, spread 25m/80ft ■ *Full sun* ■ *Deep, moist, well-drained soil; not suitable for shallow chalk*

A fast-growing upright tree with twisted, contorted stems that are most obvious in winter when the leaves are off the tree. Bright green

▲ *Malus x soulardii* 'Red Tip'

leaves are also twisted and the spring catkins are a yellow-green.

Sorbus aria, Whitebeam
Height up to 15m/50ft, spread 7m/22ft ■ *Full sun – partial shade* ■ *Moist, well-drained neutral to slightly alkaline soil*

With young leaves of a silvery grey in a rounded, cloudy shape, this is a very pretty tree. Older leaves are a dark green with white hairy undersides that show up in a breeze. White flowers appear in late spring, followed by red berries.

Syringa, Lilac
Height and spread up to 4m/12ft ■ *Full sun* ■ *Fertile, well-drained, neutral to alkaline soil*

Lilac has spikes of fragrant white, pink, magenta-red or blue-grey flowers in spring. *Syringa vulgaris* 'Mme Florent Stepman' has white flowers, 'Paul Thirion' has magenta-red flowers, and 'Charles Joly' has deep purple-blue flowers.

▼ *Syringa palibiniana*

(continued from opposite)

Tease out some of the thick roots that have run around inside the edge of the pot if planting a container-grown tree.

Place the tree in the hole and put a cane across the hole to check that the soil mark on the tree matches the soil height. Fill the hole with soil, water in, and tread in firmly to ensure that there are no air pockets around the roots.

Water thoroughly and apply a 5cm/2in depth of mulch to help conserve moisture. Water in dry weather for some months until the tree is well established.

EVERGREEN TREES

Planting a tree in a tub or container

Trees grown in tubs can be used to add interest to a patio and are much less trouble than annuals. This is the only method of successfully growing larger plants on a roof garden or balcony.

Choose a container larger than the pot the tree comes in and at least 30cm/12in in diameter. If using a ceramic pot check that it is frost-proof. Insert a drainage layer at the bottom before adding a layer of compost. Where weight is not a priority use heavy, loam-based compost for stability.

Remove the tree from its pot and tease out some of the larger roots. Stand it on the new compost and trickle more compost around the sides and up to the original height of the soil on the trunk.

(continued opposite)

A round-the-year outline to the garden is provided by those trees and hedges that keep their leaves. They can provide a valuable screen as well as a constant form. Those that clip well, for example box, holly and privet, make neat, sculptured hedges and some can be shaped to form decorative and fun topiary shapes. Evergreens come in a wide range of shapes and with many different leaf forms, textures and colours to choose from. Some also have aromatic leaves. Cones and berries add further interest.

Buxus sempervirens, Box
Height up to 5m/15ft spread 5-6m/15-20ft ■ *Partial shade* ■ *Fertile, well-drained soil*
This small, bushy tree has glossy, dark green leaves and is ideal for clipping to form a hedge or for topiary, particularly in the forms *Buxus sempervirens* 'Handsworthensis' or *B. sempervirens* 'Suffruticosa'. Variegated varieties are *B. sempervirens* 'Marginata', with a golden edge to the leaves, and *B. sempervirens* 'Elegantissima', which has white leaf margins. Select dwarf box for edging.

Cryptomeria japonica, Japanese cedar
Height up to 25m/80ft, spread 6m/20ft ■ *Full sun – partial shade* ■ *Fertile, moist, well-drained soil but will tolerate most well-drained soils, including chalk*
A cedar that grows as a tall, cone-shaped column with glossy green leaves that take on a warm russet tint in autumn. The bright orange-brown bark shreds attractively and the female flowers produce small brown cones.

Eucalyptus gunnii, Cider gum
Height 9-25m/30-80ft, spread 6-15m/20-50ft ■ *Full sun* ■ *Fertile, neutral to slightly acid soil*
Rounded leaves are silvery grey-green when young, turning lance-shaped and blue-green later. They have an aromatic smell when crushed. *Eucalyptus gunnii* can grow large, so cut it back regularly to encourage young leaves and maintain a bushy, compact shape in a small garden. Cream flowers appear in summer. The grey bark

▲ Box tree clipped in spiral shape

peels away to reveal yellow-grey new bark below, sometimes flushed with pink or orange.

Ilex aquifolium 'J.C. van Tol', Holly
Height up to 6m/20ft, spread 4m/12ft ■ *Full sun – partial shade* ■ *Moderately fertile, moist, well-drained soil*
Hollies are slow-growing, neat and compact. This columnar female holly with shiny, plain green, rounded leaves, is self-fertile, so if only one tree is grown it is still able to produce a mass of bright red berries. 'Golden van Tol' has golden edges to the spineless leaves.

Juniperus scopulorum 'Skyrocket', Rocky mountain juniper
Height up to 6m/20ft, spread 50-60cm/20-24in ■ *Full sun – lightly dappled shade* ■ *Well-drained, sandy, chalky or dry soil*
This juniper, as its name suggests, forms a tall, slender spire and provides a strong, sculptural shape that fits neatly into a small garden. It can be used to provide a good contrast with lower-growing plants. Its leaves are grey-green.

Laurus nobilis, Bay
Height up to 12m/40ft, spread 9m/30ft ■ *Full sun – partial shade* ■ *Fertile, moist, well-drained soil*
The aromatic, glossy, dark green leaves of bay are commonly used in cooking. Bay can also be clipped into topiary shapes. In spring small balls of tiny creamy yellow flowers appear. Clip well. The plant is suitable for a container.

▼ *Cryptomeria japonica*

▲ *Laurus nobilis*, Bay, in flower

Ligustrum lucidum 'Excelsum Superbum', Chinese privet

Height and spread up to 9m/30ft ■ *Full sun – partial shade* ■ *Any well-drained soil*

A cone-shaped privet with yellow-edged, glossy green leaves, and white flowers in late summer and early autumn. It is suitable as a specimen tree or for hedging.

Ligustrum ovalifolium 'Aureum', Golden privet

Height and spread up to 2m/6ft ■ *Full sun to partial shade* ■ *Any well-drained soil*

This bushy privet is grown for its sunny, golden variegated foliage and is suitable as a specimen tree or to grow as hedging.

Magnolia grandiflora, Bull bay

Height up 6-18m/20-60ft, spread 15m/50ft ■ *Full sun – partial shade; needs shelter from strong winds* ■ *Fertile, moist, well-drained, preferably acid to neutral soil*

A dense, conical evergreen with decorative, dark glossy green leaves that have a paler green underside, usually with rusty hairs. Large, fragrant flowers appear in late summer and early autumn.

Photinia x fraseri 'Red Robin'

Height and spread up to 5m/15ft ■ *Full sun – partial shade; needs winter shelter in frost-prone areas* ■ *Fertile, moist, well-drained soil*

A compact, globe-shaped tree with bright red new leaves in spring.

Grow it as a specimen tree or grouped with other trees or shrubs.

Prunus laurocerasus, Cherry laurel

Height and spread up to 5m/15ft ■ *Full sun – partial shade* ■ *Moderately fertile, moist, well-drained soil but not shallow chalk*

Dense and bushy, the cherry laurel has shiny green leaves and can be cut back to keep its shape. Fragrant white flowers appear in upright spires in mid- and late spring, followed by cherry-like red fruit. Use this shrub as a specimen or for a hedge.

Quercus ilex, Holm oak

Height up to 25m/80ft, spread up to 20m/65ft ■ *Full sun – partial shade* ■ *Deep, fertile, well-drained soil*

Slow-growing and rounded in shape, the evergreen holm oak has holly-like, glossy green leaves that are silvery-grey when young. It bears short, oblong acorns.

Taxus baccata, Yew

Height up to 10-20m/33-65ft, spread

▲ *Taxus baccata*, Yew, with berries

up to 9m/30ft ■ *Sun – deep shade* ■ *Fertile, well-drained soil, including alkaline and acid soils*

A slow-growing, long-lived tree with needle-like, dark green leaves and bright red autumn berries. Yew creates a fine hedge and wonderful topiary shapes but it is very toxic.

▼ A colourful border based on carefully chosen mixed conifers

(continued from opposite)

Work the compost firmly down around the root ball to make sure that the tree will remain stable in wind. Water well, and make sure the plant has adequate moisture, even when it is well established.

ARCHITECTURAL PLANTS

Training a tree to the shape you want

For a multi-stemmed tree or one with branches close to the ground buy a plant with shoots along the length of the trunk. Prune out only those branches that are badly positioned or crossing others. Shorten the remaining sideshoots to within 5-10cm/2-4in of the trunk. Do this only once.

For a tree with a clear trunk and a spreading top cut back all new shoots on the trunk and above the branching head to about 10-15cm/4-6in during the summer. When the tree is dormant, cut the shoots right back to the stem.

(continued opposite)

W here shape is all-important these plants are the stars. They stand out on their own to form a living sculpture and provide a strong focal point. Alternatively, you can use the bold shape, texture or stunning colour of one of these plants as a contrasting feature to highlight softer, more muted effects created by other plants positioned around it.

Acer palmatum, Japanese maple
Height up to 8m/25ft, spread up to 10m/33ft ■ Sun – partial shade; needs shelter from cold winds and frost ■ Fertile, moist, well-drained soil

A deciduous tree with beautiful, fringed, fine-fingered green leaves that curl delicately earthwards and turn a wonderful rich red in autumn. Some are variegated, such as *Acer palmatum* 'Filigree', with pale green, cream-mottled leaves that turn golden; *A. palmatum* 'Garnet' has leaves that are very finely fingered and deep crimson in colour. This tree is suitable for a large container.

Cordyline australis 'Torbay Dazzler', New Zealand cabbage palm
Height 3-10m/10-33ft, spread 1-4m/3-12ft ■ Sun – partial shade; needs shelter from cold winds and frost ■ Fertile, well-drained soil

A palm with long, slim, sword-like leaves that arch to form a rosetted head. The green leaves are margined in cream and have cream stripes along their length. *Cordyline australis* 'Atropurpurea' has leaves

▲ *Acer palmatum,* Japanese maple

flushed with purple at the base and purple streaks along the veins on the underside.

Cornus alternifolia 'Argentea', Pagoda dogwood/ Green osier
Height and spread up to 15m/50ft ■ Sun – partial shade ■ Fertile, well-drained, neutral to acid soil

This softly layered tree is often described as being shaped like a wedding cake, because of the way it displays its white-margined leaves in clearly defined tiers.

Cornus controversa 'Variegata'
Height and spread up to 15m/50ft ■ Sun – partial shade ■ Fertile, well-drained, neutral to acid soil

A shapely tree with branches that are arranged in tiers. The green leaves are strongly marked with creamy white margins.

Fatsia japonica, Japanese aralia/ fatsia
Height and spread 1.5-4m/5-12ft ■ Sun – light, dappled shade ■ Well-drained soil

▼ *Cornus controversa* 'Variegata'

This is a very striking plant with its large, leathery, toothed, hand-shaped, dark green leaves, which are up to 40cm/16in in size. Fist-like knobs of creamy white flowers appear in autumn, followed by small, round, black fruit. Suitable as a container plant.

Festuca glauca, Blue fescue grass
Height up to 30cm/12in, spread up to 25cm/10in ■ Full sun ■ Poor to moderately fertile, dry, well-drained soil

Grasses, with their tufty, long, slim, arching leaves, provide a stunning contrast to low-growing and earth-hugging plants. This blue-green evergreen perennial grows in cushion-like hummocks and produces violet-flushed, blue-green flowers in summer.

Liquidambar styraciflua, Sweet gum
Height up to 25m/80ft, spread up to 12m/40ft; ' Golden Treasure' grows to height 10m/33ft, spread 6m/20ft ■ Full sun ■ Moderately fertile, moist, well-drained, acid to neutral soil

▼ *Festuca glauca*

▲ *Stipa gigantea*, giant feather grass

Grow this sweet gum as a specimen where its vibrant autumn colour can be clearly admired. The glossy green, hand-shaped leaves turn a wonderful rich red and orange. *Liquidambar styraciflua* 'Golden Treasure' is a slow-growing alternative which has green leaves with yellow margins.

Phormium tenax, New Zealand flax
Height up to 4m/12ft, spread up to 2m/6ft ■ Full sun, with protection from frost ■ Fertile, moist, well-drained soil

The long, slim, sword-shaped leaves of New Zealand flax, folded into a V-shape at the base, grow to form striking, spiky, rosette-shaped plants. The more compact hybrid *P. tenax* 'Dazzler' has stunning red, orange and pink stripes.

Rhus typhina 'Dissecta', Stag's horn sumach
Height up to 2m/6ft, spread up to 3m/10ft ■ Full sun ■ Moderately fertile, moist, well-drained soil

The velvety textured, red shoots of this deciduous shrub look like stag's antlers, giving it its common name. Long, curving fronds of lance-shaped leaves turn a brilliant orange-red in autumn and the furry flower buds turn into red, nobbly flowerheads. On female plants these are followed by hairy red fruit.

Stipa gigantea, Giant feather grass/ golden oats
Height up to 2.5m/8ft, spread up to 1.2m/4ft ■ Full sun ■ Moderately

fertile, medium to light, moist, well-drained soil

Dense tufts of tall, arching, blue-green leaves up to 30cm/12in long quiver in the breeze on long stems and are highlighted in summer by silver panicles of taller feathery flowers with a hint of purple that go golden as the seeds ripen.

Yucca filamentosa 'Bright Edge', Adam's needle
Height up to 75cm/30in, spread up to 1.5m/5ft ■ Sun ■ Any well-drained soil

Rigid, long, spiky leaves that are dark green with broad golden yellow margins form clump-like rosettes on 'Bright Edge', which appears to be bathed in constant sunlight.

▲ *Yucca filamentosa* 'Variegata'

BAMBOOS

The delicate, arching stems and curving, feathery leaves of bamboos make these a wonderful contrast to the bolder and firmer leaf shapes of many other architectural plants.

Nandina domestica, Heavenly bamboo
Height up to 2m/6ft, spread up to 1.5m/5ft ■ Sun ■ Moist, well-drained soil

The mid-green leaves of heavenly bamboo curl downwards to show off their striking, serrated shape, which is highlighted by reddish-purple winter colour. Star-shaped white flowers appear in spring, followed by long-lasting clusters of red fruit.

Phyllostachys nigra, Black bamboo
Height 3-5m/10-15ft, spread 2-3m/6-10ft ■ Full sun – light, dappled shade; give shelter from frost and cold wind ■ Fertile, moist, well-drained soil

The arching, slender, green canes of black bamboo grow in clumps and in their second or third year turn an eye-catching shiny black shown off by the many lance-shaped green leaves.

Pleioblastus pygmaeus var. *distichus*, Pigmy bamboo
Height up to 1m/3ft, spread up to 1.5m/5ft ■ Full sun ■ Fertile, moist well-drained soil

This low-growing, upright, woody bamboo has mid-green, hollow canes and hairless, long, slim leaves.

▼ *Phyllostachys nigra*, Black bamboo

(continued from opposite)

For a tall and upright tree with a dominant central leading shoot, make sure that it has not developed two leaders. If so, prune one of them back to its point of origin, leaving the more upright leading shoot to continue growing upward.

GREY AND SILVER FOLIAGE PLANTS

Pruning grey-leaved shrubs

To prevent them becoming unattractively straggly, small plants like *Santolina pinnata*, cotton lavender, and *Helichrysum italicum serotinum*, curry plant, need to be pruned every spring.

Cut back close to the base, to a point where new shoots can be seen. If plants are pruned regularly this may be only 10cm/4in from the ground. A neglected plant will shoot higher up.

The plant will look rather bare immediately after pruning but new shoots will soon begin to grow.

(continued opposite)

Beautiful effects can be created by mixing foliage shape, texture and colour so that a garden never looks dull at any time of the year. Grey-green foliage acts as a highlighter, showing up as a haze of silvery light against the dark green leaves of its neighbours. Alternatively these plants, displayed together, can form a very decorative silver-grey border.

Armoracia rusticana 'Variegata', Variegated horseradish
Height up to 1.2m/4ft, spread up to 2m/6ft ■ Full sun ■ Fertile, well-drained soil

This is a perennial closely related to the horseradish with roots which are used for the hot and spicy sauce. It grows in clumps and has long stalks with green, serrated leaves which are splashed with decorative white markings. Clusters of white flowers appear on the plant from spring to late summer.

Astelia chathamica
Height up to 1.2m/4ft, spread up to 2m/6ft ■ Sun – partial shade ■ Moist, fertile, peaty soil

A clump-forming plant, this perennial produces arching leaves of an interesting silver-green which have a metallic and woolly texture on the upperside. This plant is not frost-hardy: in frost-prone areas grow it in pots and take indoors during winter.

Ballota pseudodictamnus
Height up to 45cm/18in, spread up to 2m/6ft ■ Full sun ■ Well-drained soil

This low-growing, mound-shaped shrub has silvery, egg-shaped leaves that curl upwards on erect, white, woolly stems. In late spring to early summer it has unusual, pink-flushed, white flowers with funnel-shaped green calyces.

Brachyglottis Dunedin hybrids/ Senecio
Height up to 1.5m/5ft, spread up to 2m/6ft ■ Full sun ■ Fertile, well-drained soil

This bushy shrub has scalloped green leaves with white hairs that create an overall silvery effect. Loose clusters of yellow, daisy-like flowers

appear from late summer and on into the autumn.

Buddleja crispa, Buddleia
Height and spread up to 3m/10ft ■ Full sun ■ Fertile, well-drained soil

A deciduous shrub with arching stems and woolly white young shoots and leaves. Mauve, fragrant flowers appear in mid- and late summer. *Buddleja davidii* 'Harlequin' has mid-green leaves with creamy coloured margins.

Dianthus species, Pinks
Height 25-45cm/10-18in, spread 30-40cm/12-16in ■ Full sun ■ Fertile, well-drained alkaline soil

Pinks form a decorative edging for the front of a border or alongside a path. They grow to form mounds of slim, silvery foliage topped by a huge range of fragrant flowers, mostly in shades of pink and white, some with petals edged in a second colour, and others with 'eyes' of a different shade.

Elaeagnus angustifolia 'Quicksilver', Oleaster
Height and spread up to 4m/12ft ■ Full sun ■ Fertile, well-drained soil; tolerates dry soil and coastal winds

A very decorative deciduous

▲ *Buddleja crispa*

shrub which shows off its silvery shoots and slim, silvery leaves to perfection in spring. Even the flower buds are silvery, opening into small, fragrant, creamy yellow flowers in early summer.

Helichrysum italicum serotinum, Curry plant
Height up to 40cm/16in, spread up to 75cm/30in ■ Full sun ■

▼ Grey and silver plants generally thrive in dry, sunny places

▲ *Dianthus deltoides*, Maiden pink

Moderately fertile, neutral to alkaline soil

An evergreen, low-growing shrub, the curry plant has narrow, silvery leaves and a strong aroma of the mixed spices it is named after. Yellow daisy-like flowers appear from summer through to autumn.

Ilex aquifolium 'Silver Milkmaid', Holly
Height and spread up to 4m/12ft ▒ *Full sun* ▒ *Fertile, well-drained soil; tolerates dry soil and coastal winds*

This holly forms a spreading, open shape, rather than the dense bush usually associated with hollies. It has sharply spined dark green leaves which are strongly marked, with an uneven silvery-white centre.

Lavandula species, Lavender
Height and spread up to 1m/3ft; Lavandula lanata has height 75cm/30in, spread 90cm/36in ▒ *Full sun* ▒ *Moderately fertile, well-drained soil*

The silver-grey foliage of most lavenders forms a complementary background to the strongly aromatic blue-mauve, pink or white flowers, according to species. Flowers are dried to scent linen or pot-pourri and the essential oils are used for both cosmetic and medicinal purposes. *Lavandula lanata* has the lightest coloured foliage. Some lavenders are only half-hardy and need to be grown in a protected spot in frost-prone areas.

Perovskia atriplicifolia, 'Blue Spire', Perovskia
Height up to 1.2m/4ft, spread up to

1m/3ft ▒ *Full sun* ▒ *Poor to moderately fertile, well-drained soil; tolerates coastal conditions and dry, alkaline soils*

This tall plant with its silvery, furry stems and deeply divided silver-grey leaves is topped by clusters of violet-blue flowers in late summer and early autumn.

Salix exigua, Coyote willow
Height up to 4m/12ft, spread up to 5m/15ft ▒ *Full sun* ▒ *Deep, moist, well-drained sandy soil; does not tolerate shallow, chalky soil*

This beautiful, upright, spherical shrub, with slender shoots bearing long, grey-blue leaves that are covered in silvery grey hairs when young, is ideal for use as a focal point in a small garden. Striking grey-yellow catkins appear with the leaves in spring.

Santolina pinnata, Cotton lavender
Height up to 75cm/30in spread up to 1m/3ft ▒ *Full sun* ▒ *Poor to moderately fertile, well-drained soil*

Keep this decorative, round and

▲ *Lavandula* 'Bowles' Variety'

low bushy shrub in a neat shape by pruning hard in spring. It will then provide good ground cover or can be used to form a low hedge. It has deeply indented and slightly aromatic silvery leaves. In summer creamy white to lemon-yellow flowers rise above the leaves.

▼ *Border with mixed coloured and silver foliage planting*

(continued from opposite)

By summer a compact, well-clothed shrub will have been formed. *Santolina pinnata*, cotton lavender, is illustrated here.

GOLD AND BRIGHT GREEN FOLIAGE PLANTS

Taking heel cuttings

This method works well for *Elaeagnus* x *ebbingei* 'Gilt Edge' as well as elders (*Sambucus*), rhododendrons and azaleas.

Pull off the cutting to leave a sliver of bark at the end. Pull downwards so that the sliver of bark comes away at the base. This is where the hormones that stimulate rooting are most concentrated.

Using a sharp knife, trim off the long 'tail' close to the base of the cutting and at an angle, then insert the cutting in compost in a pot and cover with a polythene bag or use a cold frame or propagator.

In the colder wintertime, or when the weather is dull and uninviting, plants with golden coloured foliage create bright spots in the landscape and give a hint of sunnier days. They also look very effective in a special bed mixed with plants that have sunny flower colours of yellow, rust or orange. Alternatively, mix them with white for a fresh, clean look or blue for a striking contrast.

Carex hachijoensis 'Evergold', Sedge
Height up to 30cm/12in, spread up to 35cm/14in ■ *Sun – partial shade* ■ *Fertile, moist, well-drained soil*

The long, slim, grass-like leaves of this evergreen, clump-forming sedge are decoratively striped in green and yellow. In spring spikes of small brown flowers appear on 15cm/6in-long stems.

Catalpa bignonioides 'Aurea', Indian bean tree
Height and spread up to 10m/33ft ■ *Full sun* ■ *Fertile, moist, well-drained soil*

Giant, lime-yellow, pointed, heart-shaped leaves adorn this slow-growing and shapely deciduous tree, which appears as a haze of gold when the young leaves first unfold. Very decorative, white, foxglove-shaped flowers with throats of yellow and purple appear in summer, and these are followed by slim, trailing seed pods. Indian bean tree needs shelter from strong winds and young trees should be protected in frost-prone areas.

▼ *Euonymus fortunei* 'Emerald 'n Gold'

Choisya ternata 'Sundance', Mexican orange blossom
Height and spread up to 2.5m/8ft ■ *Full sun* ■ *Fertile, well-drained soil*

This dome-shaped evergreen shrub with its attractive divided and slightly aromatic golden yellow leaves provides a sunny feature, even in the gloomiest months of the year. The white orange blossom-scented flowers which appear in spring on other Mexican orange blossoms are rarer and less abundant on 'Sundance'. A sunny position gives the best colour. Provide shelter from frosts.

Elaeagnus x *ebbingei* 'Gilt Edge'
Height and spread up to 4m/12ft ■ *Full sun – partial shade* ■ *Fertile, well-drained soil*

This dense and slow-growing evergreen shrub provides round-the-year brightness with its colourful, pointed leaves, dark green in the centre and surrounded by a wide margin of bright creamy yellow. Slightly smaller, *E.* x *ebbingei* 'Limelight' provides more subtle colour with silvery young leaves that later become marked with yellow and pale green at the centre.

Euonymus fortunei 'Emerald 'n Gold'
Height and spread up to 90cm/36in ■ *Full sun* ■ *Moist, well-drained soil*

This low-growing, bushy evergreen shrub has leaves of bright green edged with a wide margin of sunny yellow that becomes tinged pink in winter. A sunny position gives the best colour.

Hedera colchica 'Sulphur Heart', Persian ivy
Height and spread 5m/15ft; H. helix 'Buttercup' 2m/6ft ■ *Full sun*

▲ *Eleagnus* x *ebbingei* 'Gilt Edge'

■ *Fertile, moist, well-drained, preferably alkaline soil*

This is a vigorous climbing ivy with large, elongated, mid-green leaves splashed liberally with yellow. Full sun produces strongest coloration. An alternative choice is the small-leaved ivy *Hedera helix* 'Buttercup', which needs full sun to bring out its brilliant yellow colouring.

▼ *Hedera helix* 'Buttercup'

▲ *Hosta fortunei* 'Aureo Marginata'

Hosta 'Gold Standard', Plantain lily/hosta

Height 65cm/26in, spread 1m/3ft; 'Sum and Substance' height 75cm/30in, spread 1.2m/4ft ▪ Partial shade ▪ Fertile, moist, well-drained soil

Clump-forming hostas are grown for their colourful and shapely leaves. 'Gold Standard' has golden, strongly veined leaves edged with bright green. Funnel-shaped, lavender-blue flowers appear on tall stems in mid-summer. An alternative is 'Sum and Substance', which has heart-shaped, glossy, yellow-green leaves and bell-shaped, pale lilac flowers. Prone to slug and snail damage hostas need good mulching as they will not tolerate drought.

Humulus lupulus 'Aureus', Golden hop

Height up to 6m/20ft, spread up to 2m/6ft ▪ Bright sun – partial shade ▪ Moderately fertile, moist, well-drained soil

◄ *Sambucus racemosa* 'Plumosa Aurea'

This fast-growing and vigorous climber is best trained over a fence, through a tree or up a tall frame, where its golden foliage can be seen to advantage. It dies down in winter and produces fresh growth in spring. The plant needs full sun to produce its best colouring.

Ilex aquifolium 'Golden Milkboy', Holly

Height up to 6m/20ft, spread up to 4m/12ft ▪ Sun ▪ Moderately fertile, moist, well-drained soil

The spiny leaves of this holly are mainly a creamy gold, highlighted by an outer dark green marking. The plant is dense and upright with purple-green stems. A position in full sun produces best colour.

Lonicera nitida 'Baggesen's Gold'

Height and spread up to 1.5m/5ft ▪ Full sun – partial shade ▪ Any well-drained soil

The long, arching shoots of this evergreen, bushy shrub produce small, bright yellow leaves and minute, creamy white flowers in spring. Grown in partial shade the plant is less prone to aphids but it needs sun for the best colouring.

Philadelphus coronarius 'Aureus', Mock orange

Height up to 2.5m/8ft, spread 1.5m/5ft ▪ Partial shade ▪ Moderately fertile, well-drained soil

This deciduous shrub is a shade-happy plant that displays leaves that are golden yellow at first, turning golden green later.

Sambucus nigra 'Aurea', Golden elder

Height and spread of up to 6m/20ft ▪ Full sun –partial shade ▪ Moderately fertile soil

This deciduous shrub is related to the common elder whose flowers are used to make elderflower cordial and the fruit for elderberry wine. *Sambucus nigra* 'Aurea' is a very decorative form of the shrub, with bright golden yellow foliage developing from bronze new leaves on pink-flushed leafstalks.

▲ *Ilex aquifolium* 'Argentea Pendula'

▼ *Choisya ternata* 'Sundance' (middle right), mixed with other foliage plants

VIGOROUS BACKGROUND CLIMBERS

Pruning a rambler rose

After flowering and in late summer cut out very old, dead and diseased shoots right to the base. Leave all the young and healthy shoots.

On the remaining main shoots go along the length and prune all sideshoots, cutting them down to between two and four pairs of leaves from the main stem.

These vigorous climbers have a wide range of uses. They will quickly clothe a pergola or archway or cover an arbour. Alternatively use one to hide an unsightly building or train up trellis to screen a bin, coal bunker or garden shed. Grown up a wigwam or obelisk they can soon obscure an upright eyesore. Some of these climbers rely on leaf colour for decorative effect, others form a fine curtain of flowers for part of the year, and a number provide fragrance too. All spread generously, in proportion to their height.

Actinidia kolomikta
Height to around 5m/15ft ■ *Sun, with shelter from strong wind* ■ *Fertile, well-drained soil*

The green leaves of this twining climber have tips strongly splashed in pink and white to give a colourful cover to walls, fences or the branches of a tree, until the leaves fall in autumn. Full sun gives the best colour variegation.

Ampelopsis brevipedunculata 'Elegans'
Height to around 5m/15ft ■ *Sun – partial shade, in a sheltered position* ■ *Fertile, moist, well-drained soil*

Divided leaves of dark green mottled with pink and white decorate this deciduous climber. Small, inconspicuous green flowers appear in summer, and these are followed by decorative, marbled, pink and purple fruit that eventually turn blue in late autumn. It makes an ideal plant for clothing a wall, fence, pergola or tree.

Hedera colchica 'Dentata', Persian ivy
Height to around 10m/33ft; Hedera helix *'Goldheart' grows to around 5m/15ft* ■ *Sun – full shade* ■ *Fertile, moist, well-drained soil*

This ivy has dark green, elongated, heart-shaped leaves with stems and leafstalks flushed purple. It makes excellent ground cover or can be used to conceal a wall or fence in the shade. Its blue-black winter berries are poisonous. A variegated ivy that also grows well up a wall in shade is *Hedera helix* 'Goldheart' which has green leaves that are brightly splashed with creamy gold in the centre.

▲ *Actinidia kolomikta*

▼ *Parthenocissus quinquefolia,* Virginia creeper

Hydrangea petiolaris, Climbing hydrangea
Height to around 15m/50ft ■ *Shade, in a sheltered position* ■ *Moderately fertile, moist, well-drained soil*

This hydrangea is a vigorous climber, clinging to its support by aerial roots. It will grow over a shady wall or structure, and in summer it produces small, creamy white flowers with flower heads similar to those of a lace-cap type. Leaves turn yellow in autumn.

Jasminum humile 'Revolutum', Yellow jasmine
Height to 2.5m/8ft, spread to 3m/10ft ■ *Sun – partial shade, in a*

▲ *Vitis coignetia*

red in autumn. The small, blue-black grapes are not edible.

Wisteria sinensis, Chinese wisteria

Height to around 8.5m/28ft ■ *Sun – partial shade* ■ *Fertile, moist, well-drained soil*

This twining climber needs a firm support for its vigorous growth. In late spring to early summer it is covered by trailing, pendent streamers, up to 30cm/12in long, of scented, pea-shaped, lilac or white flowers. 'Alba' has white flowers, and 'Sierra Madre' has very fragrant lavender-violet flowers.

▶ *Wisteria sinensis* is grown over a pergola to show off its lilac flowers

sheltered position in cold areas ■ *Fertile, well-drained soil*

Grow this bushy shrub to screen an unattractive view. The delicate, pointed, slim, dark green leaves are semi-evergreen. Masses of fragrant, buttercup-yellow flowers add colour from late spring right through to early autumn.

Parthenoncissus quinquefolia, Virginia creeper

Height to 15m/50ft ■ *Sun – partial shade* ■ *Fertile, well-drained soil*

To provide quick cover for a wall, fence, or even a large tree, use this creeper with its serrated green leaves that turn a glorious warm, golden russet in autumn.

Schizophragma integrifolium

Height to around 12m/40ft ■ *Sun – partial shade* ■ *Moderately fertile, well-drained soil*

The large, dark green leaves of this plant, which climbs by aerial roots, are almost obscured in mid-summer by the unusual, creamy white, fragrant flowers which have long, eye-catching, creamy bracts around the edges.

Vitis coignetiae, Crimson glory vine

Height to 15m/50ft ■ *Sun – partial shade* ■ *Well-drained, neutral to alkaline soil*

Climbing by tendrils, this hardy vine has large, heart-shaped green and strongly veined leaves that turn brilliant yellow, orange and scarlet

RAMBLER ROSES

These vigorous roses will soon clothe a sunny wall or fence, or clamber through a tree. They only flower once but the mass of clustered, sweetly scented flowers more than makes up for this. Most roses prefer sun and moderately fertile, moist but well-drained soil.

Rosa 'Albertine'

Height to 5m/15ft, spread up to 4m/12ft

An old and vigorous rambler with prickly red-green stems, mid-green leaves and rusty-orange buds that turn into very sweetly scented, light salmon pink, cup-shaped flowers in mid-summer.

Rosa filipes 'Kiftsgate'

Height up to 10m/33ft, spread up to 6m/20ft

Huge clusters of small, open, creamy white, fragrant flowers cover this exceptionally rampant rambler in summer.

Rosa 'Paul's Himalayan Musk'

Height and spread up to 10m/33ft

Large clusters of double, pale-pink, rosette-shaped, pleasantly fragrant flowers cover the trailing shoots of this climber in summer.

▲ *Rosa filipes* 'Kiftsgate'   ▼ *Rosa* 'Albertine'

CHAPTER 8

PLANTS FOR COLOUR AND DECORATIVE DETAIL

Part of a garden's charm is the way it changes through the seasons. New plants come into flower and take centre stage, creating a different colour scheme from those that are on their way out, and adding new shapes.

Long-season flowers provide continuing colour. Bulbs fill in the spaces, and ground-cover plants introduce more colour and hide patches of bare soil. Annuals and bedding plants provide instant colour for containers and areas of the garden where it is needed. Scented leaves and flowers play a vital role in the enjoyment of the garden, while other specially chosen plants create a natural, integrated look for the pond. Herbs and vegetables not only provide fresh produce but, if chosen carefully, can introduce both colour and decorative leaf shapes too.

In this chapter plants are chosen to cover all these categories, with tips on sowing seeds, planting, pruning and how to prolong flowering.

BULBS FOR ALL SEASONS

Planting bulbs in grass

Many bulbs create colour and a very natural effect if they are planted in grass. Where bulbs are planted, leave mowing the grass until the foliage has died back completely after flowering.

Slice through the grass with a spade or edging iron around the area to be planted. Then use the spade to slice beneath the turf and fold it back for planting.

Scatter the bulbs randomly for the most natural effect, having forked over the soil first to loosen it and added some slow-release fertilizer. Just press small bulbs into the loosened surface. Plant larger bulbs with a trowel to a depth twice that of the bulb's size.

(continued opposite)

Not only do bulbs produce wonderful colour and exotic flower shapes but some species flower at times of the year when few other plants are in bloom, then die back to allow shrubs, trees and annuals to take pride of place. Not all have to be grown in beds: for example, crocuses or daffodils can be planted in grass, and the larger lilies look very effective grown in a container and placed in a prominent position when the flowers come into bloom. They can later be moved to take a back seat as the leaves die back.

Where planting depths are not mentioned, plant bulbs to a depth that is twice as deep as the bulb itself.

Allium 'Purple Sensation'
Height up to 1m/3ft, spread 8cm/3in ▪ *Plant 5-10cm/2-4in deep* ▪ *Full sun* ▪ *Fertile, well-drained soil*

A relative of the onion, *Allium* 'Purple Sensation' has a globe-shaped head made up of 50 or more star-shaped, deep violet flowers on a tall stem in summer.

Anemone blanda
Height and spread up to 15cm/6in ▪ *Plant 8-10cm/3-4in deep* ▪ *Full sun – partial shade* ▪ *Light, sandy, well-drained soil*

Solitary daisy-like flowers, in deep blue, pink or white depending on variety, appear in spring above the decorative and deeply cut green leaves. These ground-hugging plants quickly spread and multiply to form large clumps.

Crocus vernus, Dutch crocus
Height 10-12cm/4-5in, spread 5cm/2in ▪ *Plant 8-10cm/3-4in deep* ▪ *Full sun* ▪ *Gritty, poor to moderately fertile, well-drained soil*

This crocus species, of which there are numerous cultivars, looks most at home grown in grass, where it will flower from early to late spring. The flowers are about 3-6cm/1.25-2.5in long and come in white and shades of purple and lilac, sometimes decoratively streaked as in *Crocus vernus* 'Pickwick'. There are numerous other varieties of crocus to choose from, including *Crocus tommasinianus* f. *albus*, which has slim white petals and a golden centre, and 'Ruby Giant', which quickly naturalizes to form clumps, and produces flowers in the rich purple-red of a ruby.

▲ *Crocus 'Remembrance'*

Cyclamen repandum
Height 10-12cm/4-5in, spread 5cm/2in ▪ *Plant 8-10cm/3-4in deep* ▪ *Full sun* ▪ *Gritty, poor to moderately fertile, well-drained soil*

This cyclamen, with rich red flowers that appear in mid- to late spring, also has pretty, dark green leaves marbled with a pale grey-green. For autumn colour there is *Cyclamen hederifolium* 'Album', which has pure white flowers.

▼ *Cyclamen repandum*

Fritillaria imperialis, Crown imperial
Height up to 1.5m/5ft, spread 25-30cm/10-12in ▪ *Plant 8-10cm/3-4in deep* ▪ *Full sun* ▪ *Fertile, well-drained soil*

This is a very decorative, tall, lily-like plant that flowers in spring. Stems and leaves grow rapidly and the bud opens to produce a cluster of around 5-7 downward-hanging, bell-shaped flowers that can be deep red, orange or yellow. Above the flowers there is a crowning tuft of short, strap-like leaves.

Fritillaria meleagris, Snake's head fritillary
Height up to 30cm/12in, spread 5-8cm/2-3in ▪ *Full sun to light shade* ▪ *Fertile, damp, well-drained soil*

The small, delicate, bell-shaped flowers of this plant appear in spring in white or a pinkish purple marked with a subtle snake-skin pattern. These fritillaries grow well in grass.

Fritillaria persica
Height up to 1m/3ft, spread 10cm/4in ▪ *Plant 8-10cm/3-4in deep* ▪ *Full sun and a hot site* ▪ *Fertile, well-drained soil*

As many as 30 green-brown to deep purple, bell-shaped flowers make up the long flowering spike of each stem in early spring.

Galanthus 'S. Arnott', Snowdrop
Height 20cm/8in, spread 8cm/3in ▪ *Plant 3.5cm/1.5in deep* ▪ *Full sun* ▪ *Fertile, well-drained soil*

The large, white, honey-scented hanging flowers of this vigorous and tall snowdrop appear in very early

▲ *Fritillaria imperialis,* Crown imperial

spring among long, slim, grey-green leaves. The central inner tepals of the flowers are edged with green.

Iris reticulata

Height 10-15cm/4-6in, spread 6-8cm/2.5-3in ▨ *Full sun – light, dappled shade* ▨ *Moderately fertile, well-drained soil, from slightly acid to slightly alkaline*

This pretty iris has blue-purple, fragrant flowers with a yellow central ridge in late winter to early spring. Iris reticulata 'Cantab' has pale blue flowers with an orange-yellow central mark; I. reticulata 'J. S Dijt' has deep purple-red flowers with an orange-yellow streak.

Lilium regale, Regale lily

Height up to 2m/6ft, spread 5-8cm/2-3in ▨ *Full sun to light shade* ▨ *Well-drained soil; unlike most lilies, L. regale tolerates lime*

From deep red buds the beautiful, fragrant flowers of the regale lily open in mid-summer to reveal petals streaked white and pink on the outer side and white on the inside, with yellow stamens and a yellow-flushed throat. These are wonderful plants for pots on the patio.

Muscari neglectum, Grape hyacinth

Height 10-20cm/4-8in, spread 5cm/2in ▨ *Plant 10cm/4in deep* ▨ *Full sun* ▨ *Moderately fertile, moist, well-drained soil*

Fragrant cones of blue-black flowers with almost closed, white mouths appear in spring. Grape hyacinths will soon spread.

Narcissus 'Spellbinder'

Height up to 50cm/20in; N. bulbocodium is 10-15cm/4-6in ▨ *Full sun and a sheltered site* ▨ *Moist, well-drained soil; plant N. bulbocodium in acid soil, to 1.5 times its depth*

This daffodil has bright saffron-yellow flowers up to 11.5cm/4.5in across. The trumpet-shaped centre fades gradually to white, with whitish green at the mouth. The hoop-petticoat daffodil, *Narcissus bulbocodium* is a wild hybrid with cone-shaped, bright yellow flowers.

Scilla sibirica 'Spring Beauty', Siberian squill

Height 20cm/8in ▨ *Plant 8-10cm/ 3-4in deep* ▨ *Full sun – partial shade* ▨ *Moderately fertile, well-drained soil*

AUTUMN-FLOWERING SPECIES

Colchicum speciosum 'Album', White autumn crocus

Height up to 18cm/7in, spread 10cm/4in ▨ *Plant 8-10cm/3-4in deep* ▨ *Full sun* ▨ *Fertile, damp, well-drained soil*

This autumn crocus produces large, pure white, goblet-shaped flowers which have bright yellow anthers. The flowers, which appear in autumn before the leaves, have good resistance to bad weather.

Eucomis bicolor, Pineapple lily

Height 30-60cm/12-24in, spread 20cm/8in ▨ *Plant 15cm/6in deep* ▨ *Full sun* ▨ *Fertile, well-drained soil*

This unusual plant is borderline hardy, so avoid growing it in frost-prone areas, or grow it in pots which can be moved indoors. In

▲ *Lilium regale*

The bell-shaped, deep blue flowers of this plant are produced in spring at the same time as the broad, strap-like leaves.

▲ *Nerine bowderii*

late summer tall, maroon-flecked stems hold up pineapple-like multi-flower heads of pale green which are edged and striped at the neck with purple.

Nerine bowderii

Height up to 45m/18in, spread 8cm/3in ▨ *Plant with tip exposed* ▨ *Full sun* ▨ *Well-drained soil*

Fine-petalled, star-shaped, scented pink flowers appear late in the year. There may be up to 7 or more on one stem. *Nerine flexuosa* 'Alba' has white flowers that are sometimes flushed faintly pink. In cold areas, mulch the plants well in winter.

◄ *Colchicum speciosum* 'Album', White autumn crocus

(continued from opposite)

Fold the grass flaps back over the planted area, firming them carefully with your hand so that the grass remains level.

For large bulbs use a bulb planter to make individual holes. Remove the core of soil, position the bulb, crumble some soil over the bulb and press the plug back into the planting hole.

COLOURFUL CLIMBERS

Planting a climber

Fix the support for the climber to grow up first, then dig a hole large enough to take the root ball comfortably. Position this at least 45cm/18in away from a wall or fence, where the roots will be able to obtain water.

Fork over the soil in the base of the hole and add plenty of well-rotted manure or garden compost. Position the plant so that it leans towards the wall. Use a stick to check that the soil lines are level on the plant and the surrounding soil.

(continued opposite)

Climbers with a showy display of flowers bring a brilliant splash of colour to walls, fences, archways, pergolas and arbours. Many can be grown over a tree or around a pillar to create extra interest or add a focal point, while trained to cover trellis, they can do a wonderful job in hiding an eyesore. Many of the climbers described below also bring fragrance to the garden.

Akebia quinata, Chocolate vine

Height up to 10m/30ft ■ *Sun – partial shade* ■ *Fertile, moist, well drained soil*

This twining semi-evergreen climber from eastern Asia has leaves that turn softly purple in winter. The fascinating open cup-shaped flowers are an unusual purple-brown with a spicy fragrance and fall in short, pendulous streamers in early spring, to be followed by 10cm/4in-long sausage-shaped purple fruit. A warm spring and a long, hot summer are necessary for a good supply of fruit. Although this plant is frost-hardy late frosts may spoil the flowers.

Campsis radicans, Trumpet creeper

Height up to 10m/33ft ■ *Full sun (will tolerate more shade in warm climates)* ■ *Moderately fertile, moist, well-drained soil*

A deciduous climber hanging onto the wall surface with aerial roots, the trumpet vine is covered in clusters of up to 12 brilliant orange, slim trumpet-shaped flowers from

▼ *Rosa 'Constance Spry'*

late summer to early autumn. For golden flowers choose *Campsis. radicans* f. *flava* 'Yellow Trumpet'. In frost-prone areas grow the plant against a warm wall.

Cobaea scandens, Cathedral bell/ Cup and saucer plant

Height up to 10-20m/33-65ft ■ *Sheltered site in full sun* ■ *Moderately fertile, moist, well-drained soil*

The large green buds, wonderfully teacup-like, frilly-edged mauve and white flowers, and big seed heads make this a very decorative climber. Although this is a perennial you will probably need to treat it as an annual in frost-prone areas and start it from seed each year. The large, single, slightly scented flowers appear from late summer to early autumn. *Cobaea scandens* f. *alba* has white flowers.

Ipomoea lobata, Spanish flag

Height 1-2m/3-6ft ■ *Full sun* ■ *Moderately fertile, well-drained soil*

This is another perennial climber that is usually grown as an annual. The narrow, scarlet flowers, which change to orange and then white, appear on erect, one-sided spikes from summer through to autumn.

Jasminum nudiflorum, Winter jasmine

Height 3m/10ft ■ *Full sun – partial shade* ■ *Fertile, well-drained soil*

This arching, slender-stemmed, deciduous shrub adds colour to the winter and early spring months with a mass of small, open, sunny yellow flowers that appear along the stems prior to the small, dark-green leaves.

Passiflora caerulea, Passion flower

Height 10m/33ft ■ *Sun – partial*

▲ *Cobaea scandens,* Cathedral bell

shade ■ *Fertile, moist, well-drained soil*

Deeply divided green leaves cover this fast-growing climber, which in

▼ Climbing roses, 'Meg' (front), and 'Albertine' (background)

▲ *Passiflora caerulea,* Passion flower

(continued from opposite)

summer has saucer-shaped white flowers tinged with pink, with purple streaks and a ring of fine, purple-blue filaments with nail-shaped stamens, said to portray Christ's crown of thorns – hence the common name. Flowers are sometimes followed by orange, lemon-shaped fruits. Grow the plant against a sheltered wall.

Rosa, climbing, Climbing roses
Height up to 3m/10ft ■ Most roses prefer full sun ■ Moderately fertile, moist, well-drained soil

'Climbing Ena Harkness' has huge, hybrid tea roses of a wonderful deep, velvety, wine red, and is very fragrant. Many modern climbing roses are repeat flowering rather than providing one stunning display in the way that rambler roses do (see page 161 for rambler roses). All the following roses flower from summer through to autumn. Handel is an urn-shaped, double rose in creamy white, edged with deep crimson pink, and is slightly fragrant. Height and spread up to 2.5m/8ft. 'Zephirine Drouhin' has carmine-pink double flowers and grows to height 3m/10ft, and 'Golden Showers' has open, double, fragrant, butter-yellow flowers and also grows to height 3m/10ft.

Solanum crispum, Chilean potato vine
Height up to 6m/20ft ■ Full sun ■ Fairly fertile, moist, well-drained, neutral to slightly alkaline soil

A scrambling climber with terminal festoons of purple-blue

flowers, each with a bright yellow centre. Grow against a warm wall for protection from frost.

Trachelospermum jasminoides, Confederate jasmine/ Star jasmine
Height 9m/30ft ■ Full sun – partial shade ■ Fertile, well-drained soil

Pure white flowers with frilled

▲ *Solanum crispum,* Potato vine

edges, the shape of old-fashioned children's windmills, appear on this twining, evergreen climber in mid- to late summer. It has another benefit too, as the dark green leaves turn a rich bronze-red in winter. Grow the plant against a warm wall to give protection from frost.

CLEMATIS

Sun – partial shade ■ Fertile, moist, well-drained soil

The showy, colourful flowers of clematis make this one of the most popular climbers. There is a huge choice, from those with large, open, single or double flowers to those with small bell- or tulip-shaped blooms. The wide range allows you to pick clematis that flower from early spring through to autumn and those listed are good examples. In spring the tiny, brilliant blue, open bell-shaped flowers of *Clematis alpina,* with their crisp white centres, are in evidence, soon to be followed by the huge, pale

▼ *Clematis alpina*

▲ *Clematis* 'Percy Picton'

pink, deeper pink-streaked flowers of *C.* 'Nelly Moser'. In mid-summer the brilliant burgundy pink flowers edged with a deeper red of *C.* 'Ville de Lyon' are on show, and these are followed by the deep purple-blue open flowers of *C.* 'Jackmannii'. Finally, late summer to early autumn brings the tiny, yellow, bell-shaped, scented flowers of *C. rehderiana*. Plant clematis with their roots shaded, away from early morning sun.

Tease out some of the roots from the root ball, then replace the soil in the hole. Firm well to ensure that there are no air pockets around the roots. Water thoroughly.

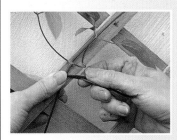

Untie stems from any supports the plant arrived with and train the stems to the wall supports, taking them out horizontally as well as vertically to spread them well.

WINTER COLOUR

Pruning dogwood

Dogwood needs pruning annually in spring, or at least every other year, if it is to produce the bright red young stems which provide winter colour.

Prune in early spring before the leaves appear. Cut back each stem to an outward-facing bud about 5cm/2in from the stump of hard wood at the centre.

(continued opposite)

It is in the winter months that we especially appreciate plants that flower or have leaves or stems that provide colour, for this is usually a less than hospitable time of the year. These plants are not as difficult to track down as could be imagined. Many winter flowers are also scented, providing an added bonus when they are cut and brought into the house.

Berberis thunbergii f. atropurpurea, Berberis

Height up to 1m/3ft, spread up to 2.5m/8ft ▨ Sun – partial shade ▨ Well-drained soil

A dense shrub that is excellent for a hedge, this deciduous berberis has dark purple-red leaves that turn a bright red in autumn. Pale yellow flowers appear in spring, and these are followed by glossy red autumn and winter berries.

▲ *Berberis thunbergii* f. *atropurpurea*

Chaenomeles japonica, Japanese quince/Japonica

Height up to 1m/3ft, spread up to 2m/6ft ▨ Sun – partial shade ▨ Moderately fertile, well-drained soil, including alkaline

A spreading, thorny shrub that can be trained against a wall. In early spring japonica is covered with small, brilliant orange to red flowers. These are followed in late summer by yellow, edible, aromatic fruits that often stay on the bush all winter. Some garden varieties have pink or white flowers.

Chimonanthus praecox, Wintersweet

Height up to 4m/12ft, spread up to 3m/10ft ▨ Sheltered position in full

sun ▨ *Fertile, well-drained soil*

The pendent, fragrant, yellow winter flowers of this deciduous shrub appear along the bare stems long before the large and glossy mid-green leaves open. The variety *Chimonanthus praecox* 'Luteus' has lemon-yellow flowers; *C. praecox* 'Grandiflorus' has deeper yellow flowers with red centres.

Cornus alba, 'Sibirica', Dogwood

Height and spread up to 3m/10ft ▨ Sun – partial shade ▨ Fertile, well-drained, neutral to acid soil

This deciduous upright shrub is grown for its bright red winter stems. To encourage colourful stems it is important to prune at least every second year in spring. Autumn colour is provided by the leaves. which turn red. (See also *Cornus stolonifera* and *C. alba*, page 148.)

Cotoneaster 'Cornubia', Cotoneaster

Height and spread up to 6m/20ft

▼ *Cornus alba* 'Sibirica', Dogwood

▲ *Chaenomeles* x *superba* 'Ernst Finken'

▨ *Sun – partial shade* ▨ *Moderately fertile, well-drained soil*

This arching semi-evergreen shrub provides interest around the year. Clusters of small white flowers appear on branch ends in summer, and these are followed by red autumn berries. Finally the green leaves turn a rich bronze in winter.

Daphne laureola, Spurge laurel

Height 1m/3ft, spread up to 1.5m/5ft ; D. bholua has height 2-4m/6-12ft, spread up to 1.5m/5ft ▨ Sun – partial shade ▨ Moderately fertile, well-drained, preferably slightly alkaline soil

Most of the daphnes produce clusters of intensely fragrant winter flowers. *Daphne laureola* is a bushy evergreen shrub which has scented yellow to pale green flowers in late winter to early spring, and the related *D. bholua* produces its fragrant white to purplish pink flowers in late winter. In both species the flowers are followed by blackish-purple fruit.

▲ *Daphne bholua*
Jaqueline Postill'

▲ *Daphne laureola,* Spurge laurel

(continued from opposite)

Hamamelis x *intermedia,* 'Diane', Witch hazel

Height and spread up to 4m/12ft ■ *Full sun – partial shade* ■ *Acid to neutral soil*

The dark red, fragrant winter flowers and orange-red autumn foliage make 'Diane' a must for winter colour. The earlier flowering 'Jelena' has yellow-orange flowers that appear on the bare stems in winter. 'Pallida' has clusters of large yellow flowers. (See also page 149.)

Helleborus niger, Christmas rose

Height and spread up to 45cm/18in ■ *Dappled shade* ■ *Heavy, neutral to alkaline soil*

In winter, from amongst the large, serrated, 7-8 fingered leaves, stems rise to produce saucer-shaped white

▼ *Prunus subhirtella,* 'Autumnalis', double form, Autumn cherry

or greenish cream flowers that flush pink with age.

Lonicera fragrantissima, Winter honeysuckle

Height up to 2m/6ft, spread up to 3m/10ft ■ *Sun – partial shade* ■ *Fertile, moist, well-drained soil*

Grow this honeysuckle against a protective wall if you want it to provide you with a good supply of small but very fragrant creamy white flowers. These appear in late winter or early spring.

Mahonia x *media* 'Charity'

Height up to 5m/16ft, spread up to 4m/12ft ■ *Full or partial shade* ■ *Moderately fertile, moist, well-drained soil*

Ideal for a shady situation, this tall and striking evergreen shrub is another winter-flowering plant with sweetly scented flowers. The tiny yellow flowers come in clusters of upright, then spreading, streamers forming sunny festoons above the sharply toothed green leaves.

Prunus subhirtella 'Autumnalis', Higan cherry/ Rosebud or Autumn cherry

Height and spread up to 8m/25ft ■ *Sun – partial shade* ■ *Moderately fertile, moist, well-drained soil*

This decorative, spreading deciduous tree produces white flowers tinged with pink on its bare branches continuously from autumn until spring, although if the weather becomes very cold it may cease to flower temporarily.

Viburnum tinus 'Eve Price'

Height and spread up to 3m/10ft ■ *Sun to partial shade* ■ *Moderately fertile, moist but well-drained soil*

This dense and bushy evergreen shrub displays pink buds which open into tiny white flowers arranged in hydrangea-like heads. Flowers continue over a long period in late winter and early spring.

▼ *Hamamelis* x *intermedia* 'Diane'

The pruning looks frighteningly severe when it is completed as the shrub will be only about 30cm/12in high. However, it will not be long before new shoots appear.

LONG-SEASON FLOWERS

Tips for prolonging flowering

Dead-heading Removing the heads of flowers as they die considerably prolongs the flowering period as they are unable to set seed and need to produce more new flowers for survival.

Feeding Feed roses annually in spring or early summer. Follow the application rate recommended by the manufacturer and sprinkle the fertilizer around the edge of the plant. Avoid the leaves. On dry soil, water the fertilizer in well.

(continued opposite)

W here space is at a premium, flowers that last, or are produced over a long period, are especially valuable as they provide almost constant colour without taking up a lot of space to do so.

Campanula, Campanula

Sun – partial shade ■ Moist, well-drained soil

Apart from the spreading and clump-forming campanulas there are also trailing and upright species. *Campanula glomerata* 'Superba', the clustered bellflower, needs fertile soil and grows to 60cm/24in, with large, spherical heads of deep purple-violet flowers. *C. garganica* 'W.H. Paine' is a spreading variety only 5cm/2in high, with deep lavender-blue, white-centred flowers. *C. carpatica* 'Bressingham White' is pure white and clump-forming, growing to 15cm/6in with a spread of 60cm/24in. The trailing white or pale blue *C. isophylla* is ideal for hanging baskets and window boxes, and *C. persicifolia*, with its delicate, single, harebell-like flowers in white and blue, forms clumps 90cm/36in high with a spread of 30cm/12in.

Eryngium giganteum, Sea holly

Height up to 90cm/36in, spread 30cm/12in ■ Full sun ■ Poor to moderately fertile, dry, well-drained soil

The tall, mound-shaped heads of masses of tiny, silvery, metallic-blue

▲ *Campanula persicifolia*

flowers rise from silver-grey bracts to create a prickly but very decorative effect. Valuable for dried flower arrangements, in which case pick stems just before the flowers open fully.

Fremontodendron californicum, Flannel bush

Height 6m/20ft, spread 4m/12ft ■ Full sun, with shelter from wind ■ Poor to moderately fertile, well-drained neutral to alkaline soil

An evergreen shrub with showy,

▼ *Fremontodendron californica*

saucer-shaped, yellow flowers up to 6cm/2.5in across, right through the summer from late spring to early autumn. Grow the plant against a sunny, sheltered wall.

Omphalodes cappadocica 'Cherry Ingram', Navelwort

Height 15cm/6in, spread 40cm/16in ■ Partial shade ■ Moderately fertile, moist soil

This shade-loving, evergreen ground-cover plant has bright azure blue flowers through spring and summer. It is similar in colour and shape to forget-me-not but each flower has a white central eye.

Osteospermum, Osteospermum/African daisy

Height 15cm/6in, spread 90cm/36in ('Nairobi Purple'); height and spread 60cm/24in ('Whirligig') ■ Full sun, warm, sheltered site ■ Light, moderately fertile, well-drained soil

These ground-covering plants have large daisy-like flowers from late spring through to autumn. Those of 'Nairobi Purple' are striped pink and purple, flushed white on

▲ *Rosa* 'The Fairy'

the reverse. 'Whirligig' has most unusual white flowers with crimped and spoon-shaped petals with blue centres and blue on the reverse.

Pelargonium, Pelargonium/Geranium

Height and spread various ■ *Full sun in a warm, sheltered site; regal pelargoniums prefer more shady conditions than other types* ■ *Light, moderately fertile, well-drained soil*

These well-loved, long-flowering plants have flowers in a wide range of sizes and in every shade of pink, apricot and red, as well as white and purple. 'Apple Blossom Rosebud' is pink and white and is of the traditional 'geranium' type known as zonal. 'Attar of Roses' is a scented-leaved pelargonium with clusters of mauve flowers. 'L'Elegante' is ivy-leaved with clusters of white flowers and silver-green leaves, and 'Leslie Judd' is a large-flowered regal pelargonium with apricot flowers, feathered in wine-red. Pelargoniums are not frost-hardy. In frost-prone areas lift and store under cover.

Penstemon, Penstemon

Height 6ocm/24in, spread 45cm/18in ('White Bedder'); height 5ocm/2oin, spread 45cm/18in ('Stapleford Gem') ■ *Full sun – partial shade* ■ *Fertile, well-drained soil*

The tubular, bell-shaped flowers of penstemon come in pink, red, mauve, yellow, and white and appear from mid-summer through to mid-autumn. 'White Bedder' has white flowers becoming pink-tinged. 'Stapleford Gem' has streaked pink and purple flowers with white throats decorated with purple streaks. Protect from frost with dry winter mulch.

Phuopsis stylosa

Height 15cm/6in, spread 5ocm/2oin ■ *Sun – partial shade* ■ *Gritty, moist, well-drained soil*

A low creeping and mat-forming perennial with star-shaped leaves and spherical heads of tiny pink flowers produced throughout most of the summer.

Phygelius 'Africa Queen'

Height and spread 1.5m/5ft ■ *Full sun* ■ *Fertile, moist, well-drained soil*

This plant's long, slim, pale red tubular flowers have yellow mouths and appear like streamers from tall stems throughout summer and often into autumn. They need protection from frost.

Romneya coulteri, Tree poppy

Height 1.2-2m/4-6ft ■ *Full sun* ■ *Fertile, moist, well-drained soil*

The poppy-like, scented flowers of this perennial are white with bold sunny yellow centres and continue through most of summer. Grow the tree poppy against a warm, sunny wall in areas prone to frost.

Rosa species, Roses

■ *Full sun, with shelter from wind* ■ *Fertile, well-drained soil*

Repeat-flowering roses usually continue with a display from early summer into mid-autumn. The spreading rose 'The Fairy' is a ground-cover shrub rose with masses of scented pale pink flowers. It grows to 75cm/3oin with a spread of 1.2m/4ft. *R. x odorata* 'Mutabilis' will climb if it is supported, and has single flowers of light yellow turning to copper-pink and then to deep pink, with height 1.2m/4ft, and spread 1m/3ft. As a climber it grows to 3m/1oft with a spread of 2m/6ft. *R.* 'Little White Pet' is a low-growing shrub rose with pink buds and

rosette-shaped creamy white flowers. It grows to 45cm/18in with a spread of 55cm/22in.

Salvia, Salvia

■ *Full sun – light, dappled shade* ■ *S. guaranitica needs light, moderately-fertile, moist, well drained soil. S. uliginosa needs moist soil.*

The 1.5m/5ft-tall spikes of tubular flowers of *Salvia guaranitica* 'Blue Enigma' are of a deep purple-blue and each flower head is up to 5cm/2in long. *S. uliginosa* is a moisture-loving plant with sky-blue flowers, that grows to 2m/6ft.

Scabiosa caucasica 'Miss Willmott', Pincushion flower/Scabious

Height 9ocm/36in, spread 6ocm/24in ■ *Full sun* ■ *Moderately fertile, well-drained, neutral to alkaline soil.*

Attractive to bees and butterflies, this is a large, white, open-flowered scabious that flowers in mid- and late summer. Other *Scabiosa caucasica* varieties have lavender or pale blue flowers.

(continued from opposite)

Mulching To suppress weeds and conserve moisture, apply a layer at least 5cm/2in thick of an attractive organic material such as chipped bark. Apply when the soil is wet.

▼ *Pelargonium quercifolium,* Oak-leaved geranium

TEMPORARY COLOUR

Sowing annuals where they are to flower

First prepare the ground by raking it to break down any large lumps of earth so that the seeds have fine soil in which to germinate.

Mark out the area where they are to grow using sand or grit. Use a hoe to take out shallow drills at a spacing appropriate to the type of seed. To stop the planting looking too regimented, alternate the direction of the drills.

(continued opposite)

Annuals and bedding plants allow you to provide a burst of colour in any part of the garden when it happens to look dull, and at almost any time of the year. They also create more splashes of bright colour when grown in hanging baskets, window boxes and tubs.

Most of the plants listed below are easy to grow from seed, making them very economical to produce.

Ageratum houstonianum, Ageratum
Height and spread 15-20cm/6-8in ▨ *Full sun* ▨ *Fertile, moist, well-drained soil*

For a patch of bright lavender-blue these compact, mound-forming bedding plants are ideal, with their flowers borne from mid-summer until late autumn, or the first frosts. Pink and white forms of ageratums are also available.

Begonia hybrids, Begonia
Height up to 60cm/24in, spread 45cm/18in ▨ *Partial shade* ▨ *Fertile, well-drained, neutral to slightly acid soil*

Tuberous begonias with their mix of small female flowers and larger, more showy male flowers provide colour for more shaded parts of the garden in summer. Tubers can be lifted in the autumn and dried ready for planting again the next spring. Trailing varieties are also available. 'Anniversary' has large, wavy-edged, multi-petalled, golden yellow flowers. 'Apricot Delight' is similar but with apricot flowers, while 'Roy Hartley' has pink flowers. 'Bridal Cascade' is a pendent begonia with white flowers, which grows to only 10cm/4in high but has the same spread as the others.

Cosmos bipinnatus 'Sea shells', Cosmea/Cosmos
Height up to 1.5m/5ft, spread up to 45cm/18in ▨ *Full sun* ▨ *Moderately fertile, moist, well-drained soil*

The unusual flowers of this cosmos rise above the feathery leaves in pink, crimson or white throughout the summer until the first frosts. Each of the many petals is rolled into a delicate cone, which makes the colour appear shaded and deeper on the inside.

▲ *Begonia* 'Non-stop Orange'

Lavatera trimestris, Lavatera
Height up to 1.2m/4ft, spread up to 45cm/18in ▨ *Full sun, with shelter from cold winds* ▨ *Light, moderately fertile, well-drained soil*

This annual has open, funnel-shaped, showy flowers in soft pale pink, strong pink or white. Some varieties, such as *Lavatera trimestris* 'Pink Beauty', which is pale pink, are decoratively streaked, in this case with purple.

Myosotis sylvatica, Forget-me-not
Height 12-30cm/5-12in, spread 15-30cm/6-12in ▨ *Full sun – partial shade* ▨ *Moderately fertile to poor, moist, well-drained soil*

The small, saucer-shaped, bright-blue flowers, each with a yellow eye, appear in dense clusters to herald the start of summer. *Myosotis sylvatica* 'Snowball' has white flowers and *M. sylvatica* 'Victoria Rose' has pink flowers.

Petunia Surfinia Series, Trailing petunia
Height 23-40cm/9-16in, spread 30-90cm/12-36in ▨ *Full sun, with*

▼ *Tropaeolum majus* 'Alaska', Nasturtium

▲ *Tagetes patula* in yellow and gold

▲ *Verbena* 'Aveyron'

(continued from opposite)

Sow the seeds as evenly as possible, label each section, then gently rake the soil level to cover the seeds.

Water well and continue to do this whenever the weather is dry and until all the seedlings have germinated. Thin seedlings out where necessary to allow the young plants to bush out.

shelter from wind ▨ *Light, well-drained soil*

This large, trailing petunia is ideal for hanging baskets and window boxes. The showy, trumpet-shaped flowers of these many-branching petunias appear throughout summer if you dead-head them regularly. Flowers come in a wide range of colours – in shades of pink, magenta, white, lavender and blue.

Platycodon grandiflorus, Balloon flower
Height 60cm/24in, spread 30cm/12in ▨ *Full sun – partial shade* ▨ *Deep but light, fertile, moist, well-drained soil*

Balloon-shaped buds open in late summer to display bell-like flowers of purple-blue, veined with a darker blue. *Platycodon grandiflorus* f. *albus* has blue-veined white flowers; *P. grandiflorus* 'Perlmutterschale' has pale pink flowers.

Tagetes 'Lemon Gem', Signet marigold
Height up to 23cm/9in, spread 30cm/12in ▨ *Full sun – partial shade* ▨ *Deep but light, fertile, moist, well-drained soil*

From spring to early autumn signet marigolds open their single sunny yellow or orange heads above the fern-like, feathery leaves. 'Lemon Gem' has five-petalled lemon heads. These plants are ideal for containers or to edge a border. French marigolds, *Tagetes patula,* are used in companion planting for their strong scent which helps to keep aphids at bay.

Tropaeolum majus, Nasturtium
▨ *Full sun* ▨ *Moderately fertile, moist, well-drained soil*

Easy to grow from seed, nasturtiums may be trailing, climbing or bushy. *Tropaeolum majus* 'Peach Melba' is a dwarf, bushy annual with semi-double pale creamy yellow flowers that have orange-red centres; it grows to 23-30cm/9-12in with a spread of up to 45cm/18in. The 'Alaska' series are similar but have leaves that are green, marbled white. *T. peregrinum,* canary creeper, is a climber which produces smaller, deeply divided bright yellow petals that are fringe-edged. It grows to 2.5-4m/8-12ft.

Verbena x *hybrida,* Verbena
Height up to 45cm/18in, spread 30-50cm/12-20in ▨ *Full sun* ▨ *Moderately fertile, moist,*

▼ *Viola* (purple garden hybrid)

well-drained soil

Ideal for the edge of a border, the brightly coloured, sometimes scented flowers of these verbenas come in white, pink, red, yellow or purple and appear in summer and autumn. Other more spreading varieties are also suitable for hanging baskets.

Viola x *wittrockiana,* Pansy
Height 16-23cm/6-9in, spread 23-30cm/9-12in ▨ *Full sun – partial shade* ▨ *Fertile, moist, well-drained soil*

These pansies come in plain blue, white, yellow, orange, pink, red and purple, as well as bi-coloured and centrally streaked. Flowering occurs mainly in spring and summer but smaller-flowered cultivars are also available which provide winter and early spring colour.

GROUND COVER

Planting in spaces in paving

If there are no ready-made spaces chisel out a few to a depth of at least 5cm/2in. Add loam-based compost, leaving space to plant.

If using small seedlings trickle more compost around the roots as you plant them, then firm them in gently to remove any pockets of air around the roots.

(continued opposite)

Low-growing plants, whether mat, clump-forming or spreading, are the best method of providing a decorative edge for a border. Planted in cracks and spaces, they soften a low wall or an area of paving. They are also a very attractive alternative to a mulch as, once established, the low spread of leaves keeps weeds at bay and helps to conserve moisture in the soil.

Ajuga reptans, Bugle
Height 15cm/6in, spread 60-90cm/24-36in ■ Partial shade ■ Any moist soil

This spreading, evergreen perennial with its deep purple foliage creates colour not only when it is flowering. In spring to early summer deep blue flowers appear in whorls up the stems. According to variety leaves may be silvery, with a wine-red tinge, as in 'Burgundy Glow', marked with cream and pink, as in 'Multicolor' or splashed with cream, as in 'Variegata'.

Alchemilla mollis, Lady's mantle
Height 60cm/24in, spread 75cm/30in ■ Sun – partial shade ■ Any moist and fertile soil

This perennial plant is most commonly grown for its attractive foliage. The silky-haired, round, scalloped leaves have a serrated edge and young leaves are concertina-like before they open. They look their best after rain when the water droplets remain to decorate the surface. A haze of multi-headed flowers of a pale yellowish-green decorate the plant

▼ *Armeria maritima, Thrift*

for a long period from summer to early autumn.

Armeria maritima, Sea pink/ Thrift
Height 20cm/8in, spread to 30cm/12in ■ Full sun ■ Poor, moderately fertile, well-drained soil

Slim, grass-like green leaves form tufted hummocks from which, in early summer, rise stiff stems topped with bright pink, globe-shaped flower heads. Show sea pinks off by growing them at the front of a sunny border or planted in a rock garden or trough.

▲ *Alchemilla mollis, Lady's mantle*

Asarum europaeum, Wild ginger
Height 60cm/24in, spread 75cm/30in ■ Partial – full shade ■ Moderately fertile, moist, well-drained, neutral to acid soil

A creeping, evergreen perennial, which enjoys shade and produces almost heart-shaped and strongly veined, dark glossy green leaves. Concealed beneath the leaves unobtrusive, small bell-shaped, greenish-purple flowers appear in late spring.

Bergenia 'Bressingham White', Bergenia
Height 30-45cm/12-18in, spread 45-60cm/18-24in ■ Full sun – partial shade ■ Fertile, moist, well-drained soil

The leathery cabbage-like leaves of bergenias take on a range of colours in winter, particularly if grown in an exposed position and in poor soil. Flower heads of pink, red or purple are most common but 'Bressingham White' has white flowers in mid- and late spring.

▲ *Cotoneaster horizontalis* 'Variegatus'

Chamaemelum nobile 'Treneague', Chamomile

Height 10cm/4in, spread 45cm/18in ▪ Full sun and an open site ▪ Light, sandy, well-drained soil

The plants of this chamomile, with their feathery leaves, need to be placed close together when they create a lawn-like effect that is suitable for lightly used paths and grassy seats. 'Treneague', unlike other chamomiles, does not flower but its foliage is strongly scented.

Cotoneaster horizontalis, Cotoneaster

Height up to 1m/3ft, spread 1.5m/5ft ▪ Full sun ▪ Moderately fertile, well-drained soil

A spreading and low-growing cotoneaster, with small dark green leaves that turn red in autumn. Pink-tinged white flowers appear in late spring, followed by bright red berries loved by birds.

Galium odoratum, Sweet woodruff

Height 45cm/18in, spread indefinite ▪ Sun – partial shade ▪ Any moist and fertile soil

A member of the bedstraw family, woodruff was once strewn over floors to sweeten the home. Sweet woodruff, with its hay-scented fragrance has star-shaped, white, scented flowers that appear from late spring through to mid-summer and are very attractive to bees.

Hedera helix, Ivy

Spread up to 10m/33ft ▪ Sun – light shade (tolerates full shade) ▪ Tolerates most soils but prefers moist, well-drained, alkaline soil

The variegated forms of the common ivy will brighten a shady part of the garden, although the variegation will be stronger in sun. They can also trail to provide good ground cover. *Hedera helix* 'Angularis Aurea' has lemon-yellow

▼ *Pulmonaria angustifolia*, Lungwort

▲ *Sedum selskianum*

edged and speckled leaves and *H. helix* 'Adam' had larger two-green marbled leaves edged in white.

Lysimachia nummularia 'Aurea', Creeping Jenny

Height 5cm/2in, spread 23-45cm/9-18in ▪ Sun – partial shade ▪ Fertile, moist, well-drained soil

A fast-growing and spreading evergreen perennial with golden lime-green leaves that are small and rounded. In summer it produces cheerful upturned, cup-shaped, bright yellow flowers.

Pulmonaria, Lungwort/ Soldiers and sailors

Height 30-35cm/12-14in, spread 45cm/18in ▪ Full – partial shade ▪ Fertile, moist soil

A low-growing perennial with green leaves spotted and splashed with white. Bell-shaped flowers in mixed blue and pink open in early spring on 'Lewis Palmer', while 'Beth's Pink' has deep coral pink flowers and 'Sissinghurst White' has white flowers.

Sedum selskianum, Stonecrop

Height 10cm/4in, spread 60cm/24in ▪ Sun – light shade ▪ Moderately fertile, well-drained, neutral to slightly alkaline soil

A mat-forming evergreen perennial, ideal for the rock garden with branching stems and spoon-shaped, tooth-edged mid-green leaves that are fleshy and succulent-like. In summer clusters of star-shaped bright yellow flowers appear.

(continued from opposite)

If using seeds, sprinkle the seeds over compost, then cover with a little more compost.

Using a spray, water carefully to avoid washing away any compost. Water regularly in the same way until the plants are well established.

PLANTS FOR SCENT

Using scented plants to best effect

Near doorways and windows
Scented plants growing around a door or window will perfume the house as well as the garden.

In pots on patios
Pots of scented plants make sitting on the patio even more relaxing.

Fragrance is, to many of us, one of the most important ingredients of a flowering plant. To grow sweet-smelling varieties close to a gate or doorway or around a window gives pleasure to both visitors and those inside the house while scented climbers transform sitting in an arbour or under a pergola into a sensual as well as a relaxing experience.

Chimonanthus praecox 'Grandiflorus', Wintersweet
Height up to 4m/12ft, spread up to 3m/10ft ▪ *Full sun* ▪ *Fertile, well-drained soil*

A deciduous shrub that adorns its bare branches in winter with pendent bright yellow flowers that are very fragrant.

Choisya ternata, Mexican orange blossom
Height and spread up to 2.5m/8ft ▪ *Full sun* ▪ *Fertile, well-drained soil*

A compact, evergreen shrub with large, finger-like, green leaves, Mexican orange blossom has hydrangea-like heads of small white flowers in late spring with a scent similar to that of orange blossom. A second, though less prolific, flowering often occurs in late summer to early autumn.

Daphne odora, Daphne
Height and spread up to 1.5m/5ft ▪ *Sun – partial shade* ▪ *Moderately fertile, well-drained, slightly alkaline to slightly acid soil*

▼ *Hesperis matronalis,* Sweet rocket

▲ *Lilium candidum,* Madonna lily

Like most daphnes this species is a bushy shrub that bears fragrant deep purple-pink and white flowers in clusters in winter to early spring. These are followed by round red fruit. The very hardy evergreen variety *Daphne odora* 'Aureomarginata' has creamy edged leaves and deep purple-pink flowers with white interiors. Mulch daphnes to keep their roots cool.

Hesperis matronalis, Sweet rocket/ Dame's violet
Height up to 90cm/36in, spread up to 45cm/18in ▪ *Sun – partial shade* ▪ *Fertile, moist, well-drained neutral to alkaline soil*

In late spring to mid-summer this hardy but short-lived perennial plant supports large heads of small pale pink, purple or white flowers that are very fragrant in the evening. Sweet rocket self-seeds and is attractive to bees and butterflies.

Lilium candidum, Madonna lily
Height 1-2m/3-6ft ▪ *Sun – partial shade* ▪ *Fertile, moist, well-drained neutral to alkaline soil (most lilies need neutral to acid soil)* ▪ *Plant this lily just below ground level*

In mid-summer set atop long stems the very fragrant white trumpet-shaped flowers of the madonna lily open to show bright yellow anthers. *L.* 'Journey's End' is another fragrant, but slightly shorter, lily that has large turkscap

▼ *Choisya ternata,* Mexican orange blossom

Osmanthus delavayi

owers which are a deep pink ith maroon spots and white, avy petal margins.

Mahonia aquifolium, Oregon grape

eight 1m/3ft, spread 1.5m/5ft ■ un – partial shade ■ Moderately ertile, moist, well-drained soil

This low-growing but bushy ahonia has densely clustered eads of small, bright yellow flowers hich scent the spring air. The right green, spiny leaflets often irn red-purple in winter.

Nicotiana alata, Tobacco plant

eight up to 1.5m/5ft, spread ocm/12in ■ Sun – partial shade ■ Fertile, moist, well-drained soil

Little betters the evening agrance of these tobacco plants ith their funnel-shaped white owers. A group of these plants rown as annuals in a container will cent both the house and outdoor itting area when placed beside an pen window. There are also many arieties in reds, pinks, creams and ellow, including an attractive and nusual greenish-yellow.

Osmanthus delavayi, Osmanthus

leight 2-6m/6-20ft, spread 4m/12ft ■ Sun – partial shade, shelter from vind ■ Fertile, well-drained soil

In mid- and late spring clusters of

white tubular flowers give off their heady orange-scented fragrance on this bushy shrub. Blue-black fruit adorn the plant later.

Paeonia lactiflora hybrids, Peonies

Height 75cm/30in, spread 1m/3ft ■ Sun – partial shade ■ Moist, fertile, well-drained soil

These peonies have a flowery fragrance which scents the air around the plants in late spring and early summer. 'Duchesse de Nemours' is creamy white and 'Sarah Bernhardt' pink. Grow the plants where early morning sun will not shine on them and cause damage in periods of late frost.

Sarcococca hookeriana var. humilis, Sweet box

Height 60cm/24in, spread 1m/3ft ■ Deep – partial shade ■ Moderately fertile, moist, well-drained soil

This dwarf, evergreen shrub has clusters of fragrant, pink-tinged white flowers in winter, and can be grown as an ornamental low hedge.

▲ Mahonia aquifolium, Holly-leaved barberry

Viburnum x burkwoodii, Viburnum

Height up to 2.5m/8ft, spread 3-4m/10-12ft ■ Sun – partial shade ■ Deep, moist, well-drained soil

This viburnum has very fragrant, pinky white, waxy, tubular flowers opening from deep pink buds in mid- to late spring. In mild areas the leaves are evergreen. Grow it where the flowers will not be in early morning sun, which causes damage if there is frost.

SCENTED CLIMBERS

Lathyrus odoratus, Sweet pea

Height 2m/6ft ■ Full sun – lightly dappled shade ■ Fertile, well-drained soil

This annual climber with its clinging tendrils produces decorative, scented, pea-type flowers through from early summer to early autumn. The more regularly you pick them the longer flowers will continue to appear. This old-fashioned sweet pea has dark blue-red petals and purple wings and is deeply scented but many cultivars have been developed to produce flowers in a huge range of wonderfully co-ordinated colours, such as deep to salmon pink, lavender to mid-blue, scarlet, and white.

Lonicera periclymenum 'Graham Thomas', Honeysuckle

Height up to 7m/22ft ■ Partial shade ■ Fertile, moist, well-drained soil

▲ Lonicera periclymenum 'Graham Thomas'

A scented climber that grows well in partial shade, this variety of the common honeysuckle is twining and vigorous. It produces white buds often flushed with red that open into white flowers which gradually turn to cream and then yellow. The scent is at its best in the evenings. Flowers are later

followed by small, cylindrical, bright red berries.

Rosa 'Climbing Blue Moon'

Height up to 3m/10ft ■ Full sun – light shade ■ Moderately fertile, moist, well-drained soil

An unusual and very fragrant climbing bush rose that has lilac-mauve, double, heavily scented flowers from summer right through to the autumn.

WATER PLANTS

Keeping the water clear

Oxygenators help to keep pond water clear by absorbing the underwater food supply and so starving out the algae.

Lagarosiphon, Curly water thyme

■ *Full sun* ■ *Grow underwater in baskets in loamy soil*

A vigorous oxygentor with curly, whorl-like, spiral leaves. It is easily removed if it becomes too prolific. Simply pull out older stems.

Myriophyllum aquaticum, Water milfoil

■ *Full sun* ■ *Grow underwater in baskets at a depth of 1m/3ft*

This is an attractive water plant, with its bright green feathery foliage. Bright yellow flowers appear in spikes rising up from the submerged parts of the plant.

▲ *Myriophyllum aquaticum,* 'Parrot's feather', Water milfoil

For the best effect ponds require both plants that survive in deep water with leaves and flowers floating on the water surface on long stems, and margina plants that like to grow in shallow water to break up the hard edges of a garden pond. Plants that grow close to a pond also need to enjoy the local damp conditions. Apart from the pleasing effect of visually attractive plants, some plants are required for the practical job they do in creating a balanced pond with clear water. Water lilies, by shading the water with their large leaves, help to keep down the algae that create green water, as do oxygenating plants which absorb the food supply otherwise available to algae. Creatures such as water snails are a very valuable addition as they rasp away at the algae as well as gobbling up decomposing plant material. Water fleas, daphnia, will quickly clea green water but this method only works if there are no fish in the pond, as they quickly devour the fleas. If blanket weed algae occurs remove this by hand.

For the bottom of the pond

Aponogeton distachyos, Water hawthorn/Cape pondweed

Spread up to 1.2m/4ft ■ *Grow in soil on the bottom of the pond or in baskets at 30-90cm/12-36in deep*

The oblong green leaves of water hawthorn float on the water surface to be joined in spring and autumn by spikes of striking white flowers with dark, almost black anthers. The flowers are faintly scented.

Eichhornia crassipes, Water hyacinth

Height and spread 45cm/18in ■ *Full sun*

A floating plant, with decorative purple-green roots that hang beneath the surface. In summer tall spikes of pale blue flowers with yellow markings appear. In areas prone to frost lift plants and overwinter them in loamy soil in a shallow bowl kept in a light position. Return to the pond when all chance of frost is past.

Marginal plants for shallow water

Caltha palustris 'Flore Pleno', Marsh marigold/ Kingcup

Height up to 23cm/9in, spread 30cm/12in ■ *Full sun* ■ *Water's*

▲ *Aponogeton distachyos,* Water hawthorn

edge or bog; prefers very shallow water but will grow in water up to 23cm/9in deep

The waxy, bright yellow spring flowers of kingcups are well-known to most country people who pass by streamsides and boggy areas. *Caltha palustris* 'Flore Pleno' has double yellow flowers, while *C. p.* var. *alba* has single-headed white flowers with bright yellow centres. Restrict roots by growing in aquatic baskets.

Iris pseudacorus, Yellow flag

Height 1-1.5m/3-5ft ■ *Sun – partial shade* ■ *Moist to wet, deep, humus-rich acid soil*

A plant of bogs and shallow water, yellow flag has long, ribbed,

▼ *Caltha palustris* 'Flore Pleno', double-flowered Marsh marigold

▲ *Astilbe* 'Sprite'

Planting a water lily

A washing-up bowl makes an ideal container – alternatively use a special planting basket. Fill the bowl with poor soil or a special aquatic compost and plant the lily in the centre.

Add oxygenating plants around the edge if you use a bowl, just pushing the ends into the soil. Alternatively plant in separate containers.

Cover the surface of the soil with gravel. This helps both to anchor the plants and to keep the soil in place.

Lower the container into the pond. If the leaf stems are not long enough, stand it on bricks and remove the bricks as the stems grow longer.

strap-like leaves and tall stems of bright yellow flowers, typically iris in shape. Each is decorated with violet or brown markings. The flowers appear in summer, a number flowering in turn on each stem.

Mentha aquatica, Watermint
Height 15-90cm/6-36in, spread 1m/3ft or more ■ *Full sun* ■ *Poor, moist soil, submerged to a depth of 15cm/6in*

A stream-side plant that grows happily in the shallow water of a pond margin. The green, hairy leaves have the typical strong scent of other mint species. Tubular lilac flowers are produced in dense spherical heads in summer.

For the edge of the pond or a bog garden

Aruncus dioicus 'Kneiffii', Goat's beard
Height up to 1.2m/4ft, spread 45cm/18in ■ *Full – partial shade* ■ *Moist, fertile soil*

Tall streamers of white feathery flowers top the arching stems of this waterside plant in early and mid-

▲ *Iris pseudacorus,* Yellow flag

summer. The attractive leaves are fine and fern like.

Astilbe 'Sprite', Astilbe
Height 50cm/20in, spread 1m/3ft, 'Purpulanze' and 'Irlicht' are taller ■ *Sun – partial shade* ■ *Moist, humus-rich soil or boggy conditions*

Ideal for the pond edge, this plant

requires fairly damp conditions and is very decorative with bright green, divided leaves, and streamers of fluffy pink flowers in summer. 'Purpulanze' has taller spikes of deep purple-pink flowers and 'Irlicht' has plumes of white flowers.

Darmera peltata, Umbrella plant
Height up to 2m/6ft, spread 1m/3ft ■ *Sun – partial shade* ■ *Moist, well-drained soil*

A decorative, large-leaved waterside plant, the umbrella plant shows its early clusters of white to deep pink flowers before the large umbrella-like leaves unfurl.

NYMPHEA, WATER LILY

A 'must' with almost everyone who has a pond are water lilies, with their exotic, floating heads and large, saucer-shaped leaves. They come in a wide range of sizes and colours with spreads to suit most ponds, even tiny tub ponds.

Nymphea 'Albida' has pure white flowers with a bright yellow centre, and has a spread of 1-1.2m/3-4ft.

Nymphea 'Escarboule' has flowers of a beautiful vermilion-red with lighter coloured outer petals and yellow-orange and pink stamens. It also has a spread of 1-1.2m/3-4ft.

Nymphea tetragona 'Helvolva' is a good choice for a tiny pond, with its pale yellow flowers with star-shaped petals and deeper yellow centre. Its a spread is 25-40cm/10-16in.

▼ *Nymphea* 'Escarboule'

HERBS AND DECORATIVE VEGETABLES

Making a herb wheel

First mark out a circle. Use string pulled taut from a central stake to mark the shape. Then excavate the circle to a depth of about 15cm/6in.

Around the edge of the circle lay bricks at an angle to create a dog-tooth effect. You may need to adjust the diameter of the circle slightly for a close fit. Compact the earth around each brick, checking the height with a spirit level.

Add lines of bricks to form 'spokes' to the wheel. It is not essential that bricks meet exactly at the centre as you can use a plant, ornament or herb in a pot to disguise this.

(continued opposite)

There is always space for herbs and vegetables in the smallest garden and nothing compares with the pleasure and taste of food freshly picked. Decorative food plants earn a space amongst the garden flowers in the time-honoured way that was used in the English cottage garden. Many herbs and vegetables are also suitable for growing in containers against a sunny wall. Alternatively you can create a small wheel-shaped bed as a decorative herb potager (see the steps, left and opposite).

Decorative vegetables

Beta vulgaris, Swiss chard

Height 23cm/9in, spread 45cm/18in ▩ Sun – partial shade ▩ Rich, light, moisture-retaining soil

Easy to grow and very decorative, this member of the spinach family has arching, crinkled leaves with white, pink or bright red ribs and sometimes the leaves themselves are also a deep wine-red, as in *Beta vulgaris* 'Feurio'. Swiss chard is drought tolerant and can be cropped over a long period.

Brassica oleracea var. *gongylodes,* Kohlrabi

Height 1m/3ft, spread 60-75cm/24-30in ▩ Sun – partial shade ▩ Fertile, well-drained soil

A fast-growing vegetable with a flavour like turnip, kohlrabi produces a tennis ball-sized bulb part way up the stem and this is the part to eat. The leaves may be

▼ *Brassica rapa chinensis,* Pak choi

▲ Rhubarb chard

purple with deeper purple veins or green with purple veins.

Brassica rapa, Pak choi

Height and spread 10-45cm/4-18in ▩ Sun – partial shade ▩ Fertile, well-drained soil

An oriental vegetable, pak choi has stiff, upright, outward-curling, bright green leaves with white veins, and broad white leafstalks that are widest where they overlap each other at the base.

Brassica rapa var. *nipposinica,* Mizuna

Height 23cm/9in, spread 23-38cm/9-15in ▩ Sun – partial shade ▩ Fertile, well-drained soil

A very decorative Japanese vegetable with strongly dissected dark green leaves that have white leafstalks. Both parts are edible. Mizuna does best in the cooler months of the year and if sown in late summer and early autumn will be available for use in the winter.

Cucurbita pepo, Courgette

Height 1m/36in, spread 75cm/30in ▩ Sun ▩ Rich, moisture-retentive soil

These miniature marrows, simply marrows picked while still young, fill a sunny space with their large, ornate, serrated leaves and bold bright-yellow flowers. They can also be grown in large containers. Picked regularly the fruit will supply a demand over several months.

Lactuca sativa, Lettuce

Height 15cm/6in, spread 23cm/9in ▩ Sun – partial shade ▩ Rich, light, moisture-retaining soil

Lettuces with ornamental leaves can form a decorative low-growing border at the front of a bed. Red-leaved cos lettuces such as 'Little Leprechaun' can be interspersed with green-leaved varieties such as 'Little Gem'. Alternatively use the loose-headed 'salad bowl' lettuces in the same way, mixing green 'Lollo' and red 'Lollo Rossa' or red and green oak-leaved lettuces. With the loose-headed type, leaves can be cut, and the plant will continue to grow, soon to provide new leaves which are often more strongly coloured than the first.

Phaseolus species, Climbing beans

Height up to 2.5m/8ft ▩ Sun, with protection from strong wind ▩ Rich, very fertile soil

Climbing runner beans are ideal for the small garden, as they take up little ground space and can also look decorative on a trellis, wig-wam or pergola. *Phaseolus coccineus* 'Painted Lady' has bi-coloured flowers of red and white. French beans, *Phaseolus vulgaris,* also come in varieties that climb. 'Purple

Podded' has deep purple pods, which turn green when cooked.

Pisum sativum, mangetout or sugar pea

Height up to 1.28m/6ft ■ Sun, with protection from strong wind ■ Rich, very fertile soil

These small, sweet-tasting peas that are picked when young and eaten along with their pods come in climbing as well as bush varieties.

Herbs

Allium schoenoprasum, Chives

Height 30-60cm/12-24in, spread 5cm/2in ■ Sun – light shade ■ Fertile, moist, well-drained soil

Lightly tasting of onion, chives are traditionally used in cooking and salads and as an edging herb in decorative herb gardens. Remove the stalks of the pretty purple-pink spherical flower heads if you want to continue cutting back the leaves for culinary purposes or allow some to flower for decorative effect. *Allium tuberosum*, Chinese chives, have star-shaped, fragrant white flowers. All parts of chives – leaves, buds and flowers – are edible.

Foeniculum vulgare, Fennel

Height up to 2m/6ft, spread 45cm/18in ■ Full sun ■ Fertile, moist, well-drained soil

The tall stems and large feathery leaves of this aromatic herb ensure that it is a beautiful plant to grow in

▲ *Foeniculum vulgare*, Fennel

any sunny part of the garden. The leaves are used in cooking or added to salad, and provide an attractive background in any natural-looking garden flower arrangement.

Levisticum officinale, Lovage

Height up to 2.m/6ft, spread 1m/3ft ■ Sun ■ Deep, moderately fertile, moist, well-drained soil, but tolerant of most soils

A tall, decorative, divided-leaved perennial which dies back in the autumn to re-emerge each spring. The mildly celery-tasting leaves spice up an ordinary salad.

Rosmarinus officinalis, Rosemary

Height and spread up to 1.5m/5ft ■ Full sun ■ Poor to moderately fertile, well-drained soil

▲ *Rosmarinus officinalis*, Rosemary

An evergreen shrub with fine, needle-like, very aromatic leaves and small, two-lipped, funnel-shaped, purple-blue or white flowers in spring to early summer. Apart from the use of the leaves as a culinary herb, rosemary can also be grown to make an attractive low, informal hedge.

Thymus vulgaris, Garden thyme

Height 15-30cm/6-12in, spread 40cm/16in ■ Full sun ■ Well-drained neutral to alkaline soil

This low-growing aromatic evergreen shrub likes well-drained soil and is an ideal plant to grow in cracks in paving on the patio or in a path. Bees cluster to enjoy the whorls of summer pink-purple or white flowers. A wide range of other thymes is readily available.

(continued from opposite)

Top up the soil between the spokes with a loam-based potting compost or good garden compost. Plant up the spaces with the herbs of your choice, planting several plants of each species in a group.

Use a decorative mulch of cocoa shells, stone chippings or ornamental bark to cover the soil and finish off the bed.

Planting between the spokes of a wooden carriage wheel makes an attractive, small-scale alternative to a brick-built herb wheel and is ideal in a country setting.

▼ *Allium schoenoprasum*, Chives

▼ *Thymus* x *citriodorus*, Lemon-scented thyme

CHAPTER 9

PLANTS FOR PROBLEM AREAS

Almost every garden has problem areas where few plants thrive. These may consist of shaded patches where the soil never dries out, or, conversely, shady places where the soil is always much too dry, such as under a tree or large shrub, next to the house or close to a hedge, wall or fence. Equally, few plants can survive in sun-baked areas, which go with dry conditions, while in exposed areas harsh, cold winds can burn leaves, break stems and damage flowers.

Luckily there are plants which can survive each of these problems and some of the best are described in the following pages. Something can also be done to improve the situation. Soil can always be made more fertile (see pages 102-105), shade can be provided from strong sunlight, and shelter from wind.

PLANTS FOR SHADE

Most plants find it difficult to flourish in the extremes of very moist or very dry shade. You can offer some aid to plants in these inhospitable conditions if you dig in lots of bulky organic matter, which helps to improve the soil's structure, retaining water and nutrients within the soil while improving drainage. On dry soil, after watering well, add mulch, which will also help to stop the soil drying out so quickly in the future. In the end the most successful results will be obtained if you choose those plants which are most able to cope with the conditions or when the soil is wet after rain.

Ferns

Many ferns are ideal for damp, shady conditions and their arching, verdant leaves create beautiful effects. Some suitable species are *Asplenium nidus*, Bird's nest fern and *A. scolopendrium*, Hart's tongue fern. Both are evergreen and very decorative with their long, lance-shaped leaves.

In a shady corner ferns can be grown by a pond, to be reflected in the water. Moss will gather and add more shades of green.

Plants for moist shade

Dicentra formosa, Bleeding heart
Height 45cm/18in, spread 60-90cm/24-36in ▪ Partial shade ▪ Moist, humus-rich, neutral to slightly alkaline soil
In late spring and early summer arching stems of beautifully spaced pendent flowers appear above the fern-like green leaves. The unusual, almost heart-shaped flowers are pink fading to white.

Epimedium pinnatum ssp. colchicum Barrenwort/Bishop's mitre
Height 30-40cm/12-16in, spread 4m/12ft ▪ Partial shade ▪ Humus-rich, moist, well-drained soil
With its evergreen, hairy leaves barrenwort makes an excellent ground-cover plant for areas of

▼ *Epimedium pinnatum subsp. colchicum, Barrenwort/Bishop's mitre*

▲ *Dicentra formosa, Bleeding heart*

shade under trees and shrubs. In spring spikes of yellow, open, four-petalled flowers with pretty brown-flecked spurs are produced.

Mimulus luteus, Yellow monkey flower/Monkey musk
Height 30cm/12in, spread 60cm/24in ▪ Sun – light, dappled shade ▪ Fertile, humus-rich, very moist soil
The ornate trumpet-shaped flowers of this spreading perennial appear in late spring to summer and are yellow, spotted with purple-red on the petals and within the throat. Other species come in red, apricot, pale and deep pink.

Symphytum, Comfrey
Height up to 1.5m/5ft, spread up to 2m/6ft ▪ Sun – partial shade ▪ Moderately fertile, moist soil
Comfrey provides excellent ground cover in a shady area, with its large, coarse and hairy green leaves. In late spring to summer small groups of drooping purple-

violet, pink or creamy yellow flowers add extra interest.

Tellima grandiflora, Fringe cups
Height up to 75cm/30in, spread 30cm/12in ▪ Partial shade ▪ Moist, humus-rich soil
On this shade-loving plant pretty serrated leaves are topped from late spring to early summer by tall stems of tiny, greenish white to white trumpet-shaped flowers.

Uvularia grandiflora, Merrybells
Height 75cm/30in, spread 30cm/12in ▪ Partial – deep shade ▪ Fertile, moist, well-drained soil
Hanging, bell-shaped, yellow flowers appear in mid- to late spring amongst the drooping, green, sword-shaped leaves of this unusual shade-loving plant.

▼ *Symphytum grandiflorum, a small, neat, spreading comfrey*

Plants for dry shade

Alchemilla alpina, Alpine lady's mantle
Height 8-12cm/3-5in, spread 50cm/20in ▪ *Sun – partial shade* ▪ *Humus–rich soil*

This mat-forming ground-cover plant has very divided, finger-like leaves with silvery-haired undersides. Tiny yellow-green flowers appear in summer.

Bergenia cordifolia, Bergenia
Height up to 60cm/24in, spread 75cm/30in ▪ *Sun – partial shade* ▪ *Humus-rich soil*

The strongly veined, large, tough, rounded heart-shaped deep-green leaves of bergenia are tinted purple in winter. In late winter to early spring pale rose to deep pink flowers appear on long red stalks.

Digitalis purpurea, Foxglove
Height 1-2 m/3-6ft, spread 60cm/24in ▪ *Partial shade* ▪ *Humus-rich soil*

The tall spikes of purple, pink or

▲ *Bergenia cordifolia*

▼ *Digitalis purpurea*, Foxglove

white foxglove flowers are produced in early summer. The flowers are hooded and trumpet-shaped, and beautifully maroon- or purple-spotted inside. Foxgloves often re-seed themselves. Alternatively you can grow them annually from seed.

Euphorbia amygdaloides var. robbiae, Mrs Robb's bonnet
Height 60cm/24in ▪ *Light, dappled shade* ▪ *Moist, humus-rich soil*

A spreading plant with dark green spoon-shaped leaves with red undersides. These are topped in late spring to early summer by large torches of small lime-yellow flowers.

Geranium phaeum, Mourning widow
Height 75cm/30in, spread 15cm/6in ▪ *Sun – partial shade* ▪ *Well-drained, neutral to slightly acid soil*

Unusual white-centred flowers in dark purple-black, deep maroon, violet-blue, light mauve or white appear in summer on this member of the cranesbill family.

Iris foetidissima, Stinking iris
Height 30-90c/12-36in, spread 3m/10ft ▪ *Full sun – partial shade* ▪ *Well-drained soil*

A beardless iris with tough, sword-shaped dark green leaves

that have an unpleasant smell if crushed. Insignificant pale purple flowers, touched with yellow, appear in early summer, and these are followed in autumn by seed capsules that split open to reveal bright orange-red seeds.

Vinca major, Periwinkle
Height 45cm/18in, spread indefinite

▼ *Geranium phaeum*, Mourning widow

▲ *Vinca major* ssp. *hirsuta*

▪ *Sun – partial shade* ▪ *Any but very dry soil*

The open white, deep mauve or blue flowers of the evergreen periwinkle appear in spring and can continue right through until autumn. *Vinca major* 'Variegata' has white-edged green leaves that add light to a shady spot.

▼ *Iris foetidissima*, Stinking iris

PLANTS FOR FULL SUN AND DRY CONDITIONS

Planting a rock garden

Before you start, place the plants in their pots in position among the rocks and check you are happy with the effect. Move them around if you are not satisfied. Water plants well.

Knock each plant out of its pot as you plant it. Invert the pot, while holding your hand over the root ball. If necessary tap the edge of the pot on a rock to loosen it.

(continued opposite)

An exposed site in full sun often goes with light, dry soil that drains quickly. Some plants can survive these conditions, but most quickly wilt. To increase the choice of suitable plants, improve the soil by regularly digging in lots of bulky organic matter such as well-rotted manure and compost. Mulch with a thick layer of ornamental bark or compost and, best of all, grow ground cover plants to help to retain moisture within the soil. Never mulch soil that is already dry as this will only make matters worse. Instead wait until there has been a good shower of rain, or water well first.

Cistus hybrids, Rock rose
Height and spread 1.5m/5ft (C. x cyprius); C *x* purpureus *and* C. x skanbergii *both have height 1m/3ft* ■ *Full sun* ■ *Poor to moderately fertile, well-drained soil*

The open summer flowers of rock roses, with their paper-thin petals, come in a range of pinks or white with bright yellow centres and striking contrast markings. *C. x cyprius* has white flowers with deep purple marks, one on each petal, towards the centres, while *C. x purpureus* has dark pink flowers with maroon marks and *C. x skanbergii* has pale pink flowers.

Dianthus hybrids, Garden pinks
Height 25-45cm/10-18in, spread 30-40cm/12-16in ■ *Full sun* ■ *Well-drained, neutral to alkaline soil*

Pinks look decorative bordering a sunny bed or trailing over the edge of a container. They are renowned for their silver foliage and clove-scented, often bi-coloured flowers. 'Alice' is very striking with white, semi-double flowers and a large splash of dark crimson. 'Doris' is pale pink with a dark pink centre, and 'Musgrave's Pink' is an old-fashioned pink with single white flowers which have a green eye.

Diascia species/ Diascia
Height 15-25cm/6-10in, spread 50cm/20in ■ *Full sun* ■ *Fertile, moist, well-drained soil*

Ideal for a sunny bank or a rock garden, diascias have a long flowering season from summer to autumn and pretty trumpet-shaped flowers. *Diascia* 'Blackthorn Apricot' has clusters of apricot-coloured

flowers, while *D. rigescens* has tall spikes of deep pink flowers.

Euphorbia polychroma, Euphorbia
Height 40cm/16in, spread 60cm/24in ■ *Full sun* ■ *Light, well-drained soil*

This clump-forming perennial is topped by a mass of short-stemmed and tight-headed lemon-yellow

▲ *Cistus* 'Sunset'

flower-like bracts from mid-spring to mid-summer.

Gaura lindheimeri 'The Bride'
Height up to 1.5m/5ft, spread 90cm/36in ■ *Full sun* ■ *Fertile,*

▼ Pinks in a sunny border

▲ *Diascia barberae*

...oist, well-drained soil.

From late spring to early autumn ...e butterfly-like white flowers of ...his pretty plant open at dawn from ...ale pink buds, and then change ...ter to pink again.

...nula helenium, Elecampane
...eight 1-2m/3-6ft, spread 1m/3ft ■ ...ull sun ■ Deep, fertile, moist, well-...rained soil

This tall perennial becomes a ...ass of striking bright yellow daisy-...ke flowers with very fine petals in ...id- and late summer.

...ris sibirica
...eight 50-120cm/20-48in ■ Full sun ■ Well-drained, moist, neutral to ...lightly acid soil

The deep purple-blue flowers of ...his iris, which appear in early ...ummer, have white markings and ...arker veining. The foliage, which ...rows up in spring is an attractive ...ass of slim, grass-like leaves.

...nautia macedonica
...eight 60-75cm/24-30in, spread ...5cm/18in ■ Full sun ■ Moderately ...ertile, well-drained soil, preferably ...lkaline

In mid- to late summer the dark ...rimson-scarlet flowers of this ...igorous perennial appear, to last ...ver a long period. *Knautia arvensis* ...as lilac-blue flowers.

...avandula species, Lavender
...eight and spread 30-50cm/12-20in ...L. x intermedia); L. latifolia has ...eight 1m/3ft, spread 1.2m/4ft ■ Full ...un ■ Moderately fertile, well-...rained soil

Lovers of sunshine, lavenders with their mauve, fragrant flowers and silver-grey foliage form an ornamental edge or low hedge for an open border. *L. x intermedia* has spikes of light blue to violet flowers, while the taller *L. latifolia* has mauve-blue flowers.

Leycesteria formosa, Pheasant's eye
Height and spread 2m/6ft ■ Full sun – partial shade ■ Moderately fertile, well-drained soil

The deep wine-red bracts interspersed with tiny white bell-shaped flowers appear from summer to early autumn on this deciduous shrub. They trail decoratively amongst the pointed green leaves and the flowers are later followed by purple-red berries.

Sanguisorba minor, Salad burnet
Height and spread about 15-20cm/ 6-8in ■ Full sun – partial shade ■ Moderately fertile, moist, well-drained soil

A wild plant grown in gardens for its tiny deeply-toothed leaves with a hint of cucumber that provide a tasty addition to a salad. In summer it has pretty red bobble-like flowers.

Santolina chamaecyparisus, Cotton lavender
Height 50cm/20in, spread 1m/3ft ■ Full sun ■ Poor to moderately fertile, well-drained soil

This attractive plant has fine-leaved silver foliage and pretty

▲ *Santolina chamaecyparisus*, Cotton lavender

button-shaped bright yellow flowers. These appear in mid- and late summer, making this a delightful plant to grow in a rock garden, as ground cover or edging, and even as a low hedge.

Verbascum chaixii 'Album', Nettle-leafed mullein
Height 90cm/36in, spread 45cm/18in ■ Full sun ■ Poor, well-drained, alkaline soil

Tall spires of creamy white flowers with decorative deep mauve centres appear in mid- to late summer. A relation of the bright yellow wild mullein, this is a plant to show off in a herbaceous border or a wild or woodland garden.

▼ Lavenders enjoy the baking conditions of a sunny patio

(continued from opposite)

Use a narrow-bladed trowel to make a hole a little larger than the root ball. Trickle some gritty soil around the roots, making sure that the crown of the plant is not buried too deeply.

Firm well, then trickle coarse grit around the plant, keeping it off the leaves. Firm and level the grit with your hands to create a neat finish.

PLANTS FOR WIND AND POOR SOIL

Creating artificial windbreaks

When wind hits a solid object such as a wall or fence it goes over or around it, often causing severe turbulence a short distance from it on the leeward side. This can be very damaging to plants. Planting a hedge is the solution.

Hedges and screens of tall shrubs and trees make the most efficient windbreaks, because they reduce the velocity of the wind while causing less turbulence than a solid windbreak such as a wall or fence.

Moulded plastic windbreak nets give some protection to plants for up to ten years, or even longer. They are a very useful temporary addition to help while more natural windbreaks such as hedges and other living screens are becoming established.

F ew plants can be expected to cope well with cold winds and poor soil. Although the plants listed here, some of them used in coastal conditions, will do better than most others in these situations, even they grow better in less exposed conditions and in more fertile, well-drained soil. By following the tips to cut down wind turbulence, described on page 122 and in the column left, and by improving the soil condition you can introduce a wider range of plants.

Agapanthus, Agapanthus
Height 60cm- 1.2m/2-4ft, spread 60-45cm/18in ▪ Full sun ▪ Preferably fertile, moist but well-drained, soil

These eye-catching plants have huge globes of closely packed deep blue, bell-shaped flowers that top each tall stem in mid- to late summer. The long, dark green, strap-like leaves appear in early spring and arch decoratively outwards.

▼ *Allium*, Allium species

Allium, Allium species
Height up to 1.5-2m/5-6ft, spread 15cm/6in (A. giganteum); A. 'Globemaster' has height up to 75cm/30in, spread 20cm/8in; A. caeruleum has height up to 60cm/24in, spread 2.5cm/1in ▪ Full sun ▪ Preferably fertile, well-drained soil

Ping-pong balls of colourful, tiny flowers rise on tall stems on these decorative members of the onion family. *Allium giganteum* has strong pink-purple flowers in summer, A. 'Globemaster' has deep purple-

blue summer flowers and A. caeruleum has silvery blue flowers which appear in early summer.

Alstroemeria, Alstroemeria
Height 50cm-1m/20in-3ft, spread up to 60cm/24in ▪ Full sun – partial shade ▪ Preferably fertile, moist but well-drained soil

In summer the trumpet-shaped flowers of alstroemerias appear in colours of pink, red, apricot and yellow, each with its own decorative tiger-like throat markings. *Alstroemeria hookeri* has soft creamy apricot flowers with yellow and brown markings and brown stamens, and A. *pelegrina* has magenta pink petals, white at the throat, also with the characteristic yellow and brown flecks. A. *aurantiaca* is bright orange or red, streaked in dark red.

Cortaderia sellowana 'Sunningdale Silver', Pampas grass
Height up to 3m/10ft, spread up to

▲ *Alstroemeria aurantiaca*

▲ *Agapanthus campanulatus*

2.5m/8ft ▪ Full sun ▪ Preferably fertile, well-drained soil

This is a plant for a prominent position. With its tall silver-white plumes towering above the long, grass-like leaves it makes a striking display in late summer.

Crambe maritima, Sea kale
Height up to 75cm/30in, spread up to 60cm/24in ▪ Full sun ▪ Preferably fertile, well-drained soil

The thick and leafy stems, which are forced for use as a vegetable, bear fragrant flower heads in early summer. These are made up of masses of tiny white flowers.

Griselinia littoralis
Height up to 8m/25ft, spread up to 5m/15ft ▪ Full sun ▪ Light, fertile, dry, well-drained soil

A bold, evergreen shrub that is grown for its glossy, bright apple-green leaves. In 'Dixon's Cream' the leaves are strongly marked with creamy yellow centres.

▲ *Cortaderia sellowana,*
Pampas grass

Kniphofia, Red hot poker
*Height 1.2m/4ft, spread up to
75cm/30in (K. 'Atlanta'); K.'Bees'
Sunset' and K. 'Erecta' have height
90cm/36in, spread up to 60cm/24in*
◼ *Full sun – partial shade* ◼ *Prefers
fertile, moist, well-drained soil*

A striking plant when in flower,
Kniphofia 'Atlanta' has yellow, red-
topped poker heads of tiny pendent,
tubular flowers in late spring and
early summer. K. 'Bees' Sunset'
flowers later in the year, during

summer, and produces brilliant
yellow-gold heads, while *K.* 'Erecta'
has flaming orange heads in late
summer and early autumn. These
appear in tall, slim cones that widen
at the top.

Potentilla fruticosa, Potentilla
*Height 1m/3ft, spread up to 1.5m/5ft
(Potentilla fruticosa 'Elizabeth' and
P. fruticosa 'Farrer's White'); P.
fruticosa 'Princess' has height
60cm/24in, spread up to 1m/3ft* ◼
Full sun ◼ *Poor to moderately
fertile, well-drained soil*

The dainty, rose-like, single, open
flowers of these potentillas come in
shades of pink, red, yellow, and
white and flowers appear over a
long period from late spring to early
autumn. *Potentilla fruticosa*
'Elizabeth' has lemon-yellow
flowers, *P. fruticosa* 'Farrer's White'
has white flowers and *P. fruticosa*
'Princess', which is slightly smaller,
has pink flowers with yellow centres.

Stipa calamagrostis
*Height up to 1m/3ft, spread up to
1.2m/4ft* ◼ *Full sun* ◼ *Prefers
medium to light, moderately fertile,
well-drained soil*

This densely tufted grass with
arching blue-green leaves has

silvery, purple-tinted, feathery
flowers from early summer to
autumn. The flower stems form
decorative additions to flower
arrangements.

Tamarix ramosissima 'Pink Cascade', Tamarisk
Height and spread up to 5m/15ft
◼ *Full sun* ◼ *Well-drained soil near
coast, moister soil inland; also
needs some protection from cold
winds inland*

An ideal shrub or small tree to
grow as a windbreak or hedge in
coastal areas. Tamarisk 'Pink

▲ *Potentilla fruticosa*

Cascade' has bottle-brush spikes of
pretty, feathery, deep-pink flowers in
late summer and early autumn.

Zantedeschia aethiopica, Arum lily
*Height 90cm/36in, spread
60cm/24in* ◼ *Full sun* ◼ *Prefers
humus-rich, moist soil*

The large, pure-white, upstanding
trumpet flowers of arum lily appear
above the glossy, bright green,
arrow-shaped leaves in succession
from late spring to mid-summer.

▼ *Kniphofia,* Red hot poker

▼ *Zantedeschia aethiopica,* Arum lily

INDEX

ACKNOWLEDGEMENTS

Key TL=top left; TC=top centre; TR=top right; CL=centre left; C=centre; CR=centre right; BL=bottom left; BC= bottom centre; BR=bottom right

Gay Search's portrait, page 7, © BBC Books

Special photography
Dr Bob Gibbons • 01202 675 916
8-9, 14-15, 15, 16TL, BL, 17TL, TR, BL, BC, 22-23, 30TL, BL, 31TL, TR,34-35, 38, 39TL, TR, BL, BC, 42TL, BL, BC, 43TL, TR, 46TL, BL, 47TL, TR, C, 48-49, 49, 52TL, 53TL, TR, BR, 56TL, BL, 60CL, TC, BL, C, 61TL, TC, TR, 64BL, 65TL, TC, BL, BC, 69BR, 72, 73TL, TR, BL, 75, 78, 79, 82, 83TL, TR, BL, BR, 94-95, 98-99, 100-101, 106BC, 108BL, 109BR, 110TR, 116CL, BL, 117TC, BL, 118, 119TL, BL, 120BL, BR, 122BR, 125TL, 132BR, 134TR, BR, 139TR, 149BC, 150BR, 156BR, 159BR, 161TR, 162-63, 173B, 181BC, 184BL, 186BR, 187B

Peter Wilson 86TL, BL, 87TL, TC, TR, BR

A–Z Botanical Collection Ltd
127TC, Mrs W Monks; 127BL, A Stenning; 129BC, BR, Adrian Thomas Photography
Agriframes Ltd • 01342 310 000
132TC
Malcolm Birkitt
26TL, 27TL, TR
Brookbrae Ltd • 0181 876 9238
137TC
Capital Garden Products Ltd •
01580 201 092
137BL
Croft Studios/Designer: Caroline Russell-Lacy
01384 393 389 39CR, 137TL
Garden Answers/EMAP
17CR, 112, 113TR, CR, BR, 126TR, 129TR, 143
Gloster Furniture Ltd •
01117 931 5335
4TL, 140TL, BL, 144TR
Jean Goldberry • 01803 712 611
60TL, 61BL, BC, BR, 64TL, 65TR, 68TL, 69TL, TR
David Goode, Sculptor •
01865 717 966
137TR
Houses & Interiors
142, 144BL Victor Watts, 145T

Hozelock • 01844 291 881
110BL, 111TL, BL
Marley Building Materials Ltd/Marley Paving •
01675 468 400
57TL, right hand column: 1-4, 116TC, BR, 119TC
Marston & Langinger Ltd • 0171 824 8818
4-5, 145CR
Natural Image/Robin Fletcher
64C, 87BL, 109CR, BC, 148BR, 151BC, 153TL, 156TR, 157TL, 167TC, 177B, 182-3
Natural Image/Dr Bob Gibbons
2, 7, 26BL, C, 27BL, BC, 30C, 31BL, BC, 42C, 43BL, BC, 46C, 47BL, 52BL, C, 53BL, C, 56C, 57BC, 68BL, C, 69BL, BC, 73BC, 83BC, 86C, 87BC, 109TR, TC, 120TR, 124CR, 125TC, 146-47, 148TC, 149TL, TC, 150TR, 151TL, TC, 152BR, 153TC, 154TC, BL, 155TL, TC, B, 157TC, 158BC, 159TC, 160TR, BR, 161BR, 164TC, BC, 165TL, TC, C, BC, 166TR, BC, 167TL, C, BC, 168TR, BC, 169TL, TC, BL, BR, 170BL, 171TL, BR, 172TC, BR, 173TL, TC, 174TR, BL, 175TL, TC, B, 176TC,

BC, BR, 177TL, TR, 178L, TR, BR, 179TC, BC, 180TC, BC, 181TL, TC, BL, 183R, 184, BC, BR, 185TR, BC, BR, 186TR, 187TC, 188TR, CL, BC, 189TL, TR, BR
Natural Image/Liz Gibbons
16C, 124TC, BC, 125BC, 161TL, 170TR, 184TC, 185TL
Natural Image/Peter Wilson
154BR, 159TL, BC, 161CR, 185BL, 187TL, 189BL
Natural Wood Products Ltd/ The Jolly Roger House Company •
01268 511 551
139BL
OSMO-GARD (Ostermann & Scheiwe UK Ltd •
01895 234 899
113TL, 114-115, 121TL, BC, 122TC, 123TL, TC, BL, BC, 131TC, 133C, 138, 140TR, 141BR, 145BR
Pots & Pithoi • 01342 714 793
126BC, 134BC
Pedro Prá-Lopez
3, 6, 57 right hand column: 5, 65BR, 108CR, 113BC, 119BC, 121TC, 128, 129TL, 130, 131TL, BC, 135TL, TC, BR, 136, 137BC, BR, 141TL, TR, 152TC, 153B, 157B, 158BR, 166BR, 176TL, BL,

179TL, 181BR, 184TL
Redwood Stone •
01749 677 777
1, Tim Mercer
Tim Sandell
74-75, 90-91

Some of the photographs in this book have previously appeared in *The Practical Gardening Encyclopedia*, © Abbeydale Press, 1996

Garden plan illustrators
Jean Goldberry 17, 21, 40-41, 58, 59, 62-63, 67, 70-71, 76-77, 80-81
Joanne Hipshon 10, 11, 12, 25, 28-29, 33, 36-37, 44-45, 50-51, 55, 84-85, 88-89, 92-93, 96-97

Every effort has been made to trace copyright holders. Any unintentional omissions or errors will be corrected in any future editions of this book.